MW01121203

CEPPETO

PRAISE FOR *CEPPETO*

"Tuscany is a magical place of sight, sound, food, wine, and wonder, all caught in lyrical style by Richard Hadar. But the true magic is the journey between Mr. Hadar, an urbane, pragmatic New Yorker who buys Ceppeto, an old villa in Chianti, and Pasquale, a poor Albanian immigrant, as unlikely a pair as you could find in fiction let alone real life, who form a very special bond as they create a paradise on a Tuscan hilltop."

—Bill Persky, five-time Emmy Award–
winning writer, director, and producer and
author of *My Life Is a Situation Comedy*

"An enchanting, humorous, ultimately inspiring story of two men, polar opposites in every way, who forge a friendship out of their shared passion for a forgotten piece of land in one of the most beautiful corners of Europe."

—Bill Mesce Jr., author of
The Advocate and *Precis*

CEPPETO
(chep~pay'~toe)

A Tale of Two Strangers
Lost and Found in Italy

R I C H A R D   H A D A R

iUniverse books may be ordered through booksellers or by contacting:

iUniverse
1663 Liberty Drive
Bloomington, IN 47403
www.iuniverse.com
1-800-Authors (1-800-288-4677)

Because of the dynamic nature of the Internet, any web addresses or links contained in this book may have changed since publication and may no longer be valid. The views expressed in this work are solely those of the author and do not necessarily reflect the views of the publisher, and the publisher hereby disclaims any responsibility for them.

Any people depicted in stock imagery provided by Thinkstock are models, and such images are being used for illustrative purposes only. Certain stock imagery © Thinkstock.

ISBN: 978-1-4917-5130-5 (sc)
ISBN: 978-1-4917-5132-9 (hc)
ISBN: 978-1-4917-5131-2 (e)

Library of Congress Control Number: 2014918997

Printed in the United States of America.

iUniverse rev. date: 11/4/2014

To Mica Bagnasco Hadar, my loving wife, who has
shown me the wonderful Italian way to live life

In memory of Liane Revzin, who, with our friends,
shared many memorable times at Ceppeto

Liane Revzin with Fumo, 1999

I say: liberate yourself as far as you can, and you have done your part … He who overturns one of his limits may have shown others the way and the means.

—Max Stirner, *The Ego and Its Own*

CONTENTS

Part IV: Rebuilding Eden

ACKNOWLEDGMENTS

Special thanks to Bill Mesce, a writing professor and published author, whose guidance and editing were extremely helpful; Marcelline Block, a superb editor and published author, who tirelessly worked with me throughout the entire process; Bill Persky, who kept urging me to write this story after receiving my weekly newsletters from Ceppeto; and my wife, Mica, who found Ceppeto, without which there would be no story to tell. And, of course, to Pasquale, an Albanian Muslim man with indefatigable optimism and energy, who transformed Ceppeto and the lives of all those who have had the good fortune to spend time in our *paradiso*. His story is one that I have pieced together over the years from the countless conversations we have had. His story includes the factual episodes of his life, but I had to construct the surroundings and personalities of the characters based on his descriptions and research into those areas of Albania and Italy. In certain instances, I have combined two characters and events into one for the ease of storytelling. Instead of quoting monetary amounts in the local currency, I have converted all into US dollars for ease of understanding.

INTRODUCTION

Ceppeto is pronounced "chep-pay'-toe." It is derived from the Italian word *ceppo*, which means "log." Ceppeto is located in an area of Chianti that was covered with forests and that was, for well over a century, the hub of a furniture-making industry using the vast supply of trees from the region. Today, that industry has all but vanished, and the area is now predominately dedicated to making wine and olive oil. These vineyards and olive groves are carved out from the thick forests that still cover a good part of the rolling hills for which Chianti is known.

Ceppeto was founded over six hundred years ago in the 1400s, before America was discovered, a fact that still amazes me today. It is called a *podere*, which means "farm" in Italian. I use the word *farm* in this book, but that conveys an image to most readers of a typical farm found in America with wood structures. A *podere* in Italy is quite different, usually having a large stone house and buildings. Although wood is plentiful, stones found in the typical rocky Italian soil, particularly in Tuscany, are the preferred building material. Roofs are made from terracotta curved tiles, like pipes cut in half, so the whole architecture is quite different from an American farm.

The land was owned by wealthy aristocrats and cultivated under a tenant farming system called *mezzadria*, in which the landowner paid for the building of the farmhouses and all expenses for the farm and the crops and profits were then shared equally. It was under this system that Ceppeto was first founded. There were good and bad landowners, but from all accounts, the landowners in this region treated their tenant farmers fairly. Ceppeto seemed to flourish until after World War II, when the area farmers were organized and demanded that their farmhouses be modernized with plumbing, electricity, and more benefits from the farm production. An added strain on the system was felt when many farmers' grown children decided to leave and seek better lives elsewhere. These events and the poor economic times Italy was experiencing as a third world country after the war caused many landowners to go bankrupt, including the owner of Ceppeto. Many farms were abandoned, and the government eventually took them over for failure to pay taxes. Ceppeto was one of them.

Up until the late 1960s, Ceppeto was abandoned, and its once beautiful and flourishing cultivated land became overgrown with an uncontrolled wild forest. Like a number of other farms in the area, it was bought for back taxes as a vacation home for families to use in the summer. The new owners of Ceppeto were two sisters with large families, and they divided and renovated the main house into two separate units. They cleaned up the area immediately around the main house, but left much of the rest of the land abandoned.

And that was the way I found it in 1998 along with Raffaello, the caretaker. Unknown to anyone at that point was how Ceppeto, over six centuries old, would change the lives of all those who were about to become part of its long and rich history.

PART I

PASQUALE

CHAPTER 1

A NEW WORLD

Numb from the cold waters of the Adriatic, he stumbled through the dark and tumbling surf and fell to the damp sands just above the water line. He shivered uncontrollably in his wet clothes, looking up and down the beach to see if any of the other swimmers from the boat had made it to shore. In the pale moonlight, he saw two men he knew only as Federico and Giancarlo, shivering on the sand close by.

Without waiting to see how the others who'd followed them into the water had fared, the three ran straight to the woods. They shed their wet clothes and hurriedly changed into dry ones from the waterproof bags that they had tied to their waists before diving into the icy sea. It took an interminable amount of time—or so it felt—because they could not stop shaking or get their cold-numbed fingers to move.

They dressed the best they could and then ran to the edge of the woods along the highway that paralleled the beach. About a quarter mile down the road they saw a car with a taxi light on the roof parked on the shoulder. While staying under the cover of the trees, they made their way to the car. The trunk was open, and two men were lifting a tire jack out.

As the three men ran up opposite the car, one of the men at the taxi spotted them and yelled, in Albanian, "Get your asses over here right away!"

The three ran from the woods and quickly jumped into the trunk with their bags. One of the taxi men hurriedly threw a blanket over them and slammed the trunk closed. As the taxi drove the half hour to the train station in Lecce, the three men in the trunk huddled together for some comfort from their shared body heat, but it was not enough to stop them from shivering.

The cab continued on to a dark section of the station's parking lot; the car trunk was opened, and the three men jumped out. The man who spoke Albanian came over to the three of them and, one by one, shook their hands, saying, "Welcome, Giancarlo; welcome, Federico; and welcome, Pasquale."

It was the first time anyone had called him by the new name he had chosen for himself: Pasquale.

After boarding a train at the Lecce station and paying the four-dollar one-way ticket to Foggia, Pasquale sat in the corner of the car with his hands buried in his coat pockets, chin tucked into his coat, collar turned up, and teeth tightly clenched as he tried to stop his shivering so as not to draw attention to himself. His traveling companions, Giancarlo and Federico, had taken a bus heading farther south, away from Foggia, so Pasquale was now alone.

It was still early, and few passengers were on board, and those who were were tired themselves and not particularly aware of anyone else nearby in the car. After a while, Pasquale fell asleep for a couple of hours, waking every now and then to make sure he hadn't missed his stop. When the train slowly ground to a halt at Foggia four hours later, it took all of Pasquale's energy to stand and walk off the train.

He had an address tucked in his wallet, and with no idea of which direction to follow, he suddenly felt a wave of panic. Pasquale understood more Italian than he spoke; the Italian language had had an enormous influence on the Albanian tongue dating back centuries, and, in modern times, Italian was frequently heard on Albanian radio and TV programs broadcast from nearby Italy. But Pasquale spoke the Italian words he knew with such a heavy accent that he was afraid he'd bring attention to himself by asking a railroad worker or a station attendant for directions. He decided to walk over to a taxi driver and show him the address.

The taxi driver looked at the slip of paper and, thinking that Pasquale wanted a ride, started to take Pasquale's bag to put in the taxi. Pasquale held tight to the bag, wanting to know how much it would cost.

The driver, used to dealing with tourists who spoke little or no Italian, sensed what Pasquale wanted to know and held up five fingers for five dollars.

Pasquale held up two.

The driver then held up three on one hand and five with the other, meaning $3.50.

It was more than Pasquale could afford, but, exhausted and on the verge of collapse, he needed to get to the address quickly. Pasquale handed the cabbie his bag, and off they drove.

The ride took only twenty-five minutes. Pasquale stepped out on a gravel road that ran through an olive grove up to a farmhouse and several barns. It was now about seven thirty in the morning, and, although still dark, workers were already moving about the barns, two of whom he heard speaking Albanian.

He approached them and, speaking his native language, said, "Good morning. I heard you speaking Albanian. I just arrived from there. My name is Pasquale."

One of the workers, wearing a baseball-style cap backward, with a barrel chest and thick neck and a face that was flattened as if he had been a boxer, stepped forward with a big smile and shook Pasquale's hand while saying, "Good morning, Pasquale. This is my friend Carlo, who is also from Albania. Pasquale, that's a nice Italian name; I chose Paolo. What is your Albanian name?"

"Hyseni Fiqiri. I was told back home that they were hiring workers here." Pasquale tried not to look as tired as he was, hoping he could get to the person hiring workers immediately.

But Paolo just continued, asking him, "Where are you from in Albania?"

Taking a deep breath and mustering all his patience, Pasquale replied, "Not far from Durrës."

Paolo, acting as if they were suddenly old friends, patted Pasquale on the back and said, "Well, we are from the same area, and I am sure we know some people in common, but I know you must be exhausted, so we can talk later. Right now, let me direct you to the owner. I did hear he wanted to hire more help. There certainly is a lot of work to do here. The owner's name is Franco Masoletti, and you should be able to find him in the cantina at the end of the path behind you. Inside you'll see an office to your left; that is where the Signor Masoletti works."

Happy that there would be no more questions for now, Pasquale said, "Thanks, Paolo. Hopefully I will get hired, and we can catch up later."

"No problem; good luck."

As Pasquale walked the few hundred yards to the office, he kept repeating the few words he knew in Italian over and over again: "*Mi chiamo Pasquale. Sono un bravo operaio e sono molto forte. C'è lavoro qui per me?*" ("My name is Pasquale. I am a good worker and am very strong. Is there work here for me?")

Arriving at the cantina, Pasquale peered through an open door to a back room and saw a man seated at a desk that was covered with piles of papers. The man's head was down, and he was making notes on a legal pad. He was thin, to the point of looking gaunt, in his fifties, with sparse gray hair and a few days of an unshaven beard. When he looked up and saw Pasquale standing at the door, his dark, deep-set eyes and slightly furrowed forehead made Pasquale think he was not welcome and was about to be sent away.

Instead, the man said, "*Venga.*" ("Come in.")

Franco Masoletti had, for years, used a network of contacts in Albania to direct good workers to his farm. He was a businessman first, someone concerned with the legal niceties last, and if he could hire good workers at a fraction of what he had to pay Italian workers, he gained a substantial advantage over his competition. Of course, to have his farm filled with illegal immigrants would normally be risky, but Masoletti was well connected and paid the right people to make sure that he wouldn't be "disturbed."

Pasquale did not yet know that in the south of Italy there were ways of getting around almost any law. The illegal-immigrant trade was a business run by Mafia groups known as 'Ndrangheta in Calabria, Camorra in Campania, and the Sacra Corona Unita in Puglia—to name a few. The latter group was the one with which Franco had been working for years.

These Mafia groups had grown into internationally connected entities since the end of WWII, becoming involved in both legal and illegal enterprises reaching the highest levels of government, financial institutions, and corporations of all types. They were thoroughly entrenched in local affairs, both public and private, from the simple shop owner paying for protection to controlling the garbage collection in Naples, the fresh water supply in entire regions, and, of course, smuggling and narcotics trafficking.

The Italian Parliament had twenty-three felons representing its people, more than any other government in the Western democracies. The only Italian leader who had ever been able to control the Mafia was Mussolini, but even he famously declared, "The Italians are not difficult to govern; they are *impossible* to govern!"

For Franco Masoletti, it was worth it. For the Mafia groups, it was just another profit center. For immigration officials, some other government employees, and local police, it was a second income. Everyone came out a winner—except for the immigrants working for poverty-level wages.

As Pasquale stood in front of Franco Masoletti's desk, he only had to say, "*Mi chiamo Pasquale.*"

Franco had a good idea of the ordeal Pasquale had just gone through and said, "Pasquale, I do have a job for you. You can stay in one of the barns for the time being. You will be given three meals daily and paid twenty-two dollars a day. The job is assured for two weeks, after which you will either be let go or allowed to continue. To start, you will clear fields, getting them ready for spring planting for wheat, our main crop. We also cultivate olive trees and produce olive oil, and if you are around at the end of the year, you'll work on that as well."

Pasquale didn't understand everything Franco said, but he got the gist of the conversation. The most important was "twenty-two dollars a day." Upon hearing that, he felt a wave of relief as the words slowly sank in. He knew the pay was low, but at this point, he was just happy to have work and was confident, given the chance, that he could prove himself worthy of a higher wage.

Franco interrupted his thoughts, saying, "You can get an early lunch near the main barn shortly and meanwhile can get cleaned up in the dormitory on the second floor where you will find an empty bed and a footlocker. You start work in the morning."

When Franco began working on his papers again, Pasquale knew the session had ended, and so after saying, "*Grazie,*" he turned around and left.

Tired almost to the point of total exhaustion, Pasquale had mixed feelings. He felt relief that he had survived the ordeal so far and at least had a start in Italy. But with it came the somber realization that his struggle to earn enough money to allow his wife and children to live above the poverty level was going to be a difficult task.

After a quick early lunch of sandwiches, he collapsed on his bed in the dormitory. He wrapped himself in the thin blanket provided and finally started feeling warmth return to his body. He was soon able to stop shivering and fell into a deep, deep sleep from which he did not stir until the next morning.

He awoke while it was still very dark outside. He looked at his watch and realized that it had stopped working, apparently ruined by the chilly waters of the Adriatic. Everyone around him was still asleep, so he lay there until the others started to stir, and then he got out of bed.

He found Paolo and Carlo, the other Albanians he had met the day before. After a breakfast of coffee, a piece of fruit, and some bread, Pasquale followed them to another barn where a foreman assigned them a tool and instructions as to what they were to do for the day.

Pasquale was given a *vanga* (spade) and joined a group of three other men, one of whom was Carlo. All were directed to walk to a field that was in the process of being cleared. There was lots of underbrush to be dug up and put in a pile for burning. The soil was extremely rocky, and the stones had to be removed and piled in one place.

Although it was backbreaking work, Pasquale was used to it, and he actually felt his strength returning the more he toiled and the warmer it became. February was still cool, but temperatures did get up to the high fifties and occasionally low sixties. Weather-wise, February was a transitional month for Southern Italy but was a good time to start preparing the fields for planting.

Around noon, there was a break for lunch, which consisted of a soup made from vegetables and bread served along with an apple. Coffee was again available along with more bread. It was obvious to Pasquale that the meals were too skimpy to fill the stomachs of such hardworking men.

He sat down with Carlo under a tree away from the other workers and, speaking in their native dialect, asked, "So are the meals always so skimpy? I was always hungry at home too, but I used to feed my chickens more than this. How are the dinners?"

Carlo said, "They just give us enough so our bellies feel only half empty. Ahhh! Dinner is the best meal of the day, but it too is often not enough to fill a belly, so on Sunday, our day off, Paolo and I go to a local market and stock up on additional food we can keep in our lockers, in case we get really hungry."

Pasquale quickly asked, "How much does that cost?"

"Oh, we spend anywhere between twenty dollars to, at the most, thirty. We can only buy food that will last the week in our lockers, so there is not a whole lot we can buy. Fruit, fava beans, bread—but that lasts only a few days—crackers, and some hard-boiled eggs are usually about it. Then we also buy our personal items, like shaving cream, razors, cigarettes, and clothes when we need them."

Pasquale quickly calculated how that would impact his weekly salary of $132 and realized things were going to be tougher than he had originally anticipated. Still, he felt that if he could show he was the best worker there, he would be rewarded.

Two weeks passed quickly, after which Franco Masoletti called Pasquale into his office. Sitting behind the desk, surrounded by piles of papers the same way Pasquale found him when they first met, Franco looked up at Pasquale and said, "The foreman was very pleased with your work, so you can stay on, and you will be given a raise of an additional four dollars a day."

Pasquale was able to understand "additional four dollars a day" and was pleased, although when calculating the number of hours he was working, it still came to less than three dollars per hour, which came to a little over $150 per week. But he had no choice, so he continued and kept giving his absolute all to whatever task was assigned him.

After three months, Pasquale was awakened one morning by a sharp pain in his stomach. He ignored it for several days until it got so bad that he was unable to get out of bed. Carlo, seeing how much pain Pasquale was in, ran as fast as he could to Franco Masoletti's office and breathlessly blurted in his broken Italian, "*Scusi* me, Signor, I sorry disturb you. Ma Pasquale need doctor; he in pain and no can move."

Franco appeared startled at first but after an instant jumped up from his chair and ran to the barn with Carlo close behind. As soon as he entered the room and saw Pasquale writhing in pain, he turned to Paolo, who was standing nearby, and handed him a set of car keys. He said, "Paolo, my car is in front of my office. Get over there as fast as you can, and bring it around front so we can get Pasquale in the back. We need to get him to the doctor right away."

Pasquale, in spite of the pain, could only think, *What is going to happen now? If I lose my job, I will have to return to Albania.* The pain of that thought was almost as bad as the pain in his stomach.

It took only a few minutes for Paolo to bring the car in front of the barn, and four of the workers carried Pasquale, wrapped in a blanket, and laid him onto the backseat of the car. Franco Masoletti and two of the workers drove Pasquale to a doctor's office about twenty minutes away.

Pasquale was moved into an examination room, and when the doctor entered, he was stunned to see that she was a woman. Despite his pain, Pasquale was horrified at having to be examined by a woman, as he had never been treated by a female doctor. He was uncomfortable enough around male doctors and, as a Muslim, even more so around women. In his country, female doctors were for women and male doctors for men. The two simply didn't mix. Sensing his discomfort and obvious pain, in a gentle voice she said, "Good morning, Pasquale; I am *Dottoressa* Perlino. Everything is going to be just fine. I just need to determine where your pain is, so I will have to gently touch your stomach. Just tell me when I touch the area that hurts and areas that do not. As soon as we can pinpoint where the pain is located, we will know how best to treat you."

She then went through a routine examination and arranged for him to immediately have an endoscopy. Pasquale had not eaten in almost two days, so he tolerated the procedure well and waited anxiously for the results. Meanwhile, the doctor had given him some medicine that relieved the pain somewhat. When *Dottoressa* Perlino returned, she told Pasquale, "The results are in, and you have what is called a peptic ulcer. That has resulted in a small hole in your stomach wall that is releasing bacteria into your bloodstream. This must be fixed immediately, so I have scheduled an operation for you for later this afternoon."

Pasquale, feeling panicked and understanding "operation," managed to say, "*Dottoressa*, me illegal immigrant, me must stay to work. Me must send money to my family in Albania. Cannot go home."

At that point, Franco had joined them in the room and heard what Pasquale had said. "Both the *dottoressa* and I can assure you that this will not be an issue. I have already made arrangements for the operation to be performed."

Pasquale, understanding most of what was said, looked at each of them, trying as hard as he could to trust them, knowing that he really had no choice. Smiling, *Dottoressa* Perlino said, "Please do not worry. You are not the first, nor will you be the last, illegal immigrant to need and get medical treatment here without being deported. You have my word."

Pasquale underwent the operation within hours. The operation was successful, but Pasquale was left with damaged intestines that would plague him for the rest of his life. He was told that had he waited any longer, he could have died from the complications.

He remained in the hospital for a week and then was brought back to the farm where he recovered in a small private bedroom that Franco had made available for him. Franco continued to pay Pasquale half of his regular weekly salary the entire time that he was sick. Pasquale was surprised at the care and consideration that Franco had extended to him; it was something he would never forget.

It took a month for Pasquale to get his strength back, during which time Franco made sure he was given three good meals a day. Pasquale then began working again, and after a couple of weeks, he was feeling well enough to work at his old pace.

Franco Masoletti's largesse may not have been completely altruistic. He surely couldn't help but recognize early on what a great worker Pasquale was, noting how he worked with his head down, completely focused on the task at hand, no matter how menial. Pasquale routinely finished in any given day more than three workers combined, and the quality of his work was superb. Franco had never seen anyone quite like Pasquale and didn't want to lose him.

Whatever Franco's motives were, Pasquale didn't care. He wanted to work, he wanted to prove he was worth more, and by dint of that work ethic, he hoped to be rewarded. That may have been what saved his life.

CHAPTER 2
BANKRUPTCY AND CHANGE

During Pasquale's first year after his operation, Franco continued to increase Pasquale's weekly pay. By the end of his first year on Franco's farm, Pasquale was making enough money to send home a decent amount to his wife and children in Albania, so they were slowly able to rise above the poverty subsistence level. He was still spending more money on food and personal necessities than he wanted to, but as an illegal immigrant, he had few other options. They were about to get fewer.

As the year 2000 wound down, Franco ran into financial problems and went bankrupt. Pasquale had no idea why or how it happened, only that all the workers at the farm were laid off. He was shocked at the suddenness and speed with which it all happened. No one knew for sure what transpired, but many speculated that Franco Masoletti probably became overly in debt to the Mafia. It was not uncommon for them to take over property if their debts were not repaid. For Franco, it was probably the preferred choice, considering what the alternatives likely were. A lot of land and businesses had been similarly taken over by various Mafia groups in the south of Italy. It had gotten so bad that food packages found in grocery stores were actually labeled, rather proudly, "Produced on land taken back from the Mafia."

Pasquale was beside himself. He was still checking in with the doctor every two months and was due for another appointment but didn't have the money to pay for the visit. He went to see her and said, "*Dottoressa, mi scusi*, me no have work anymore. Farm went in *bancarotta*. Me can no pay you for *exami*."

She immediately responded, "You do not have to pay me; that is okay. I will check you today, and if all is okay, you don't have to have another exam until a year from now."

She proceeded to examine Pasquale and found that he was in good shape—in fact, surprisingly good shape considering what he had been through. She thought, *It has to be from all that physical labor he does.* She said to Pasquale, "You are doing great. Just be sure to see a doctor in a year from now for an exam. In the meantime, you must eat properly—no alcohol, no spicy food, and eat regularly. Lots of grains, vegetables, and fruit. Always drink lots of water all during the day. Do you understand everything, Pasquale? If not, please ask me, because what I am telling you is very important."

She knew for illegal immigrants eating properly was always a challenge, but now that Pasquale had no work, it would be especially hard.

As Pasquale nodded and said, "*Capisco bene*," she suddenly had an idea. "I want you to speak to my husband. He hires work crews from this area for farms up north. I will be happy to recommend you."

Pasquale instantly perked up and smiled. "*Molte grazie, Dottoressa.*"

The doctor knew full well that Pasquale had to be an exceptional worker; Franco Masoletti would never have taken the time to help a worker, as he had in Pasquale's case, unless that worker was very special.

A few days later, Pasquale met Renato, the doctor's husband. Renato was the least likely person Pasquale would have thought would be married to the doctor. He had none of *Dottoressa* Perlino's gentleness but was rather gruff, and his stocky build made him look more like an enforcer than a businessman married to a doctor. Renato spoke in a somewhat-raspy voice that made him sound like an impersonator of the Godfather, which Pasquale had actually seen on television once in Albania (dubbed in Italian).

So sounding like the Godfather, Renato—looking shorter than his 5'8" height and bending over as if telling Pasquale a secret—explained, "I have a new crew of four men that I am taking to the Chianti area up north, leaving by car in two days. Housing and meals are provided, and the work will be on farms in the region, mostly vineyards. You'll be part of a crew that will be driven to and from a farm each day. Work is six days a week with Sundays off. Pay will start at $3.25 an hour for a nine-hour day, but $3.25 per day is deducted for your transportation to and from the work site. Any questions?"

Pasquale had none. He understood enough to know he would be working nine hours a day and receiving $3.25 for eight of them. That meant $156 per week—not great, but enough to keep on sending money home to his family.

One week later in Chianti, Pasquale found that he was the only foreigner in a crew of five men; the rest were all Italians from the southern part of Italy where unemployment was rampant. The crew started working one day after their arrival at local farms in the area, clearing fields and preparing them for the planting of vineyards.

While his attention was, as usual, completely focused on his work, Pasquale couldn't help but notice that Chianti was a very, very pretty place. Tall, majestic cypress trees lined many of the long driveways up to the main farmhouses, and the vineyards, olive groves, and wheat fields were planted and maintained with absolute precision. It was springtime, and the fields left fallow were covered with beautiful multicolored wildflowers. He could see that keeping everything so pristine took a lot of work—the type of work he would love to do. Yes, the place was pretty, perhaps the prettiest he had ever seen.

When Pasquale arrived in Chianti, there were a total of fifteen workers living in Renato's house. There was also a cook who took care of their meals, as well as a housecleaner to do their laundry.

Pasquale was fairly comfortable, as food this time was abundant and he didn't have to buy anything additional to eat. He was sending practically all his earnings to his wife and children, leaving a little for himself to buy a few necessities from time to time. Pasquale was frugal out of necessity. His wife was the same, but they had three growing children. Even though he was sending home about $125 a week, it didn't go very far. In those days, $125 a week would have been considered poverty level in most European countries for a family of five. As little as it was, however, it was more than he would have earned had he stayed in Albania.

He generally worked with the same four-man crew with whom he'd come up north, and it didn't take more than a few weeks for Pasquale to be recognized as a hardworking man with superstrength. Pasquale earned most of the Italian workers' respect because of this, but others still often expressed rather blatant prejudice. Their feeling was that Pasquale, as a foreigner, had taken a job away from an Italian. Although some may have harbored these prejudices, everyone still wanted Pasquale to work on their squad because they knew he worked so hard that it made it easier on them.

One day after they had just finished a project on a farm near Siena, Renato announced that Pasquale's squad would be going to a new location in the morning. Whenever a change was made from one location to another, there was always great anticipation among the crew. What would it be like working for the new owners? Would they be fair or overly demanding? Would the farm be pleasant or grim? Pasquale hoped to find someone that he could work for on his own but knew that as long as he worked for Renato, it wasn't going to happen. Without legal papers and status, he had to hope he would find someone who would take him on even as an illegal.

Early the next morning, the crew was driven to the farm to meet the owners and start work. On the drive over, Renato explained, "This could be one of the best projects any of you will ever work on up here. The job is to clear and clean up the grounds of a forty-acre farm where most of the land was abandoned not so long after the end of the Second World War. The owners are an American man and his wife, an Italian woman, who live in New York City."

One of the workers interjected with a whistle, "Is she *bella*?"

Renato, his temper flaring, said, "One more remark like that and you're fired. You can figure out on your own how to get your ass back home because I won't pay you a dime, even for the work you have already done this week. Understood?"

The man looked down at his feet, avoiding Renato's menacing glare and nodded his head. Renato screamed, "I didn't hear you! Speak up, or get off right here and now and go back south."

The man said, "Yes."

Renato, his face crimson with anger, continued to scream, "Yes is not good enough. It is 'Yes, sir.'"

The man answered, "Yes, sir."

Renato didn't stop, demanding, "Louder, so everyone here can hear you."

The man yelled, "Yes, sir!"

"Now," Renato continued, "if any of you dare say a disrespectful word to or about any of my clients, you will be fired on the spot and docked any pay for that week. I work hard to get clients so you can have work, and I won't tolerate any of you fucking it up with a foul-mouthed remark like that. Now, if you are ready to hear me continue, just sit there and listen."

Everyone nodded; most had experienced Renato's rage before and seen workers kicked out. This was the first time for Pasquale, though, and he was surprised at Renato's sudden burst of anger. He couldn't believe that he was listening to the man married to the gentle *Dottoressa* Perlino.

Renato continued, "I heard the owners are good people to work for from contractors I know that have done work there. If you all do a good job, the project will likely last a long time, even through most of the winter, when I usually have to let a lot of you go until the spring. So if you want to stick around and get paid, be sure to do a good job."

On hearing this, Pasquale realized he had forgotten about there being no work in the winter months and thought, *Oh Dio, I forgot about saving money for my family during the winter. I have to make sure I keep this job no matter what.*

CHAPTER 3

HYSENI

Pasquale's given name was Hyseni Fiqiri, and he was the fourth of six children born to a Muslim family in rural Albania.

For much of Hyseni's life, what constituted hope, the extent of his ambition, and the dreamed-for possibilities of the future amounted to nothing more than the anxious wish that there would be enough to eat that day. In that respect, Hyseni Fiqiri was no exception. Albania had long been a growth culture for hard-luck stories because the history of Albania was just that: one hard-luck story, centuries long. Albania—like the rest of the Balkans—had the misfortune of sitting along a favored route for invaders from both east and west. Invasions and occupations had left the area a checkerboard of religious and ethnic enclaves, some quite conflicting.

For centuries, it had been a part of the Ottoman Empire. In the early part of the twentieth century, Albania got one of its few breaks, declaring independence in 1912 as the withered remnants of the Ottoman realm began to crumble. In the end, however, it wasn't much of a break.

King Zog, who took power in the years after World War I, turned out to be less interested in Albania and the welfare of Albanians than he was in staying king of Albania. From 1928 on, Mussolini's Fascist Italy increasingly propped him up. Come 1939, wanting to compete with Hitler's early conquests, Mussolini went whole hog and invaded, giving Zog the boot. Thereafter, things continually went from bad to worse for the Albanians. When Mussolini's rule began to falter in 1943, the Germans took over, and when WWII ended in 1945, Albania found itself under the iron-fisted and corrupt rule of dictator Enver Hoxha, who brought the country into the Soviet Union's Eastern Bloc.

The Soviets and their Eastern Bloc puppets talked a good game about a Communist worker's paradise, but the Eastern Europe of Cold War days was a grim, oppressed, economically depressed place, and Albania—thanks to some unfortunate geography—was arguably more so than the other Iron Curtain countries. Albania was hemmed against the Adriatic by unfriendly territory on all three landward sides. To its south was Greece, allied with the West, and along its eastern and northern borders was Yugoslavia, which, although Communist, had remained free of the Soviets and was charting its own more-or-less independent course under Marshal Tito.

And then, because Albania's was a history in which things could never get so bad that they couldn't get worse, Hoxha, considered a poster boy Stalinist who was even more ruthless than his one-time idol, split with the Soviets over their de-Stalinization program in 1960. He hooked himself to the Red Chinese, who propped him up with feeble financial aid, only to cut him off eighteen years later.

No matter who was sitting in the capital, two things never changed about Albania: most of the population remained impoverished, and outside of the coastal plains and cities, the country remained ungovernable.

The country's rugged terrain—70 percent mountainous—allowed and protected an insular tribalism, with mountain villages that were minisocieties unto themselves, each with its own set of customs, each not caring a damn about whatever particular power claimed rule over the country at any given time. His entire life, Hyseni Fiqiri would hear stories about outsiders going up into the hills, never to be heard from again, and about how even heavily armed and armored Communist forces refused to go into those hills.

According to family lore, Hyseni's relatives had been living pretty comfortably around the time Albania first declared independence, but the next half century was hard going for them. By the time Hyseni was born on May 17, 1960, the family farm in Rrogozhinë—a small rural town in the southwestern part of the country—had been reduced to the house and a small patch of land around it.

Albania had always been an agrarian economy. Prior to WWII, large landowners had controlled most of the land, but under the Communists, most of the upper-class property owners had been exiled and their lands redistributed. This redistribution took the form of small parcels barely big enough to provide enough for the families living on them. Hoxha's attempts to push the country toward industrialization after World War II were disastrous, resulting in a collapse of public infrastructure, nonexistent medical assistance, and, with the Communists closing religious institutions, the disappearance of social support systems that had been important to Albania's Muslims and Christians alike. In other words, a country that had long been poor got a whole lot poorer.

The wear and tear of war, neglect, mismanagement, corruption, and sheer poverty showed everywhere in Rrogozhinë, which sat below the forest-covered foothills leading eastward to the rugged interior high country. The main streets were riddled with potholes, and the side roads were unpaved. The buildings were run down—the graceful architecture of an earlier, better time hidden under coats of grime and neglect. But even in their disrepair, these older buildings had a certain charm—albeit tragic—completely absent in the cellblock-looking apartment buildings that went up alongside them, the trademark dwellings of the Cold War Eastern Bloc. Inside these drab concrete cubes families were stacked atop each other, crammed into tiny, equally drab apartments.

Like 90 percent of Albanians, Hyseni's family was poor. The family cultivated their small patch of farmland by growing some lettuce, fava beans, garlic, and zucchini at a barely subsistence level. There was no promise of a future, and Hyseni's only memories of his early years are of the daily quest for food from either what they scratched out of the ground or could barter for.

Hyseni was enrolled in school at age five. While in first grade, he came home one day to find a group of his father's friends at the house. He was sure it was some sort of party and ran excitedly to his mother to ask what was happening. He found her in tears, and she told him his father had died that day of a brain aneurism while working in the fields.

He was so young at the time that he now has little memory of his father (who was actually his mother's second husband; her first had died in one of the many Balkan Wars). One of the few things he does know of his father was that he was Greek and had fled his home country when the Germans occupied it during WWII. Hyseni would always be quick to announce that part of his heritage to people, even years later: "Pasquale no 100 percent Albanian. Pasquale got Greek blood too!" But that never relieved the agony he suffered from the prejudice he would encounter in Italy against Albanians.

His mother was overwhelmed by raising six children on her own, embittered over having lost two husbands, and she took it all out on Hyseni, beating him with a stick for the slightest misbehavior. He would flee the house, sometimes skipping school (which he hadn't much cared for anyway) and hiding out for days—even weeks—at a time. He did small chores and ran errands for his father's friends in return for enough food and shelter to survive.

At age twelve, he was legally able to quit school, which he did, though he could barely read or write. He immediately went to work as a farmer's helper. His pittance of a pay, along with that of an older brother who worked on the rail lines, went to keeping the family fed, although this was more out of concern for their younger brother and sister (two older sisters had left home to marry) than out of any sense of allegiance to or affection for their abusive mother. From those days forward he carried a dark vow in his heart that he would not attend his mother's funeral (he kept that vow when she passed away in 2011, though he did return to Albania a few months later to visit his family and pay his respects). By the time Hyseni had quit school, his mother had remarried. Since Hyseni's stepfather was a moderate Muslim and because all the mosques had been closed under the Communists, most of what Hyseni learned about Islam came from this man.

Not knowing his biological father, Hyseni grew close to his stepfather. His stepfather was not just his teacher but also a role model. His stepfather treated him with a kindness his mother never showed him. From his stepfather, Hyseni learned what it meant to be a man. His stepfather taught him to believe in Allah and the basic precepts of the Muslim faith, one of which was first to take care of your own family. If something was left over, offer it to your neighbor. If they did not need it and something more was left over, give it to the needy. Most importantly to Hyseni, his stepfather taught him that Allah alone decides when you die and if you have obeyed Muslim law, Allah will be kind to you.

Hyseni soon found personally that Albania was a place where things were never so bad that they couldn't get worse. At the age of sixteen, Hyseni lost his surrogate dad to a brain tumor. Shortly afterward, his older brother was hit by a train and killed while working on the railroad. Along with the emotional trauma of these losses now came the full burden of having to support his family entirely alone. He worked where he could: local factories, loading trucks, and other hard labor that toughened him physically and made him incredibly strong. These factories were controlled by the Communist government, and Hyseni often thought, while performing backbreaking tasks, *The Communist system is really for people with fat brains. They pay you less than two dollars a day and tell you the system is taking care of you. Whoever believes that and accepts it as fact has to be really dumb. A dog has better sense than that.*

A year later, Hyseni was married and soon had a daughter. He was then drafted for military service, and after passing some background checks by the strict Communist government, he was able to join the Albanian navy, serving on a torpedo boat. It's hard to imagine what kind of navy a country as small as Albania could have, but at least Hyseni's service provided a monthly stipend that he could send home to his wife and daughter. His younger brother also began working and was able to bring in a small amount of money for their mother and him to squeeze by.

Hyseni was released from the navy three years later. He was

twenty-two years old and had no better prospects than when he'd gone into the service. After his return, he and his wife had another daughter, but again he was unable to support them. His only opportunity was the two-dollar-a-day factory job. They lived in one room, perhaps nine feet by nine feet, nothing more than a shack really. There was a plastic tub in one corner for washing, and they did their cooking on an open fire just outside the door. For showers and a bathroom, they used a nearby school's locker rooms. His wife took care of their two children while he desperately tried to find work.

The Communist-engineered economic disaster that was Albania had created an avalanche of illegal immigrants fleeing the country's horrendous conditions. By the early 1990s, hundreds of thousands were attempting to illegally enter Albania's comparatively prosperous neighbor to the south: Greece.

The Albania-Greece border was a replica of the no-man's-land between East and West Germany during the tensest days of the Cold War and was just as lethal. A high, electrified fence demarcated the border, and heavily armed guards were posted within easy eyesight of one another all along the barrier, with only a few breaks where the terrain was impassably mountainous. On each side of the long, winding fence, the ground had been cleared and plowed, making it virtually impossible for anyone to cross undetected.

Although the fence would come down when the Communist regime collapsed along with the other Eastern Bloc regimes in the early 1990s, the border was still heavily patrolled to stop the flow of Albanians into Greece, as well as to deal with an even bigger problem for the Greek authorities: drug trafficking. If an Albanian was caught crossing the border into Greece, the sentence could be up to a year in jail. Once caught, the person's identity was kept on file, and if apprehended a second time, the penalty was even harsher.

That was the law, but in practice, the treatment of the apprehended relied strictly on the disposition of the guards at the scene. In 1992, three Albanians attempting to cross the border were captured by Greek guards who beat them mercilessly and then tied them to the back of a tractor and dragged them through the streets of a nearby village where the residents continued to beat them. One of the Albanians died while the other two miraculously survived, only to be sentenced to prison.

Such brutality was not spontaneous but the tragically inevitable product of centuries of animosity between the two peoples and situations in which Greeks had been living for generations in Albania and vice versa. Greeks living in Albania were persecuted by the Albanian government and were not allowed to so much as speak their native language or practice any form of religion. For their part, Albanians living in Greece were also scorned in the sadly familiar way immigrant groups are often mistreated in countries around the world and for the same xenophobic reasons: fear of losing jobs to low-paid immigrant laborers, a rise in crime rates where immigrants clustered, and clashing differences in social values and mores.

The economic conditions in Albania in the early 1990s were the worst in Europe, with abject poverty gripping most of the country's inhabitants, a result of the piled-on decades of failures from one corrupt and inept regime to another. Desperate Albanians—too desperate to wait for proper immigration documentation—chanced crossing into Greece through the one sector that wasn't heavily patrolled: the Pindus Mountains on the southeast Albania-Greece border.

Not only did border crossers have to worry about the Greek border guards but also ski-masked members of Albanian gangs, armed with Kalashnikov assault rifles, who roamed the area attacking and robbing their own people. Caught by the gangs, the least the border crossers had to worry about was losing what little money and few valuables they may have been carrying with them; in the worst-case scenario, they'd be murdered, added to the countless souls who had already disappeared in the Albanian hinterlands.

The Albanian gangs were the descendants of the people who had lived in the country's mountain villages for generations, isolated from the political rises and falls affecting the cities and towns of the lands below. In their isolation, they were a government unto themselves, imposing a Mafia-style rule by warlords and their followers. Their main source of income was drug trafficking, and their route happened to be through the same passage, the Pindus Mountains, that Albanians searching for work took into Greece. Knowing all this, but with his wife and now three children to feed and no way to do so, Hyseni felt compelled to take a potentially deadly risk.

Hyseni slipped into Greece several times, and having a valid Albanian passport, he was able to return home by bus through official border checkpoints. That way, he was able to carry home the money that he'd earned in Greece.

The first time Hyseni made the trip, he spent almost a month living in the woods before finally coming across an Albanian shepherd tending his flock. Hyseni had never had trouble making friends—he was a natural charmer—and soon convinced the shepherd he could help him with his flock. In exchange, the shepherd gave him food and a place to sleep in a hut next to the flock. The shepherd worked for a farmer who owned hundreds of acres of land where he grew tobacco, cotton, and fruit trees. He introduced Hyseni to the farmer.

Despite Hyseni's inability to speak Greek, he epitomized the reputation of Albanians having a great sense of humor. Laughter kept the Albanians going in the darkest of times, and Hyseni had been able to develop his own, distinct brand of humor, which, when combined with his warm smile, inevitably charmed those he met even upon a first encounter. But his challenge now was to ingratiate himself without being able to speak the native tongue, and having no money, it was paramount he be able to connect with those who could possibly help him.

In the short time he stayed with the shepherd, he learned a few simple words and phrases—enough to say, "I am looking for a job," "I am a good worker," and "I drive tractor and do whatever you need me to do." That and his disarming manner was enough to get the farmer to hire him immediately.

On another of his crossings, he was stopped by Greek border guards. This time he knew immediately that there would be trouble. One border guard got behind him and held a rifle to his back, while the other, from about eight feet away, jumped up in the air and hit him in the stomach with a ferocious flying martial arts kick. Hyseni saw it coming and tensed every muscle in his body, thus absorbing the kick, hardly moving. He purposely showed no grimace of pain on his face, even though the pain was excruciating. The guard became visibly angrier and kicked him again. Hyseni again tensed his body. At that point, in a rage, the guard kicked Hyseni's legs out from under him, knocking him to the ground. After two more kicks to his body, the guard hissed, "When you get up, go back to Albania where you belong. If I see you again, I will shoot you," and then walked away, followed by the other guard. It took perhaps five minutes for Hyseni to stagger to his feet. He was in terrible pain and vomited blood, but he managed to head back to the Albanian border. It took days for him to recover and for the pain to subside. The blows he'd suffered could have killed a man who was not as strong as Hyseni. For Hyseni, it just meant he would have to be even more careful when—not if—he attempted another crossing. There was no other option as far as he was concerned. It was truly a matter of survival for his family.

Hyseni made one last attempt to cross into Greece in 1993. He slowly made his way through the rocky terrain, navigating the escarpments and steep slopes of the forbidding mountainsides. He waited until five in the evening or so to make his crossing; that would put the sun at his back, enabling him to see ahead while putting a blinding light in the eyes of anyone looking his way from across the border. His greatest danger at this point, he knew, was trying to cross at the same time as one of the gangs moving a drug-laden mule train through the area.

He was walking at a swift pace when he stopped, thinking he heard the sound of donkeys behind him. He quickly sought cover in the thick underbrush about thirty yards from the trail. He waited there, motionless, for over ten minutes, and then the first donkey in the caravan appeared and ambled slowly by. Hyseni remained still, holding his breath until the rest of the caravan passed.

He doubted that another donkey train would be crossing that night, and if he kept far enough back, he'd be able to follow the caravan's trail to the border. Once there, he hoped they would cross undetected. If they were stopped, he'd have to hole up in the woods (by then, he was used to living in the forest and knew how to survive on edible plants and found water) and try for a crossing another evening, something he had done on a previous occasion.

Hyseni stayed under cover until he saw the caravan and its gang return after having delivered their cargo to the cars and trucks that had been waiting for them on the other side of the border. He knew it was now safe for him to make his move.

He took off running but was surprised when three ski-masked men, brandishing Kalashnikovs, seemed to appear out of nowhere. Speaking to him in Albanian, the apparent leader, with a rifle pointed at Hyseni's head, shouted at him, "Don't move; just empty your pockets, and drop everything to the ground, including any cash and coins."

As Hyseni obeyed, one of the gang members noticed his watch, and even though it was a cheap one, he yelled, "Take that watch off, and drop it to the ground."

The last thing Hyseni had was his passport, and as he was about to reluctantly drop that to the ground, the leader said, "You can keep your passport. Now take ten steps back to that tree behind you, turn and face it, and don't move. Stay there. If we see you move, we will shoot you."

Hyseni obeyed, and while he was facing the tree, he could hear them gathering his things from the ground, and then he heard their footsteps as they walked away.

Remembering how many people had disappeared in those mountains, thinking of how much worse things could have gone if one of the three had suddenly changed his mind, Hyseni immediately bolted toward the Greek border and didn't stop running for over two hours. He knew that he faced the double threat of the Greek border guards and the Albanian gang. Each time he stopped to catch his breath, a trembling started from the pit of his stomach and then spread throughout the rest of his body. He could feel the tingling in his limbs, even to the roots of his hair. He could only make it stop by moving. So he continued to walk and jog throughout the night, wanting to put as much distance as possible between himself and the border.

He made his way to the farm where the Albanian shepherd had introduced him after his first crossing. The owner welcomed him back and, upon hearing of how he had been robbed, gave him a day's pay in advance and a place to stay in a barn. Hyseni's work ethic had ingratiated him with the farmer, and the job lasted close to two years, during which he learned to speak a little Greek and was able to send some money home—not much, but far more than he could have ever earned in Albania.

All was going well until the day the farmer told him the farm was in financial trouble and he could no longer afford to keep Hyseni on. Hyseni was saddened for losing not only the job but also the owner's friendship, as the two had forged a close relationship (in fact, they would continue to remain in contact for years afterward).

Hyseni then spent the next two years sporadically living in the woods, occasionally finding work, but never enough. It was now 1997, and he finally gave up on the idea of trying to make a go of it in Greece. But the Albania he returned to was in even worse shape than when he had left.

By that time, the Communist regime in Albania had fallen, but the economic damage done by decades of their rule was not quickly undone. Poverty and unemployment remained rife, the new government committed its own economic missteps, and 1996 saw public dissatisfaction and frustration manifest in widespread rioting. By 1997, the country seemed on the verge of collapse. The Albanian Parliament declared a state of emergency, and an international force—including a large contingent of Italians—arrived to try to stabilize the country.

Hyseni dared not try another border crossing. The deteriorating conditions in the country had forced a step-up in border security on both sides, with Albanian guards trying to keep Albanians in and the Greeks trying to keep them out.

But doing nothing was not an option.

The distance between Albania and the southeastern part of the Italian boot was less than seventy miles, depending on where one departed—almost identical to the distance from Cuba to Florida. And much as Cubans looked across a narrow band of water to a place that promised something better, so too did thousands of Albanians look to Italy.

As in any similar border situation, there were those who would smuggle anyone who could pay across the Adriatic to Italy.

Hyseni's situation was now not a question of "doing better" but, rather, a question of *survival.* He could not watch his family live in such squalor, perhaps die in it, and do nothing.

CHAPTER 4

LEAP OF FAITH

It was a biting cold February late afternoon. An already low sun cast ominously dark shadows on the dilapidated building facades lining both sides of the half-paved, half-muddy potholed street. Streetlamps appeared randomly with no apparent forethought or plan. Many had no lightbulbs, scavenged by desperate locals looking for anything of value to trade for much-needed provisions. The few lights in working order made the street more moribund rather than less. The people hurrying along the street that afternoon had the collars of their threadbare coats turned up, their chins tucked inside and heads down, trying to shield themselves from the bitter winter winds.

One man—not tall, about 5'5", slightly built—walked with a determined step. He was fit; the white puffs of breath coming from his mouth showed him breathing slowly despite his rapid pace. The dark, piercing eyes under equally dark, bushy eyebrows—framed by his upturned collar, full black mustache, and the wool ski hat pulled down over his ears—were hard with purpose.

As he turned a corner, one of the few working streetlights illuminated a storefront with blackened windows and a single solid-wood door. He stopped in front of the door and knocked lightly. It opened immediately. He entered a small room smelling of stale beer and cigarette smoke. The man who had opened the door stepped back to sit at a table, picked up his smoldering cigarette from an ashtray, and turned back to the opened newspaper he had been reading.

The room had several overhead lights casting a bluish tint over the badly painted and peeling cream-colored walls. There was a small bar with a thin, bored, balding, middle-aged bartender. The three stools in front of the bar were empty. Two men played dominoes and drank beers at one of the six tables in the room, each with a checkered tablecloth and four wooden chairs.

At another table tucked into the corner of the room Hyseni saw a broad-shouldered, barrel-chested man, his neck so thick that even with the top two buttons of his shirt undone, his collar still appeared tight. He was probably in his forties, with dark hair slicked back into a ponytail neatly tied by a gold band. He had large, drooping, nonchalant brown eyes. By the standards of fashion in that neighborhood, he was elegantly dressed, wearing a wool jacket over the open-collared shirt. The cuffs of his shirt protruded from the jacket, revealing diamond-studded gold cuff links. On the table in front of him sat a cup of coffee and a plate of biscotti.

When the man saw Hyseni enter the room, he raised a hand ever so slightly to signal him over to his table.

Hyseni nodded and stepped over. "Mr. Rigovia, I am Hyseni Fiqiri."

The man at the table nodded and gestured for him to sit.

Hyseni took off his wool cap, unbuttoned his coat, and sat at the table, never taking his eyes off Rigovia.

"I was expecting you," Rigovia said. "I'm happy to see you are punctual. Do you have the money?"

Hyseni reached into his inside coat pocket, withdrew an envelope, and pushed it across the table to Rigovia. "It's all there as requested: eight hundred dollars. You can count it if you want."

Rigovia smiled. "I'll do that later. If the eight hundred is not there, you won't be allowed on board tomorrow night. Now let me tell you how this works. You'll be at the dock tomorrow evening at 11:00 p.m. by the tea warehouse in Vlorë. Wear clothes that you'll be throwing away as soon as you land. You'll be allowed to carry one bag; I suggest it be plastic and watertight, as you're going to get very wet during the crossing. When you reach the beach near Lecce, you'll run into the woods at the edge of the beach. There, you'll get rid of your wet clothes and change into the dry ones from your bag."

Hyseni asked, "Can I keep the wet clothes?"

Rigovia replied firmly, "No. They will only slow you down. You have to get out of there as soon as possible. The area is constantly being patrolled for clandestine immigrants. The faster you move, the better it is. The clothes are worth far less than you being arrested and deported."

Rigovia patiently continued, "From the woods, you'll head toward a main highway you can't miss seeing from the woods. Wait there until you see a blue taxi pull over to the side of the road. Work your way to the taxi while staying inside the trees. By the time you arrive, he'll have opened his truck as if changing a tire. As soon as there's no traffic passing by, run and get into the trunk. There will be two other passengers joining you from the boat. The driver will cover you up and take all of you to the train station in Lecce. From there, you can catch a train to Foggia where I'm told you have a contact for work and a place to stay." Hyseni nodded, concentrating on every word Rigovia was saying.

Rigovia continued, "There'll be a total of thirty men on board with you. Each group of three men has their own instructions, so when you arrive, you'll be scattered in different directions. As you know, I have organized this on many occasions before, so we know what we're doing and how best to get through any difficulties. The two others you're being paired with are called Giancarlo and Federico; those are the Italian names they plan to use once in Italy. Do you have a name you want to use?"

Hyseni thought for a moment, not having expected the question. He remembered his father telling him that he had met a nice Italian soldier during WWII named Pasquale. "I'll use the name Pasquale."

"Okay," said Rigovia. "By the time you arrive in Italy, my contact there, who speaks Albanian, will accompany the taxi driver. He'll be expecting a Pasquale along with a Federico and Giancarlo, whom you'll meet on the boat. Do you have any questions?"

"How long will the trip take?"

"You'll be on board a thirty-two-foot Combat Rubber Assault boat with two powerful outboard engines capable of going close to twenty-five miles an hour in calm seas, which is what's expected tomorrow night. With that and no visible moon, you should make the trip in around three hours."

It all sounded simple and straightforward enough, but Hyseni was thinking, *Twenty-four thousand dollars a boatload explains those gold and diamond cuff links and I am sure a lot of other things. And you haven't mentioned the number of times your boats have capsized, killing all those on board.*

However, Hyseni had known what the odds were before he had even made plans to leave Albania, and he still considered the trip worth the risk. He also knew that Rigovia was reliable; once he accepted your money, you would be making the trip on his boat.

Hyseni got up from the table, buttoned up his coat, and shook Rigovia's hand.

Rigovia didn't stand, but he smiled and said, "Good luck, Hyseni. I hope things work out for the best in Italy."

Hyseni left, thinking, *This **better** work. I just spent eight hundred dollars, which took me two years to save. If this fails, my family will be in worse shape than they are now.*

That night, Hyseni packed his one waterproof bag. He struggled with deciding what clothes he should wear, knowing that he would be throwing them away at the end of the trip. He had never thrown away clothes before; he always wore them until they were worn out, and then he'd find some use for them in the house, such as cleaning rags. Nothing ever went to waste in that impoverished household.

The next day, he said his good-byes to his family, giving his wife and three children especially long hugs. He didn't know when he would see them again but knew it would probably not be for years. He hadn't had the heart to reveal that to his children.

His wife had seen other women's husbands make the trip, some never returning, never calling for their families again. But she also believed—*knew*—that Hyseni was different.

They had struggled practically their whole lives together and had often discussed how they could make a better life for their children. Both reached the same unspoken conclusion after Hyseni's last, unrewarding, trip to Greece. They were out of options unless they wanted to stay in Albania and literally die a slow death. He and his wife now had two daughters and a son. Their children were young enough to dream and hope for something better, and this was a chance—their only chance—to deliver on the dreams of their children.

She knew her husband, she knew his strength and determination, and she knew his devotion. He would call for them, even if it were years from now. She could be as tough as he was, and she would never stop believing in him, even when he doubted himself.

Hyseni decided to hitch a ride toward the Albanian port of Vlorë a hundred miles away rather than spend money on a bus ride. He had taken fifty dollars to hold him over until he got work once he landed in Italy. Whatever other money he had in the world he left with his wife. It wasn't much, but if she knew anything, it was how to survive and feed her family even if the meals were meager.

When Hyseni arrived at Vlorë, he had a few hours to spare and wandered down to the tea warehouse where he found a number of other men, each carrying a waterproof bag of belongings, a sure sign that they were all passengers on the same boat. He soon found Giancarlo and Federico and introduced himself as Pasquale.

It seemed strange for him to use that name, but he knew he had to start getting used to it. Hyseni was not an easy name for Italians to pronounce, especially since the letter *H* was rarely heard in spoken Italian.

Time went by quickly, and after verifying their identities, using their Italian names as passwords, all thirty men were soon herded onto a rubber craft. It was more ominous looking than Pasquale had imagined, but his time in the Albanian navy on a torpedo boat had left him no stranger to boats or the open sea. He knew enough to realize that February was a tough time to take any voyage in an open boat.

At 11:00 p.m. sharp, with Pasquale seated in the bow of the boat, the two outboard engines thrummed to life. The helmsman gave quick instructions to everyone. "Listen up, everyone. The trip should go smoothly tonight. The sea is calm, and there is no moon, so it will be difficult to spot us. For your safety during the trip, I want you all to locate the lines running along the inside of the boat. Is there anyone that can't find them?"

It took a few moments and a little shuffling in their seats, but everyone soon nodded that they saw them.

The pilot continued, "I want everyone to hold on to those lines at all times. Don't lean over the sides for any reason. Anyone needing to go to the bathroom should go now; there won't be another opportunity. If anyone gets seasick, don't let go of the lines. If you see someone get sick, pass the word back to me; I'll slow down so they can heave overboard. Companions, hold on to anyone throwing up so they don't fall overboard. No lights of any kind are to be used. If the Italian Coast Guard spots us, I'll either turn back or, if we're close enough to shore, tell you to jump overboard and swim for the beach. This rarely, if ever, happens and certainly not at this time of year when it's dark and this cold, but you all must be prepared for any contingency. There will be no time to hesitate or question. If you are going to successfully enter Italy, you must be prepared for any eventuality. Any questions?"

Someone joked and asked, "When is dinner being served?" Everyone laughed, including the helmsman. The helmsman then pulled in the docking lines and accelerated slowly, moving away from the dock.

Hyseni turned his back and leaned against the bow of the boat, facing aft toward the helmsman. He could just make out the faces of the other men seated in front of him and saw they were as nervous and anxious as he was.

The boat left the dock and proceeded slowly until it cleared the breakwater and pushed out into the open Adriatic Sea.

Hyseni felt a cold chill run up his spine as he watched the coast slowly disappear into the darkness behind him. The driver opened the throttle of both engines, and with a roar the bow of the boat lifted up and began surfing along the ocean, bouncing from tiny wave to tiny wave. Hyseni immediately felt the pounding of the rubber craft radiating through his body and thought, *I don't know if I can take this for three straight hours.* The boat picked up speed, and the icy water sprayed up and settled on everyone on board.

For the next three hours, Hyseni held on to the lines next to him with his bag of belongings between his knees. He tried to picture the faces of his wife and children to take his mind off the numbing chill and pain of the cold water showering down on him, soaking through his clothes to the skin.

Because he was facing backward, he only knew they were getting closer to land when the man seated in front of him began pointing and yelling, "There it is! There's Italy! I can see it now!"

Hyseni tried to turn himself around to take a look, but his hands were so stiff from the cold that they were locked around the line he had been holding on to for hours. His body felt frozen. He knew he had to start moving if he was going to be able to jump onto land, so he painfully, inch by inch, began to move and turn every part of his body, starting with each finger joint and working his way up his arms and down his back to his legs and feet.

The boat began to slow, and as Hyseni tried to turn to see how far they were from shore, the helmsman yelled, "Everyone overboard now! Get going! There's an Italian Coast Guard cutter coming! Swim to shore and follow the instructions given to you as soon as you get to the beach. Jump! Dammit, jump now!"

Hyseni moved instantly, instinctively, knowing that if he didn't jump, life was over for him and his family. He tied his bag of belongings around his waist as he stood up, and then he jumped.

As the water closed over him, the wintry Adriatic hit him like an electric shock. He immediately got his bearings as he broke the surface and began swimming to the shore. From the water, he couldn't tell how far he had to swim. He could see some lights but couldn't tell whether they were near or far. As he swam, numbness spread throughout his whole body. It was an effort to move his arms and legs, which were weighed down by his shoes. He was dragging all his possessions in the plastic bag tied to his waist, and it was beginning to feel heavier and heavier. He was sure this was the end.

PART II

RICHARD

CHAPTER 5

SUPERMAN

It was a crystal clear spring morning on April 12, 2001. The sun illuminated the valley before my wife and I in every exquisite detail. My farmhouse—Ceppeto—sat on the highest hilltop in this part of the Chianti region, two thousand feet above sea level, looking out over a valley stretching five miles to the other side where Radda, an ancient eleventh-century fortress, perched on another hilltop facing us. In between, spread out before us like a patchwork quilt, were rectangular vineyards, olive groves, wheat fields, patches of woods, and fields left fallow that were filled with multicolored wildflowers. Local lore had it that this was the location of the Garden of Eden. Less speculative was the fact that this was the place where Leonardo da Vinci painted the soothingly hypnotic background for his *Mona Lisa*.

Against this backdrop, promptly at 8:00 a.m., a van pulled into our driveway, and out stepped the stocky man we knew as Renato. One of the contractors my wife and I were using to refurbish Ceppeto had recommended Renato's services: supplying crews of workers on a temporary basis. In our area, Renato provided manpower for farms for cultivation and harvesting, as well as for clearing land for planting— just what we needed. We'd contacted him for a crew of five men.

They climbed out of the van behind Renato. Four were clearly Italian, varying in height from about 5'7" to 6'. All were thin, with dark eyes, black hair, and tan skin from working full days outdoors in the sun.

But the last man out of the van was short, no more than 5'5". I noticed him right away because, while the other men stepped out of the van, this one jumped to the ground as if he were jumping over a hurdle. His exaggerated leap was matched with a big grin that gleamed underneath a bushy mustache. With his baggy and soiled work pants, shoes several sizes too big, and his extra-wide stance after he landed, he looked every bit like a Charlie Chaplin imitator. Only the crumpled bowler hat was missing; in its stead, this little man wore a crumpled baseball hat.

Renato came over to me and said, "I would like to introduce the workers to you and your wife. I have instructed them to always address you as Signor Richard and your wife as La Signora. I trust that will be satisfactory for both of you." Mica and I both nodded our approval.

Renato continued, "I have also told them what generally has to be done, but they will need to be given tools and told where to begin and exactly what you want them to do. I will be back at 6:00 p.m. to pick them up. They understand when they are to take a lunch break along with two fifteen-minute breaks, one midmorning and one midafternoon."

I was impressed with how well organized Renato seemed and how the crew seemed to respect him, and I said, "Renato, my only request is that if any of the workers aren't clear on what they are to do, they are to come and ask me. No guessing. It is much easier to ask to make sure they understand what they have to do."

I spoke loud enough to make sure the workers heard me, and Renato turned to them and asked, "Did you all understand what Signor Richard just said?"

They each nodded and murmured, "*Si, capisco bene.*"

"Okay," said Renato, "then, step forward and introduce yourselves to Signor Richard and La Signora."

Before anyone could say anything, the little Chaplin-like man jumped out of the line and said in broken Italian, "Me name Pasquale. Me Albanian. Me Muslim. We all equal under same God. Me work hard. Pasquale do whatever need to do. Ask me, Pasquale do fast. Me strong like Superman!" He then flexed his arms to show his biceps, and then he literally jumped back in line.

I was very much taken aback at this, and my immediate thought was, *Oh God, whether the same God or not, here I am, a Jew, and I have a Muslim nutcase coming here to work.* In the meantime, the other men in line laughed and then simply told us their first names: Antonio, the crew leader; Roberto; Arturo; and Carlo.

Putting aside my misgivings about Pasquale, Mica and I welcomed them all. I then brought them to the garage where they met our seventy-nine-year-old caretaker, Raffaello, who handed each of them a tool with the admonishment to be sure to return it to him at day's end.

The first chore was to rake and pick up stones on the lawns surrounding the main house and guesthouses. The lawns had been dug up to install the irrigation system and the well and to put new tubes in for electrical and water lines. The area had been releveled, so this was the last step before grass could be planted. It was a priority for us, as we knew that once the area around the house had grass instead of dirt, the farmhouse would start looking more like a completed project.

Each man in the crew was armed with a rake and a bucket. They lined up in a row at one end of the large lawn, spread apart so they covered the entire width needing to be cleared. Once they got started, I went back to the house and then returned an hour and a half later.

I noticed immediately that each of the Italian workers had progressed about the same distance, while Pasquale was at least half again as far along as they were. When I arrived, the four Italians all stopped working to look at me and ask if I was happy with what they had done. But Pasquale seemed oblivious to anything around him and continued working on his hands and knees, furiously picking up stones and putting them in a bucket. When his bucket was full, he carried it off to one side to a pile that he considered his own. The others also had their own piles, but Pasquale's pile was more than four times bigger than any other one. Actually, it was bigger than the other four *combined.*

I was amazed. I didn't say anything else other than for the men to continue. I decided I would keep an eye on Pasquale to see if he was just a one-day wonder or if he really was that good.

After the lawns were cleared, Raffaello planted grass seed. Then came the hard work of clearing the woods. The crew was equipped with sickles, machetes, heavy-duty cutters, and a motor saw.

I took them to the first patch of woods to begin work. I put Antonio, the crew leader, in charge of the motor saw with instructions that he was the only one to use it, as he had experience with one from when he'd cleared forests for another company. The others were given a full set of tools to start cutting the underbrush. As that was done, Antonio would follow, cutting the thicker pieces with the saw. So I could gauge how each man did, I gave each a separate section to work.

Once again, after I watched them get started, I left for about two hours and returned to see how they were doing. It was a repeat scene from the earlier job on the lawns: there was Pasquale so deep into the woods that I could hardly see him, while the others were far behind, working at a leisurely, unconcerned pace, joking and laughing, two of them standing idly smoking cigarettes. One was even making fun of Pasquale, who was too far away to even hear them.

As each day went by, the trend was the same: Pasquale continued to work as if in a trance, oblivious to the jokes made about him as the lone foreigner among the crew.

One morning, just as the crew arrived, a delivery truck pulled up with a new refrigerator for our kitchen. Two men got out of the truck, lowered the tailgate, and asked me where the refrigerator went. I pointed them to an entrance that would take them into the kitchen.

As they prepared to take the refrigerator off the truck, Pasquale ran up and said, "*Faccio io, faccio io!*" ("I do it, I do it!") Before anyone could say a word, the refrigerator was on his back, and he carried it into our kitchen where he carefully set it in place. The deliverymen and I stood in awe as this little man carried the heavy and bulky refrigerator, which looked even bigger on his narrow back. When Pasquale turned the corner, all you could see were two ankles and shoes sticking out below the refrigerator. He looked like a huge windup toy with rapidly moving feet shod in scruffy shoes.

Again, the Italian workers laughed as they stood watching, not lifting a finger other than to bring cigarettes to their lips. After two weeks of having Renato's crew at Ceppeto, nothing had changed in the way they worked. Pasquale continued to outpace and outdo the other four in terms of the quality and quantity of his work.

One day when I went to check to see how they were doing, I found the only one working was Pasquale. I asked where the other workers were, and he told me, in his broken Italian—or rather, sign language—that they'd gone to a café. He pointed in the direction of town and threw his head back, raising his hand to his mouth, as if he were drinking a cup of coffee.

"How long ago, Pasquale?" I asked.

Again, by sign language, he held up all ten fingers three times and said, "*Minuti fa.*" That meant thirty minutes ago. So much for the fifteen-minute break—and by the time they returned, it was close to an hour.

That was it. I called Renato and said, "I have had it with all your workers except for Pasquale, who is amazing. I have never seen anyone work as he does. He is better than any three of your other workers. The rest stand around joking, smoking cigarettes, and running off to town for coffee. I am sorry, but I don't want any of them back except Pasquale. If you can work out a way for him to get here and back to your place each day, that is fine with me. If not, I can't use any other of your workers."

Renato was quick to reply, "I understand completely. I will deal with them and either transfer or fire them. I suspect part of the problem is the crew leader, Antonio."

"It may be, but at this point I want only Pasquale. It is him or no one."

"Not a problem. Starting tomorrow I will have Pasquale there promptly at 8:00 a.m."

For the next month, Pasquale was dropped off every morning at eight and worked until his ride arrived to take him back to where he was staying, usually around six o'clock. Upon his arrival, he would wait for me along with Raffaello in front of the house to receive instructions for work to be done that day. He always arrived with a smile and an attitude of sheer happiness. He obviously loved working. He would always greet me with a big *"Buon giorno!"* and I could see that he was anxious and attentive to learn what was to be done that day.

Raffaello was a bit less enthusiastic, as he seemed to consider Pasquale a threat because Pasquale was so much younger and stronger. But Raffaello, at seventy-nine years old, was a wonder himself. He was the fittest man I had ever known at that age. He could have put Jack LaLane to shame. He was a handsome man about 5'8" tall with a full head of white hair, blue eyes, and a strong dimpled chin; he had the build of a muscular but limber forty-year-old man without an ounce of extra fat on his body.

I understood Raffaello's misgivings; after all, he had been the head custodian of Ceppeto for the last fifteen years. So I told him, "Raffaello, I want you to understand that Pasquale is a temporary worker here to do the heavy work; he is not replacing you." Despite my assurances, he nevertheless still had misgivings.

Some of that might have been his prejudice against Albanians and Muslims. Most Italians looked down on Albanians as inferior troublemakers. Pasquale seemed to understand that prejudice almost from the start, and he used his unfailing sense of humor to disarm Raffaello. On any of the chores that I assigned them, I noticed Pasquale insisted on doing all the difficult work and had no problem taking orders from Raffaello.

At these meetings, I explained in detail what I wanted done. Pasquale was never satisfied until he made sure he understood my instructions 100 percent. Because his Italian wasn't very good, he insisted upon interpreting my instructions by drawing in the dirt with a stick and using the cleverest clues for words he didn't know in Italian, as if he were playing charades. He would not relent until he understood exactly what the instructions were.

I saw in this a remarkable determination that most people new to a language wouldn't have applied, choosing to instead wing it once they got what they thought was the gist (I confess that I'm guilty of that to this day if I don't understand the whole conversation). But Pasquale had to know precisely what was required of him. Cut the grass: "How high?" Clear a patch of land: "Where and what has to be cut? Underbrush? Tree branches? Move stones and where to? Use what tools? What to do with debris afterward?"

One job was to start repairing the miles of dry stone walls around the farm, many of which had collapsed over the years. The walls were not just stones piled on top of one another; rather, they were carefully fitted together to form a smooth front and flat top, including places where they artfully curved around large trees and formed small bridges over stone-lined gullies used to direct rainwater evenly around the property.

Fortunately, Raffaello was an expert at this (it is something of an art). As a young boy in the early 1930s, he had helped build some of these very walls himself. I saw immediately that he had a rapt pupil in Pasquale, who lifted all the heavy stones—some boulder size—while Raffaello instructed him where to lay them and then how to secure them in place by fitting smaller stones around them, making a tight fit that would last. Many of the smaller pieces had to be sculpted with a chisel and hammer to achieve this kind of symmetry.

I also noticed that while Pasquale was intent on learning whatever he could from Raffaello, he didn't simply take what he was told at face value. He always questioned it so he could understand the reasoning behind it.

For example, our vineyard had to be treated for disease from time to time, something Raffaello, as a former manager of a large vineyard, knew how to do. It required mixing a couple of different environmentally friendly chemicals together and spraying them on the leaves.

I was watching Raffaello prepare the solution one day while Pasquale was looking on. Raffaello took a handful of one product, then a little bit of something else, then added some water to it with a hose, and finally stirred it all together.

Pasquale asked, "How much of each you use?"

"Oh, I just know how much to add."

"No important to make *praycheese?*"

"It's not important to be precise. I just estimate the amounts."

"*Scusi* me, medicine *per un bambino* ist less den *per adulto.* Too *grande* ist danger. Deez plants *bambini* dangers to git dem too much o too little."

Raffaello looked at Pasquale and said, "I have been doing this for most of my life. I know what to do."

Pasquale didn't say more, but I could see he didn't think Raffaello was doing the right thing. Pasquale was trying to explain that it was important to measure the exact quantities being used and that the younger the plant, the less one should use. The logic was there, although the language was not. His Italian was improving, though. When Pasquale began thinking about something, there was no stopping him until he got the answers he was seeking. I was becoming more impressed every day with this little man who I had initially thought was a nutcase. He showed himself to be far cleverer and innately smarter than anyone had probably ever given him credit for … than even *I* had originally given him credit for.

After a few weeks of the morning meetings together, Pasquale began asking me questions about current events he had heard discussed at dinnertime where he was staying. As his Italian improved, I had less and less difficulty understanding him. He asked a great variety of questions:

"Is Bush good president? Me hear he no win election. Me think America had fair government and people elect president; what went wrong?"

"Milosevic was arrested. He very bad man with black heart. Why don't they just hang him?"

"Why are Palestinians always mad at Israel? Me hear Israel is very strong and Jews are very smart. How many people in Israel? How many Palestinians are there?"

"Why there new money, the euro? Me don't understand how happened."

"How many people in America? Is it big as Europe? Where you live in America?"

"Where is New York? How many people live there?"

Some of his questions I could answer; others I found myself researching on the computer. It seemed that every answer I gave only brought more questions from Pasquale the next day. I had never seen such a hunger for knowledge.

After several more weeks of working at Ceppeto, Pasquale came to me first thing on what was a beautiful August morning. The year was 2001. I was standing outside our kitchen, admiring how vivid the valley before me looked with nothing but a crystal blue sky above. This time there was no "*Buon giorno.*" He blurted out instead with a quavering voice, "Me must quit Renato. He treats me like slave. Me find out he pay his Italiani three times what he me pay. My wife and children are always hungry, and they no have enough to live on with money me send. Me send them everything me make except few dollars each week."

At this, I saw Pasquale's jaw tighten and the muscles protrude with tension; his fists were clenched, and his chest was heaving from his rapid breathing. He hissed, "Renato taking me advantage because me illegal immigrant. Me work more hard than his Italiani." If Renato had been there, I would have feared for his life. I think Pasquale could have strangled him. Bob Marley famously sang, "A hungry man is an angry man," and Pasquale, that morning, was an angry man personified, not as much for himself as he was for his hungry wife and children counting on him in their impoverished home in Albania.

He then seemed to gain some modicum of control and stopped breathing as heavily. He unclenched his jaws and fists. I think having someone to hear him and allow him to vent his anger helped him calm down. I felt such sorrow for this man who was trying to do what he felt he had to do and yet was being prevented at almost every step of the way. How he could ever smile or laugh at anything was remarkable to me, and yet that was what he often did during the time he had been working at Ceppeto. With the slightest trace of tears in his eyes, he asked, "Signor Richard, can me come work for you? If no, me return south and try find more work pays better."

At that point, Mica had joined us and had heard most of what

Pasquale had said. I replied, "We would love to have you work for us, but there would be serious repercussions for us because of our status as visitors in Italy. It is simply illegal for us to hire an illegal immigrant."

Left unsaid was that I had gotten to know Renato fairly well while his crews worked for us. He had even brought his wife, the doctor who had treated Pasquale, and their daughter to visit us for an afternoon. He was impressed with the fact that I had a company with over three hundred employees that I had started from my apartment and built into a successful business.

As we'd discussed business over the last few months, I'd learned Renato's philosophy about his workers, which was to treat them harshly. He claimed if you showed them any kindness, they considered that a weakness and would try to take advantage of you. While I could see the rationale for that when dealing with the Italian workers he had brought to Ceppeto, I wasn't convinced that was appropriate for the likes of a "Pasquale," who wanted desperately to be recognized for the hard work he did.

I also knew that the word was out that Renato was strongly connected with the Mafia. That was not unusual, as just about every business from the south of Italy, whether voluntarily or not, was connected to the Mafia. In Renato's case, that Mafia moniker didn't quite fit with his wife being an intelligent and apparently good doctor, not to mention their sweet and adorable young daughter.

In any event, I didn't want to push it, as I'd been told Renato would be decidedly upset if any of his employees skipped out on him and went to work for one of his clients. If not dealt with, he could lose many of the workers he was bringing up from the south and face the ruin of his business. I couldn't see how it would be possible to make hiring Pasquale a win-win situation for both me and Renato. Adding to the complications with Renato was the problem of hiring illegal aliens, and I had little to no options.

I therefore said to Pasquale, who was looking at me with transparent hope in his eyes, "I hope you can understand our dilemma." Then, handing him a piece of paper with our phone numbers at Ceppeto and in New York City, I said, "Here, please keep in touch, and if the laws ever change, you can come work for us then. Now just wait a moment, I want to get something for you from inside. I will be right back." I rushed into the house and got $1,000. I returned and handed it to him. "Here is some money to help tide you over until you find work."

He was surprised and, with tears in his eyes, replied, "Thank you. Thank you both." Then he took my hand and kissed the back of it. He did the same thing with Mica. He then carefully folded the money and paper with our phone numbers and inserted them into his wallet. He turned and slowly walked toward the road where one of Renato's workers was waiting to drive him to the train station.

As he walked away, his head down and shoulders slumped, both Mica and I were deeply moved. Pasquale had done everything right but was being treated unfairly by a system that lacked compassion. But I knew Pasquale well enough by then to know that he was a survivor and would figure out a way to make it. Little did I know then how much that would involve Mica and me.

CHAPTER 6

LUCKY MAN

Icame out of the army in 1963 clueless as to what to do with myself and not even all that sure there was much I *could* do. I graduated from Penn State in 1961 with a bachelor of science degree and a commission as a lieutenant in the army. I then went right into the army and was a platoon leader of an armored cavalry unit patrolling the East-West German border. Two years later, I was standing outside the gates of Fort Hamilton in Brooklyn where I'd been discharged, not sure what my college degree or army experience would do to help me get a job. I was then faced with that rather oppressive question I suppose any unsure college graduate and ex-GI deals with: *What do I do now?*

The first thing I did was hop a train for Philadelphia to see my family, and as it happened, I bumped into an old high school friend on the train I hadn't seen in years. As we caught up on what each of us had been doing, I mentioned that I had just gotten out of the army and was going to start looking for a job. A natty-looking guy sitting nearby overheard our conversation, handed me his business card, and invited me in for an interview at his office in Philly. He was the senior vice president for Scott Paper, and a week later, I was a Scott Paper salesman. Six months later, I was an *ex*-salesman for Scott Paper.

I'd had a nice salary—nice enough to move into a small apartment with my first wife—a company car, and a position Scott usually reserved for top college graduates. But those six months confirmed an almost instinctive feeling I'd had since high school when I'd worked in a warehouse and got paid less than the agreed hourly amount: I couldn't *stand* working for someone else. It didn't matter the money, the nature of the work, how nice the boss was, or the company. There was just something about being somebody's employee that weighed on me like a twenty-pound yoke.

Be that as it may, being a twenty-four-year-old dumb enough to walk out on a well-paying job at an established company with only six months' professional experience isn't the usual path to self-made success.

A friend of my in-laws was something of a wheeler-dealer (I guess the polite word is *entrepreneur*), and he took me on as an assistant. One of his many dealings was in the duty-free business. Through him, I learned how federal and state liquor-importing regulations worked, and when this guy's business folded up after a year, I saw an opportunity to put that knowledge to work. I figured out I could ship brand-name liquor from Europe to residents in the New York–New Jersey–Connecticut area at a 40–50 percent discount from retail prices.

In less than a year, I was selling more than a fifty-foot-trailer-load of liquor per week, making my company the largest liquor retailer in the United States at that time. At the age of twenty-five, I was my own boss and earning more than the president of the United States.

Five years later, I was near broke, divorced, living in a small apartment on Manhattan's West Side, and memorizing the placement of every toll booth in the tristate area so that I could navigate around them to save a few dimes while hustling here and there on the small-money consulting and freelance gigs that kept me from starving.

I lost my business for various reasons. To begin with, the retail-liquor lobbyists and the liquor importers of all those name brands that I was buying from the distillers in Europe were enraged that I was bypassing them. Not to mention the longshoremen. They were stealing lots of my liquor as it was unloaded on the docks on the West Side of New York City in those days, so I opened a warehouse far enough away that I was able to move the containers off the docks and thus evade the longshoremen. Then the Mafia started hijacking those containers, but they were stopped after I hired undercover narcs to ride shotgun on the trucks on their time off. Then there was the State Liquor Authority, which was infuriated that I was circumventing its jurisdiction. The fact that I was able to triumph over this entire group for close to five years was in hindsight a remarkable feat that necessitated some political lobbying on my part to hold them off.

They did finally get the importing laws changed, and my business was, unfortunately, legislated out of existence. Once it was over, I received a call from the president of one of the big liquor-importing companies, asking me to come up and meet with him. I did so, and when I walked into his palatial office, he said, "I just wanted to meet you and ask how in the world a young Jewish guy like you beat the retail-liquor lobby, the importers, the longshoremen, and the State Liquor Authority all these years."

I simply answered, "It wasn't easy."

As for the marriage, my two sons, and the nice house out in the Jersey 'burbs I had by then ... I'd learned by age twenty-nine what it takes all those unhappy, midlife, andropausal guys in John Cheever stories decades to learn: money doesn't buy happiness.

So after an uncontested divorce, I left my ex-wife with everything except my clothes and a thousand dollars. I wanted to start over, and I entered what I call a monkish/spartan phase in my life.

During one of my freelance jobs in Manhattan, in a graphic designer's office, I came across a picture I couldn't quite decipher. It was in full, vibrant, translucent colors and looked more like an abstract painting. I asked him about it, and he told me it was a photograph of a mineral. He went on to say that collecting minerals was one of the fastest-growing hobbies in the country.

Mighty oaks from little acorns grow.

I started a mail-order business for minerals and inexpensive gemstones. At first, I was working out of my apartment, writing the brochures myself, and my "staff"—a cleaning woman I'd hired part-time to pack orders—sent them out from a nearby post office. I also made a deal with Dr. Martin Connors, at the time the curator of gems and minerals at the Smithsonian Institution, to pay him a commission on sales in exchange for being an advisor. By the time I sold the business in 1985, I had over three hundred employees and more than sixteen million customers. And Dr. Connors had commissioned a nice house in Maryland that he flatteringly referred to as "the house that Richard built."

A top investment bank ranked the company as one of the most profitable mail-order companies in the United States. They wanted to buy the company, but I held out and was offered ever-increasing amounts from other major investment companies, until finally my attorney asked me, "Richard, why don't you sell?"

I answered, "Because I never want to work for anyone."

"You are being offered so much money you will never have to work again anyway. Besides, you owe it to your children not to turn the offers down."

So I sold the company for all cash. That certainly was the highlight of my business career. I'd done everything with the business I'd wanted to do, so it was time to move on.

It didn't take long for me to realize that I was too young to retire completely, so I began looking for something ... well, something *else*.

One of my sons suggested real estate.

The early 1990s was the right time to play in New York real estate. The Manhattan property market was in the toilet, which meant there were a lot of choice buys available for someone with money to spend, and the sale of my mail-order business had given me a nice bucket of cash to play with. By 2001, working with my sons, we'd managed to position ourselves as a major player on the metropolitan real estate scene. I suppose the deal that cemented our status was the one that brought us midtown's iconic Citicorp building.

As unseemly as I know it is to brag (and certainly my parents taught me better), I want to quote from a January 2001 story in the *New York Times* that declared that the Citicorp deal would, ahem, "catapult [the Hadar family] to the top ranks of New York City real estate families."

In practical terms, this was a three-peat in my business career.

Short of the kind of global economic meltdown that would put the industrialized world back into the Stone Age, I was set for life—as were those who were close to me.

Yes, for me the American dream had come true. My grandparents came to this country as barely literate immigrants from Eastern Europe. My parents had been so poor that when I was a kid, we were living in a cramped apartment over my grandparents' live poultry store.

But now here I was. I'd never work for anybody again. Ever. I had gotten what, I think, we all wish for: enough money to do what I wanted, when I wanted, how I wanted. Work or play, it would be at my choosing.

I would continue to work. To this day, I still work the real estate market. I still get a sense of accomplishment from turning a property that wasn't much into an oh-*wow* property or from transforming something already worthwhile into something even more valuable.

From the time I was old enough to understand the meaning of my mother's reprimanding glare, she had instilled in me the obligation to give back, so I set up a foundation—which I still manage—to help students pay their way through college.

I had a lot … but I didn't quite have it all.

CHAPTER 7

BACK TO ITALY

In 1997, I was about to launch into converting the old Studio 54 back to a theater and decided, before beginning the project, that I would head to Florence and take an intensive six-week course in Italian.

Before I left, my personal assistant notified me that she was leaving in order to start a family. With a couple of weeks left before my departure, I quickly put out the word that I was looking for a replacement and added, "It would be nice if that person spoke Italian." It would be like having an in-house tutor. It didn't take long before a friend of mine recommended Mica Bagnasco. She was a native Italian who had been living in the States for ten years and, with an eye on her acting career, had intensely trained most—though thankfully not all—of her Italian accent into submission.

She was, undoubtedly, a striking woman, a slim 5'8" blonde, with blue-green eyes and an uncanny resemblance to Uma Thurman.

And she was capable: she could type, take shorthand, knew record keeping. It didn't hurt that she was also charming as hell, especially with that last surviving bit of *Italiano* when she spoke.

But she didn't know Quicken, a computer program I used heavily. And though I was pretty sure—despite those gemlike eyes and the Uma Thurman thing—I couldn't employ her, as a courtesy to my recommending friend more than anything else, I told her I'd get in touch when I came back from Italy and maybe we'd talk again.

A few days later, I was immersed in classes at the Italian language school in Florence where only Italian was spoken, and I was struggling to understand what was being said, not to mention trying to speak it as well. It was nice that the Italians were so forgiving about these things; if I did to French what I did to Italian, I'm sure I'd be chased out of the country by a crowd of beret-wearing, baguette-swinging purists. It certainly helped that I was assigned to a language instructor who, bless her, had the patience of a saint.

On weekends, I was literally mentally exhausted from taxing the "Big Fella" eight hours a day, five days a week, plus studying until late at night. I hadn't undergone that kind of regimen since I was in college. To get out and take a break, I rented a car on weekends and got out of Florence to tour the countryside.

I had traveled to Italy some thirty-five years before, while on leave from my army post in Germany. I wondered if this Italy would be as entrancing as the Italy I remembered from three and a half decades ago.

I had little reason to worry. Italy, like any great lady, had been aging gracefully for centuries; thirty-five years was barely a second on her clock.

I was especially enamored with the Tuscan region and Chianti in particular. I found it incredibly beautiful with a terrain quite different from anything I had ever seen in the United States. I had just seen the marked differences when I flew from Rome to Florence. The land north of Rome in Umbria had mostly what I would describe as low, almost flat, rolling hills that appeared to be easy to cultivate. It looked to me much like the countryside in Pennsylvania where I grew up. These were punctuated by quite high hill towns jutting up a thousand feet or so. The most obvious was Orvieto, and others I could identify were Assisi and Todi, all of which I was able to visit before heading back to the States. Then almost like turning a page in a book to a new chapter, there were the unmistakable, more pronounced rolling hills of Tuscany and Chianti as we approached the Florence airport.

The farms I later saw on my weekend tours were as picturesque as one could imagine, and the people I met were wonderful, warm, and friendly. I began to think about buying a farm there. I had always dreamed of owning a farm, dating back to my childhood days when, for family amusement, all seven of us would squeeze into my father's car and drive for the day around the Pennsylvania countryside and see its pristine farms.

The Chianti farms were pristine in a different way. The houses and structures were all made of stone found in the surrounding rocky terrain and were so in tune with the landscape they seemed to have grown out of the ground. No two houses or structures were alike, but they all had an architecturally raw beauty that showed the innate sense of design that most Italians seem to have. Being something of a history fanatic, the fact that most of these structures were many centuries old added to the allure of the place for me.

The fields weren't marked by fences as they were in Pennsylvania but rather were defined by perfectly symmetrical vineyards lined with straight, evenly spaced rows of grapevines, which crawled over the undulating hills of Chianti. The vineyards were just part of a patchwork-quilt design that included silvery-leafed olive groves, golden wheat fields, and often fields of yellow sunflowers (called *girasole*) lined up in military-style formation, their faces always pointing in unison toward the sun. The few fields left fallow were covered with a rainbow of wildflowers. The fields were framed by dense woods that covered the surrounding hills that were too steep for cultivation. It was difficult to imagine anything more in harmony than this balanced and exquisite combination of nature and man working together.

I loved the place for its own unique beauties and charms as well as for how it melded with my childhood memories of the Pennsylvania countryside. Here, the nonstop engine that pushed me back home on to the next project … and the next … and the next, slowed, stopped, and cooled.

The idea of having something permanent in Italy began to jell in my mind.

I decided on one of my weekend forays that, the following year, I'd rent a villa in a vineyard about an hour from Florence for a few weeks. If I really intended to buy a farm there, renting a place first would make a good toe in the water.

The six weeks in Florence flew by, and I left having learned more tenses—and their permutations—than I ever believed possible. Italian makes English grammar look like *Grammar for Dummies*. Italian is a beautiful language, but one needs to get out and speak it and hear it spoken. I was always pleasantly surprised when I did converse with Italians, as they were very tolerant with my attempts, unless they spoke English, and then, as soon as they heard me speak, they knew instantly I was American and started speaking to me in English rather than Italian.

On my trip back home, I kept thinking about what my teacher had said to me: "Richard, you need to speak and hear Italian every day if you want to master the language." With that thought swirling in my head, I thought, *If only Mica knew how to use Quicken.*

CHAPTER 8

MICA

When I walked through the door of my apartment upon returning from Italy, the first thing I did, like most people, was check my phone messages. There were many, including one from Mica Bagnasco, asking if I had returned yet and when we could set up an appointment. I felt a bit uncomfortable, since I had made up my mind that I couldn't hire her, but I felt that I should meet her and tell her I would try to recommend her for a position elsewhere. I wanted to get that out of the way sooner than later, so I called her, and we made an appointment for the next day.

When she arrived and after a few minutes of my trying to speak Italian to a less-than-enthusiastic response, I began to tell her I would be happy to recommend her to several people I knew who might be in need of an assistant. She politely interrupted me and said, "I just wanted to tell you that while you were away, I learned how to use the Quicken program."

Mica Bagnasco hasn't stopped impressing me since.

One year later, in 1998, I returned to Italy. Unfortunately I had fired Mica and hired a new assistant because I had a rule that I would not get involved socially with any of my employees. After I fired her, we began dating and soon were engaged, so Mica accompanied me as my fiancée.

It was quite a party that made the journey to the farm I'd rented for two weeks: Mica and me and three other couples, our closest friends.

One friend with us that year was Bill Persky, a multi-Emmy-winning producer, writer, and director. Bill is about 5'10" tall with a full head of silver-gray hair, giving him a distinctive appearance. He has a deep melodic announcer's voice that can be heard as clearly as if he were talking into a microphone. When he said hello to me out of the blue one day at the Vertical Club, a gym on Sixty-First Street that we both frequented, I at first thought it was coming over the loudspeaker system. When I looked up from the bicycle on which I was furiously pedaling and gasping for air, there was Bill, standing in front of the bike, smiling at me. He said, "Anyone who does all the things I like to do is someone I thought I should meet. Hi, my name is Bill Persky." He was not referring to my aerobic training on the bike; Bill kept seeing me at the same vacation spots he patronized—St. Barths, Telluride, Aspen, and Sag Harbor. I later met his lovely and charming wife, Joanna Patton, who founded and ran the largest female-owned advertising agency in the country.

Bill, in turn, introduced me to Saul Waring and Joe LaRosa, who had recently sold their own successful Manhattan advertising agency. Saul is over 6' tall and has an athletic build and a full head of chestnut hair that makes him look a lot younger. He started an ad agency with Joe LaRosa that became one of the most creative agencies in the country. Joe was considered a genius and one of the top creative directors in the ad industry, with a long list of well-known advertisements he created. Joe is about 5'9", has a full head of white hair and a dimpled chin, and is a great athlete in almost any sport and a gifted artist and photographer. Saul's wife, Willa, and Joe's longtime companion, Liane, were equally charming and both extremely bright. Willa was the guru of the group who meditated every day and was in an almost permanent state of serenity. Liane was the person you could ask almost any question, no matter how trivial or complicated, and she would know the answer. All four ladies are equally gorgeous, and I must say, the eight of us made a very attractive group.

The guys all grew so close we wound up taking a suite of offices together in midtown Manhattan, as much a place to hang out together as it was for each of us to conduct whatever business we had to conduct. Joe's companion, Liane, an ad agency vet herself, christened us "The Sagency—four Sages, never a wait!"

We Sages and Sagettes (as the ladies were called) all went to Fattoria La Massa that year, the farm I had rented for two weeks. The main house was a baronial villa that grandly accommodated all eight of us.

The villa was situated in the middle of a vineyard a few kilometers from the center of Panzano, a quaint medieval village surrounded by spectacular views of farms and vineyards.

The owner, Gianpaolo Motta, was not yet as renowned as he would become a few years later for producing perhaps the best Chianti wines (called "Super Tuscans"). A warm and charming host, he provided us with one of the best vacations any of us ever had anywhere.

Mica and I decided to contact a real estate agent there, and with all the Sages and Sagettes in tow, we began looking at houses. If you ever want to get an idea of a region and the people there, go house hunting. If you have a good agent, as we did, they can be better than any tour guide.

Ours knew not only the history of the area but also all the local news and gossip not found in any Fodor's guide. In every area, there are good guys and not-so-good guys, and we learned about both as we went to villa after villa up for sale. We saw a number of intriguing ones, none quite what we wanted, but we met some very interesting— and remarkably accommodating—people.

We came on like a real estate SWAT team, arriving in a convoy of three cars that rapidly emptied as we fanned out to scout the property. Mica and I usually scouted inside the house, while Bill and Joanna, both fabulous cooks, checked out the kitchen. Saul and Willa, who loved the outdoors and nature, checked the views and landscaping. Joe, a gifted photographer who worked with some of the top photographers in the world, went about taking pictures, which he and Liane later edited for us as reminders of what we had seen. Not one of the owners was bothered in the least by this storming of their walls. Most offered us drinks and snacks. Come lunchtime, we asked the owner of the villa we were looking at if he could recommend a local restaurant; he not only recommended a good one but also joined us there for lunch.

After a few days of searching, we found what we were looking for, falling immediately in love with the house and grounds. All the Sages and Sagettes gave it a thumbs-up as well. We put a bid in, and it was accepted a few days later. We were ecstatic.

We needed a lawyer, and a friend who lived in Florence and owned a major chain of hotels in Italy referred us to her attorney. After the lawyer reviewed all the documents relating to the property, we met with him, and our hearts broke when he advised us not to buy it.

Apparently, the property was registered with a Lichtenstein company, and one of the shareholders was the agent representing the sellers. No taxes had been paid for decades, and it would be impossible to ever sell it without getting the buyer to agree to purchase the Lichtenstein company, complete with its shareholders and activities we had no way to control or check (a not unfounded concern; several years later on another matter, the same agent was convicted for fraud and sent to jail).

We were devastated, as often happens when you are house hunting and you lose what you're convinced is your dream home. We were sure anything we found thereafter was going to be a half-hearted compromise.

CHAPTER 9

FINDING CEPPETO

We returned to New York, and the following October, Mica went back to Italy to visit her family and a friend, Antonella, with whom she had gone to school in Florence. Antonella lived in the same Chianti area where we'd stayed that summer; by coincidence, she also had a friend who was a real estate broker.

They began looking at villas together. They came across one that had been on and off the market for several years. It was jointly owned by two sisters, one of whom had died the year before. The grown children of each sister were not getting along, and they kept going back and forth, trying to work out their differences. When they couldn't, they'd put the house on the market only to patch things up and take it off the market.

At this point, however, it seemed that the differences were irreconcilable, and the house had gone back on sale just days before Mica's arrival. Mica and Antonella arranged to see the farm.

At the farm, the custodian, a gracious older man named Raffaello Rulli, met them. He was born in 1922 in Lupaia, a tiny medieval hilltop village just five hundred meters from the farm. He had worked on the farm in his youth, and his older sister had lived there when it had been a working farm. Not long after the end of World War II, the owner had gone bankrupt, and the farm had been abandoned, left to decay until it was bought for back taxes by the current residents who had modernized the main house in the 1960s into a vacation home.

Raffaello proudly escorted Mica and Antonella on a tour of the property. It was situated on one of the highest hills on the rim of the five-mile-wide valley running between Radda and Ceppeto, with a commanding view of the entire valley shared with Lupaia. As they toured the property, Raffaello began telling them the history of the area. "The Etruscans were the first known settlers around Ceppeto and in the Chianti region, 2,500 years ago. The tops of the many hills you see around this valley provided excellent locations for their settlements primarily for defensive purposes, which helped the Etruscan civilization survive. Most of those hilltop settlements remain in some form today, Siena and Florence being the major ones in the area, but many smaller hilltop towns and castles dotting Chianti owe their origins to the Etruscans, including Radda and Lupaia. Besides defense, an abundant water supply was critical to their survival. When water became exhausted, the settlement vanished."

Mica and Antonella were surprised that Raffaello, who they thought was just a custodian, would know so much of the area's history. Mica asked him how he'd learned so much about the history there.

He responded, "I spent my whole life here, except for the war years, and these were the stories I heard told by the elders from the time I was a child." As they walked through the property and he continued telling Mica and Antonella the history, they were even more surprised at the many historic details he knew.

He told them, "When the Romans conquered the area, the Etruscan civilization disappeared; where they went or what happened to them is still an unsolved mystery. There are still remnants of their settlements, foundations, tombs, and small artifacts being found to this day, but no clue as to where they disappeared. Over time as royalty and the aristocratic families of Siena and Florence flourished, the search was on for places to go near the big cities, not only to flee the hot summer months but also in times of plagues and unrest. Chianti was ideally situated in the middle of both cities, which are only about thirty-five miles apart. These families took over large tracts of land and established farms on them that were cared for by tenant farmers."

Raffaello turned out to be better than any tour guide Mica or Antonella could have found that day. And he continued, "Back in the Middle Ages, Radda was head of the Chianti League, which was a string of hilltop fortresses allied with Florence charged with protecting the area from sieges by Siena over a long-disputed boundary between the two powerful city-states. Both Lupaia and Radda were used as hilltop defenses. The League's symbol was the *Gallo Nero* [black rooster], which became the trademark for all Chianti Classico wine."

He told them, "A little known fact is that water, or the lack of it, was partially credited with Florence prevailing over Siena in their city-state wars from the thirteenth to fifteenth century. Florence had an abundant supply of water from the Arno River, whereas Siena relied on underground aquifers, which were no match for the mighty Arno."

Mica was so impressed she wrote down most of this information. Later that day, she called me, very excited, to tell me what Raffaello had said. We spoke for well over an hour. She was almost breathless with excitement. "I know this is the place we were hoping to find," she told me. "The main house is all stone, with thick walls and a traditional nineteenth-century tile roof. It's almost three stories, the third story being an attic. It is really an imposing structure, and listen to this: it has eight bedrooms, six bathrooms, two kitchens, two dining rooms, a living room, and a breakfast room, with fireplaces throughout. Can you believe that?"

Mica's excitement was beginning to become infectious, and I was excited to hear all the details, which were getting better and better. "But wait," she said, "there is a huge, separate workshop you are going to love to work in, plus a laundry area, and a large garage and several smaller structures around the property once used for storing animal feed and equipment. Richard, it is just amazing! I am so excited."

I was happily stunned and said, "I am already excited. It almost sounds too good to be true."

She giggled with joy. "Believe me, it is true, and it keeps getting better. Near the main house is a large swimming pool and a lake. The area around the house, which I think is about five acres or so, has been maintained by Raffaello and looks pretty good, but the rest of the forty-odd acres of the property is abandoned and hasn't been touched since the farm went bankrupt, I think Raffaello said in the 1950s."

Then Mica told me that Raffaello led her and Antonella through some of the abandoned areas, which Raffaello knew as well as if he'd been tending them daily. With nostalgia, he told Mica and Antonella, "I was born in Lupaia, and I grew up toiling on this farm. Look at those stone walls; there are miles of them on the property. They are dry stone walls built by hand over the centuries to create terraces, which, in the farm's heyday, produced wheat as well as olive oil from over three hundred olive trees, most of which are still living in that thick, overgrown brush you see all around."

Mica said, "It was as if Raffaello was on autopilot; neither I nor Antonella could stop his unexpected narrative, even if we had wanted to. It was almost as if he had all this pent-up knowledge and was waiting for perhaps many years to tell someone." He told Mica and Antonella that when the land was cultivated, the stones pulled from the earth were put into piles. During the spring and summer months after the day's work was done and dinner finished, the men of the farm would gather and build the walls from the piled stones while they drank wine or beer and told stories. He said it had been as much a social event as a chore.

I said, "Raffaello seems like a walking history book, and you know how much I love history." I couldn't wait to meet him to learn more about things I was sure would be difficult to find in any book.

Mica said, "Yes, I know you'll love speaking with him." She said that she had askd Raffaello if he was there in those times.

He said, "Yes, I was a young boy, and I listened to their stories of the day, which usually concerned the state of the crops and animals. The prospect of selling their crops, in which they shared the profits fifty-fifty with the owner, was often a topic of conversation, as well as what they intended to do with the money they received from the sale. As far as I could tell, it was never much, and it seemed to me to be more about hopes and dreams, the way my own parents spoke.

But working with those men was how I had learned to build the dry stone walls.'"

Mica and I would later learn that Raffaello had learned well, as he was now considered one of the last remaining experts in the area.

According to Mica, Raffaello continued his guided tour and showed her and Antonella where the cows the farmers had raised for milk and cheese were brought each day for grazing and where they had been kept at night on the first floor of the farmhouse, along with all the other farm animals. The eighteen people who had lived and worked on the farm had slept on the floors above where, during the winter, the rising body heat from the animals had helped keep them warm. According to Mica, Raffaello had said with a sigh and a sense of sadness, "It's hard to imagine now, when you see the overgrowth and collapsing stone walls, what this place looked like in its prime." But what was still intact, they could all see, were the magnificent views of the valley below, and they knew full well how important location was in real estate.

The terraces had been cut from the side of the gradual slope that went down into the valley and ended at the bottom, where a brook served as a boundary for one end of the property. It wasn't as hard as Raffaello thought for Mica to see how the cultivated areas had been hewn out of the surrounding forest, which still framed the entire property with majestic, ancient trees. Although it was October, Mica could easily imagine how beautiful the area would be with the leaves in full bloom. Even now, under gray fall skies, she found the place enchanting and exhilarating.

She realized that the interior of the house was in passable shape although it needed work, especially since it hadn't been updated in over thirty years. She also could see the grounds would need considerable restoration, but the location was exquisite. She knew it would be perfect for us and that I would love it as much as she did.

Mica described all of this to me over the phone. We were both over-the-top excited. Then Mica said in a worried tone, "I really think you will find this place is exactly what we were looking for, but if we want to buy it, we should bid on it now. I know you haven't had a chance to see it, but I hope I described it enough for you to understand how really spectacular it is. We have looked at a lot of places together, and I can tell you without any doubt this is ten times better than anything we've seen before, including the place we were heartbroken not to be able to buy last year."

I trusted Mica implicitly and said, "My love, I am sure it is everything you say it is. I want you to put in a bid now," and I gave her the amount. Before I hung up the phone, I asked, "By the way, what is the place called?"

"Ceppeto, two p's and one t. I love you, and I will call you back as soon as I hear back from the broker."

After a few back-and-forth transatlantic calls and some negotiating palaver with the owners, we agreed upon a price, and without ever having seen the house in person, I sent the required deposit, and we had a deal.

Well, not quite.

In Italy, before you can close on a farm, you're required to offer it to your neighbors and give them the right of first refusal. If any neighbor wanted to buy the property at the same price we'd offered, they could buy it, and we would be out. The notice of this offering must be sent by registered mail. But the local post offices in Italy don't run quite the way they do in the States, which is a nice way of saying there's no assurance a letter you send will be delivered … *ever*. In fact, two of Ceppeto's neighbors never responded to the offering because they apparently never got the notice. So although we were ready to close immediately, we had to wait and sweat it out a bit.

A couple of months passed, and a second notice was sent. We heard from one neighbor, who declined the offer. Great: one down, one to go.

Two months went by with no response—we were now into February 1999—so we arranged to have someone go to the remaining neighbor's house personally with the offer. Finally, we received their refusal, and we made arrangements to close on the house in March.

Mica and I flew to Biella, Mica's hometown, where the closing was scheduled to take place. I had the money wired, and the house was ours. Mica and I immediately drove to Chianti, about five hours away, where we met the broker in Panzano and followed him to the property.

It was a cold, blustery afternoon, overcast. We traveled over dirt roads for a half hour, through forests looking bleak under the gray sky. In a jet-lagged funk, I took in the winter-bare trees under that pall of a sky as I headed to a house I'd only seen in pictures and had spent *un sacco di soldi* (a lot of money) to acquire, wondering, *What have I gotten myself into?*

But then we were there. After coming up the driveway to the main house, we got out of the car, I instantly saw what Mica had seen, and any anxiety I had quickly vanished. I gave Mica, standing next to me nervously waiting for my reaction, a big hug. The view across the valley, the imposing main house, and the grounds around it—with trails leading down onto the terraces below—were even better than Mica had described. It was all spectacular. No sky could ever be gray enough or a winter so harsh as to make Ceppeto ever look anything but Edenesque. This was my old childhood dream come true.

CHAPTER 10

SYLVIA GERSHENOW'S SON

My mother was born in 1916. Her maiden name was Sylvia Gershenow, and she was the fifth of six siblings.

Her parents—my grandparents—had arrived in the United States in the early 1900s. My grandfather Morris was from Vilnius, Lithuania. He'd been a tailor, and on his arrival in New York, there were garment factory representatives waiting dockside to hire tailors on the spot as they disembarked from the boats and cleared immigration. That made him one of the fortunate new immigrants to have a source of income immediately upon his arrival.

My grandmother Miriam—or Minnie, as she was called—was from Poland and had been an orphan raised by relatives. They were able to arrange for her to leave for America, where she lived with relatives in New York.

Morris and Minnie met a short time later at a family gathering, and they were soon married. They were a study in contrasts: he was over 6' tall, and she was only 4'10". He was by then a well-read man, and she was illiterate, never able to sign her name with more than an X.

Opposite in almost every respect, they did share one thing: they both had lived through the traumas of growing up surrounded by anti-Semitism.

My grandmother had suffered through pogrom after pogrom. Her guardians had been bakers, and when the Poles were raiding their shtetl, she was tiny enough to be hidden in one of the ovens where she heard the sounds of the angry Poles smashing windows and ransacking their store. It was a memory she recounted to her last days.

My grandfather fared a little better, as there was a thriving Jewish community in Vilnius, but the Russians controlled Lithuania at that time, and with the revolutions brewing, he knew the future there would be bleak. So, like thousands of other Jews from the area, he left. His first stop had been London, and then, after earning some money there plying his trade as a tailor, he bought a ticket and sailed to America.

Once married and having started a family, survival, rather than romance, was foremost on my grandparents' minds. They joined together in that common goal, and that was the glue that bound them together throughout their whole lives.

My grandfather moved the family from New York to Chicago in 1914, where he opened up a garment factory making women's clothes. My mother was born two years later. It was never clear to me why, but the factory closed down in 1919, and the family moved back east to the small town of Phillipsburg, New Jersey.

Across the Delaware River in Pennsylvania, a relative of my grandmother had a poultry farm. My grandfather opened a live poultry store in Phillipsburg, selling those chickens. That is where my mother was raised and went to school.

She was an excellent student. When she graduated, she desperately wanted to go to college, but in those days, in her family, girls didn't go to college. Despite that, she never lost her love of learning. As long as I can remember, she was borrowing books from the local public library every week, taking out the maximum allowable and religiously returning them the next week for new ones. The day she died, there were five books at her bedside that she had borrowed the week before.

All that self-education may have been why her friends and family always flocked to her for advice and counseling whenever they had issues they couldn't resolve. She was a good listener and dispensed her advice with a wisdom that showed both compassion and pragmatic reasoning. Her ethics and sense of right and wrong were beyond reproach.

She always spoke her mind. If she thought someone wasn't telling the truth, she wouldn't hesitate to use strong language as a rebuke. Her favorite was "That is just *horseshit!*"

Instead of college, she worked in the live poultry store. The worst day she ever had at the store was when she'd been left alone to mind the place and a man came in and selected six chickens he wanted slaughtered on the spot. My mother had never done the killing by herself and had great trepidation in doing so, but fearing the ire of her father if he ever found out she had lost the sale of six chickens, she gathered up her courage and did the deed.

There was a small community of Jewish families in the area, and the older children would gather for social and athletic events. At a basketball game between two area teams, she saw a handsome young man starring on one of them. She would later meet him when he was delivering some fresh produce to a store next to her family's poultry shop. They soon started dating.

It was 1935, the depths of the Great Depression, so a date was a get-together to talk or sing popular songs from sheet music they bought for five cents. Those songs were sung years later on long car trips and, yes, when my father took a shower. "Blue Moon," "Red Sails in the Sunset," and even, much to my Jewish grandmother's chagrin, "Silent Night." It was not long after that my parents became serious and married in 1936. My sister was born a year later, and I followed two years after that. Two other brothers were each born in 1944 and 1948.

My mother was a stunning woman, over 5'7", which was tall for her generation, with dark, curly hair and large brown eyes. My father was 5'10" with blond hair and blue eyes. Both were always in excellent physical shape, and they made an extraordinarily handsome couple.

My father's parents had emigrated from Russia, first arriving in Texas and then settling in Oklahoma where they sold horses to cowboys. They then made their way east to settle in Bethlehem, Pennsylvania.

My father, being the oldest son, dropped out of school when he was sixteen in 1931 during the Depression to help his struggling family. He went to work shoveling coal into the huge furnaces at the Bethlehem Steel Mills. When he arrived home, he would drink a quart of milk with the cream still on top (in those days, milk wasn't pasteurized) to wash the coal dust out of his throat. Later, he worked with his father, who had started a fresh produce business, and did that up until he was drafted into the army during World War II.

By the time I arrived on the scene, Phillipsburg—we used to call it P'burg—was already a melancholy little town. P'burg had been a major transportation hub for moving freight, particularly coal, on barges along the Delaware and Lehigh Rivers and nearby canal system. But almost as soon as the canal network had been created, the steam engine arrived, and the railroads made the canals obsolete. It was a technological revolution from which P'burg never recovered.

From my earliest memories, I heard two languages spoken at home, English and Yiddish. My grandparents spoke Yiddish most of the time, while my parents only did when in their company. Like many first-generation Jewish families who were trying to assimilate as fast as possible, Yiddish was rarely spoken after my grandparents passed away, but by that time I was a teenager. As a result much of the vocabulary has stayed with me, Yiddish words often popping up and surprising me even today. Mica loves the way they sound and seem so appropriate to describe a person or thing. *Tokhis oyfin tish* means "Put up or shut up," "Let's get down to business," or literally, "Put your ass on the table." The endless derogatory ways to describe a person are amusing because they really symbolize a person's character in one word, such as *mensch* (a good guy), although it then gets increasingly worse from there: *nebbish* (loser), *shmendrick* (the opposite of *mensch*), *shmegegee* (worse than a shmendrick—a petty or dumb loser), *shnorer* (like a sycophant, moocher, or cheapskate), and the ultimate insult is, of course, *shmuck*.

We lived over my grandparents' live poultry store in a tiny apartment. The building was a wood frame construction with a long, winding, rickety staircase from the street up to our apartment. The store fronted Main Street, the only two-lane road in town, and was sandwiched between a fruit store and a saloon. Next to the fruit store was a Lutheran Church, and next to the saloon was a Catholic Church and convent.

Some of my first memories leaving the apartment were of climbing down those distrustful-looking wooden stairs followed by our small dog, a mixed breed resembling a cocker spaniel, walking out to Main Street, and entering the front door of the poultry store. The pungent smell—well, stench, really—that hit me when I entered the store is still indelibly etched in my mind. It was enough to dissuade the dog from entering the store. He'd go around smelling the poop of other dogs, but that odor of chickens left him cowering on the sidewalk outside the door.

There were cages stuffed with live chickens stacked on top of one another and lined up in rows along either side, leaving a feather-strewn aisle big enough for people to walk down and peer into the cages in order to select the chicken of their choice. Once a bird was selected, one of my grandparents or my mother would slowly open the top of the cage, grab the condemned by the neck with one hand, and then carry it to the back of the store as it flapped its wings and screamed, trying to get free. In short order, whoever had the chicken would grab a hatchet, place the bird's head on a wooden block, then with quick and sure movements cut the head off and fling the carcass into a funnel for the blood to drain. The brutal scene was often punctuated by the headless carcass jumping out of the funnel and floundering around on the floor. That was a hell of a way for a kid to vividly learn the meaning of the expression "Like a chicken without a head." Then, an instrument that looked like a comb plucked the feathers. Afterward, the carcass was singed to remove any traces of remaining feathers.

That ever-present stench of chickens, blood, and singed feathers is hard to forget. To this day, how I can eat chicken is beyond me, but I'm sure I know exactly how young Marcel in Proust's *Combray* felt when he saw the family cook, Françoise, slaughtering a chicken while screaming, "Dirty beast! Dirty beast!" I understand the sheer horror of that moment—the realization of where his dinner was coming from—as well as how the decision whether to eat chicken ever again weighed on his conscience.

Another early memory I have is of my parents sitting next to the radio listening intently to the news of the attack on Pearl Harbor, which brought America into the Second World War on December 7, 1941, a few days before my second birthday.

Around this time, my sister, who was four years old, attended kindergarten at the Catholic Church a few doors away from our apartment. While she attended school, I was left alone and wandered during the day between our apartment and the chicken store. For a snack, I stopped in the saloon next door where I was known as "Two-Ton Tony" (the nickname for Tony Galento, Jersey's heavyweight boxer of the day) because I was quite chubby.

I was always lifted up onto a barstool and given a stick pretzel. I have no recollection of ever talking, but I sat there and enjoyed the pretzel, which, to this day, is still my favorite snack food. The saloon was a place right out of the late 1800s with spittoons at the foot rail and sawdust on the floor. The place reeked of stale beer. (It seems many of my memories are linked to my sense of smell: the chicken store, the bar, and even my grandparents' home, which smelled of freshly baked bread, cucumbers being pickled in a big barrel on the back porch, and, of course, roasted chicken.)

A year after the war began, my father was drafted into the army, and we moved from our apartment into my grandparents' home a block away. I still have vivid memories of air raid drills with Civil Defense wardens running around tapping on windows and telling people to turn off their lights. The fear of a German bombing raid was considered a distinct possibility up and down the East Coast of America. As a child, it was unsettling—to say the least—to sit there in the dark with the air raid sirens wailing.

But there were pleasant memories too. Many a summer Sunday, we would go out to the farm where our relatives raised the chickens my grandparents sold. It was a lovely ride along the back roads, taking in the sweet country air and seeing the beautiful farmland.

Sometimes we even stopped at a little airport (really just a single landing strip with a hangar off to the side) to watch in amazement the small two-seater planes taking off and landing.

At the farm, I'd play and swim in the pond with my cousins, the women would gather and cook what seemed like tons of food, and the men would sit together playing cards. There was always lots of laughter and joy. My cousins, often as many as fifteen, ranging in age from infants to nine years old, played together all day. When my grandparents looked out at their flock, they laughed, and my grandfather would say to my grandmother, "Mimi, imagine we are responsible for all this." By the end of the day all of us kids were exhausted with tummies filled with delicious homemade food, and while traveling back home in our cars, there wasn't one child that didn't blissfully fall asleep.

I have family photos of those days, time-stamped merely by looking at the way everyone dressed. The women all wore long dresses, and some also wore aprons to signify that they were the cooks. Their shoes were certainly relics of the 1940s and earlier. No style, just laced-up, clearly weather-beaten affairs with a small heel and the sides rising up to the ankles, topped by rolled-down socks. The men were better dressed, fashion-wise: most wore long pants, with many sporting sleeveless undershirts. I later wore the same type, and when I moved to a neighborhood in the country, the local kids I found there called them "tenement shirts." We children were all dressed in short pants that doubled as bathing suits. On really warm days, a few of the adults got into bathing suits as well. The women's suits covered nearly everything except for their legs. The men paired swimming trunks with the tenement-style shirt. The best time stamp of all, however, was seeing the cars parked in the background in front of the main weather-beaten, wood frame farmhouse and barn. They were all used cars, and some trucks were from the early 1930s. For any car buff, they were a delight to see. But for me, the whole rustic nature of the farm, the outdoors, the trucks, the chickens, the cows, the pond we swam in, and the open fields surrounding us, made me feel I was in another world, especially compared to our tiny apartment in P'burg.

The war years interrupted that idyllic scene. Most of the younger men, including my father, were drafted, and then everything was rationed, especially gasoline, which made it hard to travel even short distances. But as I got older, it was the memory of those times that nurtured the idea of someday having a farm of my own.

My mother, sister, and I stayed with my grandparents until the end of the war. During that time, my sister continued to attend the Catholic school kindergarten. She has fond memories of her days there and loved the nuns who were her teachers. When she started to repeat the rosary bead prayers at home, however, that was more than my Jewish grandmother could tolerate, and my sister was yanked out of the church kindergarten, never to return.

When my father returned safely home at the end of the war, we moved to West Philadelphia, hoping for something a little better than the depressed environs of Phillipsburg. My father had trouble finding work but finally got a job as a sales clerk in a haberdashery store where the specialty item of the day was the new gizmo the ballpoint pen. They were so new and novel they cost $9.95, which, in those days, was a hell of a sum of money.

Philadelphia was a big change from Phillipsburg and not just because it was bigger and more developed. While our particular street was predominately Jewish, the next block was Irish and the next Italian. The kids from the different neighborhoods all played—and fought—together.

After two years, we were evicted from our rented house in Philadelphia. This was a time of a severe housing shortage in America, and apparently someone else was willing to pay more in rent than we could afford. My sister and I went to live with relatives, while my parents and my younger brother went to live with my grandparents.

As my parents tried to find an affordable place for us all to live together, my mother's feeling was that, as comfortable as it might be, she did not want us raised in an all-Jewish, ghetto-type neighborhood. She believed that this would keep us kids from having to face the realities of being Jewish in a society that, at the time, considered Jews almost alien beings. Knowing that we would inevitably have to learn how to deal with anti-Semitism, she insisted that we move to an area where we would be the minority. Her adamancy only prolonged the time it took to find an affordable place that could accommodate us all.

I was seven years old then, and I never forgot the experience of that separation. I vowed that when I was able to, I would start working so our family could once again be reunited. I did just that, starting when I was eight years old, shortly after we were able to find a new home in what was, back then, a very rural area of Pennsylvania.

Veterans like my father were able to buy a home with no down payment and fifty dollars a month. The house was a small three-bedroom, one-bathroom home, just big enough for our family, which by then included my parents, my sister, two younger brothers, and my grandmother.

It didn't take long for us to learn the lessons my mother had been so insistent on our learning. We were the only Jewish family in what was mostly a Protestant and Catholic neighborhood. The prejudice was immediate, plain, and complete. When I'd introduce myself to other kids and tell them I was Jewish, they would say—very innocently, mind you—"Where are your horns? My parents say Jews have horns."

When my sister and I entered the local school, she in the sixth grade and me in the fourth, we were the first Jewish students ever to attend it. There were only six classrooms—one for each grade—so there weren't many students. We found that although we made friends with our schoolmates, some of their parents wouldn't permit us to enter their houses because we were Jewish.

We also lived near a Catholic school, and as word spread through our neighborhood that we were Jewish, I began to be taunted for being a "Christ killer" by the Catholic kids.

Naturally, I absolutely hated all this, and it took years before I appreciated the wisdom of my mother's decision.

My father went back into the produce business. He would leave shortly after midnight in a large truck to go to the Philadelphia docks where the early birds got the best pick of the goods being unloaded from trains and ships. When I didn't have school the next day, I would go with him and watch as he hoisted hundred-pound bags of potatoes, one on each shoulder, and carry them to the back of the truck. He would throw them into the truck, jump up, and carry them inside the trailer where I would try to help by pulling and stacking them into neat rows. He did the same with wooden crates of oranges, grapefruits, and bananas.

When he had loaded everything he needed, he drove off to deliver them to his clients, all small ma-and-pa grocery stores around the city of Philadelphia. At each stop, I would get into the back of the truck and push and shove the crates and sacks, all weighing far more than I did, to the end of the truck where my father could take them down and carry them into the store. The result of all that work was that I grew into a powerfully strong boy for my age.

The stores would call in their orders to our home phone. My mother would take down the orders after she came home from her job, while she was waiting for my father to come home for dinner. After dinner, my father went to sleep and woke up after midnight to start the whole process over again.

Sundays were spent at the dining room table, making up the bills to be given to the grocers during the next week. Saturday was the only day off, and that was when my father got his one chance each week to get a good night's sleep.

I had a red wagon in which a wooden orange crate fit perfectly. During the spring and summer, I began taking it about a mile from our house into woods that had, apparently, never been touched. The rich, black topsoil was a few feet thick. I filled up the orange crate with it, hauled it back to my neighborhood, and sold it for fertilizer. After only a few weeks, the results on the plants and lawns were so impressive that I had more orders than I could fill. At the age of eight, I had my first successful business.

It was the custom in our home to put whatever money we'd each earned on the dining room table to be collected by my mother. She was the comptroller and went about budgeting the expenses for the week. Saturday, her day off, was the day she went from store to store getting the best prices she could find for the items she needed for the house. At the end of the day, however little or much money she had, a small amount always went to charity. If she didn't have any left over, she would volunteer her time to do some charitable work. It was something that was never discussed; I always assumed that was the way it was supposed to be.

My parents felt it was important that I go to Hebrew school so that I could have a bar mitzvah when I turned thirteen. This happened at the same time I started playing on the school football team. I begged my parents to let me do both. They got permission from the coach for me to miss two practices a week so that I could go to Hebrew school, and then they did the same at the Hebrew school, allowing me to miss some of my lessons there so I could play on the football team.

The Hebrew school was a good hour and a half away. There was no synagogue in our area because there weren't enough Jewish families to attend, so I had to walk a fair distance to take a trolley car, bus, and elevated train to get to the school after my regular school was over at 3:00 p.m.

My first day at the school, the Hebrew teacher called me to the front of the class and told me to put my hands out in front of me with the palms down. He then took a ruler he was holding behind his back and hit my hands with it while shouting, "What Jewish boy would rather play football than go to Hebrew school? Shame on you!"

I was too humiliated and embarrassed to say a word, and I bit my lower lip, trying not to show any pain or shed a tear. After the whacking, I sat back down with my head bowed, not wanting to look at any of the other boys staring at me.

After that class, I went home and told my parents that I would not go back to Hebrew school and had no desire to have a bar mitzvah. They must have recognized the anger and determination in my face, because they made no objection. I never did go back, nor did I have a bar mitzvah. Despite the lack of formal religious training, I still had a traditional Jewish childhood and adolescence.

My grandmother spoke mostly Yiddish, and we observed the dietary laws—no shellfish, no mixing meat with milk—and observed all the Jewish holidays. I always considered myself a Jew and never hid from that fact.

Starting in the fourth grade at our new school, each child was offered the opportunity to play a musical instrument. The school provided all the instruments, except the one I wanted to play the most: the piano. Since my family couldn't afford to buy one, I opted to play the drums, where the only requirement was to get a pair of drumsticks.

Two years later, the head of the middle school music department came to my classroom and listened to each student play their instrument. After hearing me play the drums, he selected me to be part of his special music program. Students in the program had to start school an hour earlier every day and received an extra hour of music during the day. The music program also required that all its students take an intensive academic or precollege curriculum. Academically, it was rated one of the top education programs available in all of Pennsylvania. In that regard, I was very fortunate.

For whatever reason, it turned out that all the music students tended to be the brighter kids in their class, and 99 percent of them wound up heading for college. As my senior year came to a close, I couldn't help but notice that as I looked to my left and right, each student was going off to college somewhere. Around April, it occurred to me that with everybody else leaving for college, maybe I should start looking, but it was too late to take entrance exams.

Still, you could get into a state school without the exam if you had a B or better average. No matter. Even a state school was beyond my financial means, especially when living expenses and the cost of books were added in. I applied anyway and was accepted to Penn State University. I was also awarded a State Senatorial Scholarship, which enabled me to attend.

Then it was time to head off to college. When I arrived, I had already decided on what I wanted to major in, due to another seminal experience I'd had a few years earlier.

During high school, I'd worked after school for a packaging company that filled orders going to supermarkets. Boxes of crackers, cereals, and condiments had to be packed at night and delivered to the stores the next morning. There was one week in which a number of new supermarkets were opening, and I was asked to work midnight each night before the big openings that weekend. I agreed. During that time I got home close to one in the morning, did my homework, and, on a few hours of sleep, went to school and back to work the next day.

When it came time for me to get paid that week, I noticed I was being paid for less than the hours I'd worked. I went to my boss and asked, "Sir, I worked over forty hours after school this past week, why am I only getting paid for half those hours?"

He said, "Look, don't blame me; I thought you knew there was a limit on how many hours we can pay a part-timer. I had no idea you were working as many hours as you did, but my hands are tied. I will try to make it up to you later, but for now that is all you are going to get paid."

I was furious at the injustice that, to me, defied logic. I responded, "Don't bother. I wouldn't trust you to ever pay me for the hours I work. I quit," and I walked out and went home.

When I arrived home, my mother, seeing the anger on my face, immediately asked, "You are home early, what happened?"

I answered with what would become my mantra for the rest of my life: "I will do everything I possibly can to be my own boss so I never have to work for another person." She saw in me the same look of determination as when I refused to go back to Hebrew school and knew there was no way to change my mind.

The next day, after calming down, I was able to tell her what had happened, and she said, "Son, you are the type of person that when you set your mind on doing something, you do it. There will always be injustices in your life, but those who are successful don't let them get in their way. They just plow right through them and continue on. You have that ability, and there will be a day when you are going to be very successful at whatever you decide to do." I guess to be successful one needs to have people who believe in him or her, and for me, that started with my parents.

Unfortunately, Penn State offered no courses called "How to Become Your Own Boss." In lieu, I chose a major I naively thought would teach me how to be just that: business administration.

When I returned home after my first semester, I learned that the scholarship that had gotten me started wasn't going to last much longer. I gave it up when I learned that the representatives from the local Democratic Party that helped get me the Senatorial Scholarship were coming around and asking my parents for money.

You have to appreciate the irony of these guys asking us for money as thanks for making college affordable for me. If we'd had that money, we wouldn't have needed the scholarship in the first place! To make up for the loss, I waited tables for my board and began playing drums in a band.

My band was hired almost every weekend to play at fraternity parties. Between that and summer jobs, I was able to pay for college. Not only had my musical training starting in the fourth grade paved the way for me to apply and enter college, but it was also the major reason why I could afford to stay in school and graduate.

In those days—we're talking 1957 now—it was mandatory for male college students to take Reserve Officers' Training Corps (ROTC) classes during their first two years. After those two years, you had the option of dropping ROTC, but if you continued on, as I did, you were paid a dollar a day. That extra thirty dollars a month was compelling, and it went a long way in helping me pay college expenses. In exchange, I graduated as a second lieutenant, obligated to serve a total of seven years active and reserve duty in the army.

I graduated college in 1961 with a bachelor of science degree in business administration and was then ordered to Fort Knox for armored training. I became close friends with a lot of guys with whom I trained, and we stayed in touch for years. One of them in particular became a lifelong friend, and I eventually became the godfather of his children. But a number of trainees had never seen a Jew before, and once again, mostly out of ignorance, I encountered prejudice. The value of my mother having pushed us to live in a mixed neighborhood paid off. In whatever form the prejudice appeared—whether rabid in-your-face hatred, casual insensitivity, or blithe ignorance—I could deal with it.

That summer, the Berlin wall was erected, and I was assigned to active duty on the East-West German border for two years. The home station for the unit was in Bindlach, Bavaria, with the assigned task of patrolling the border from the point where the East-West German border met Czechoslovakia and then west a few hundred kilometers. My platoon—which consisted of a tank, three jeeps, an armored personnel carrier, a mortar carrier, and twenty-one men—occupied a farmhouse a short distance from the border. From that position, patrols were sent out 24-7.

What with seventeen years of building Cold War paranoia, Cuba having recently fallen to Castro, and now the Berlin Wall going up, war with the Soviet Union seemed possible and maybe even inevitable. Sometimes, we could hear the Soviet T-34 tanks rumbling around on the other side of the border, especially during the Cuban Missile Crisis when massive amounts of Soviet tanks and armaments were assembled on the other side of the border facing us. If war had broken out, our job was to delay their advance. But in reality, with just twenty-one guys, I'm not sure how much good we could have done before we were steamrolled by the Russian hordes.

Because there was such a fast buildup of American forces in Germany that year, there wasn't sufficient housing available for us officers. Instead we were given a monthly stipend and told to go out and rent a place near the base. I chose an apartment in Bayreuth. I was rarely there because of the border duty to which I was assigned. Somehow the landlord discovered I was Jewish, and the next thing I knew I was being evicted from the apartment, on claims I was having loud parties there—an absurd claim considering that I slept there infrequently and never entertained anyone there. On the day I left, I noticed an older woman looking at me from the window of her apartment, and when I looked up at her, she began making all sorts of faces and mouthing, in German, "Go away, Jew."

I then rented some rooms in a house of a German family nearby, and to avoid any issues, I told them immediately that I was Jewish.

They were fine with that, and I moved in around Christmastime. They had a daughter, and because they had tragically lost a son the year before and were still in mourning, they couldn't have a Christmas tree in their section of the house. They asked if I would mind if they put one in the section I was renting, for their daughter. Without any hesitation I agreed, and that cemented what turned out to be a cordial relationship.

I never had a Christmas tree before, so this was a unique experience for me. The freshly cut tree was decorated with candles that they lit each evening I was there. As long as the tree was fresh, it was not in danger of catching fire. It actually smelled quite good, like the air fresheners of today. Having the Christmas tree also gave me the chance to share drinks of American whiskey with the owner, Herr Damphler. He was in his midforties, about 5'8", tall, and very slim. His graying hair barely covered his scalp, and his thick-lensed glasses made him look professorial. Through him I got insight into life during World War II. The propaganda that was produced during those years was astonishing to me. Most books that had the slightest criticism of Germany were burned, leaving the German people only what the Nazis wanted them to know. Herr Damphler showed me some of those books and pointed out that every great invention of the world was invented by a German: the automobile, train, electricity, telephone, radio, airplane ... you name it, Germans invented it. He then showed me a book that had a detailed drawing of the city of Nuremberg in 1400, which illustrated its many streets, bridges, roads, and buildings. Next to that was a drawing of America as it looked in 1400, pointedly showing that there were no cities or structures. The conclusion was that Germany was hundreds of years more advanced than the primitive United States.

The daughter was in fifth grade, and one night I asked her to show me her history book. I wanted to see what they were teaching her about the war years. I found a couple of sentences on it that read, "In 1933 Hitler came to power. From 1933 to 1945 was a bad time for Germany." It was obvious from all this that Germans were not yet ready to address the atrocities of the war.

I discussed all this and the plight of the Jews in Bayreuth with Herr Damphler. He and his wife both claimed they knew the Jews were being taken away but thought they were only being relocated so they could work for the war effort. He said, "Everyone was being asked to do something for the war. My wife and I joined the Luftwaffe." He introduced me to the only remaining Jewish families still living in the area. These two families were young and said they had no contacts anywhere else, so after being released from a concentration camp while still in their late teens, they returned to Bayreuth where the government gave them a stipend. I found it difficult to comprehend how they could do that, but given all that they had been through, I didn't want to push that subject with them. It appeared that Herr Damphler was on good terms with both families.

I spent many an evening with Herr Damphler, him speaking German and me part German and part Yiddish along with the assistance of the dictionary, some American whiskey, and cigarettes. Whatever it took, we were able to communicate, and I really think I was able to enlighten him enough that he began to question some of that propaganda fed to him in the war years. For a German and an American Jew, it was a start.

When my assignment on the border was over, I became a short-timer, with less than three months left on my tour before going home. It was the beginning of summer, and I was put in charge of the American officers' club in Bayreuth.

The club was in a beautiful early nineteenth-century manor right next to the Festspielhaus (Festival House) where the Wagner Fest performances were—and still are—performed to this day. The place had been used as an officers' club since the end of WWII and, in all that time, had never made a profit. The building was solid but was in shabby condition. The grounds had been, at one time, replete with formal gardens and fountains but had been left unattended since the war.

Perhaps the most unique aspect of the manor was that it had been where Hitler had stayed whenever he came to Bayreuth to hear Wagner, his favorite composer, performed in the Festspielhaus, which was just a short walk away on the property next door. Hitler's bedroom had been in the basement of the building. To get to his bedroom, you had to pass through a foyer with iron doors. When you entered the foyer, the entry door would slam shut, and you found yourself facing another iron door, which opened into Hitler's bedroom. It was designed so that if an intruder entered that foyer, the iron doors would seal the chamber airtight and deadly gas could be forced into it, killing the trespasser. In addition, inside the bedroom, there was a large picture on the wall, behind which was the entrance to an escape tunnel that led about a hundred yards into the woods nearby.

That officers' club became my first bit of real estate renovation. I had a squad of soldiers clean up the gardens, get the fountains working again, and manicure the entire property, which quickly began flowering in the early summer. I had the interiors repainted and began holding events in the ballroom. I hired a chef and started a dining service. Gambling was permitted, so I activated slot machines in the bar and lounge area. The place already had a thriving bar, but what put it over the top was that I went to the Festspielhaus right next door and invited all the performers over for cocktails each evening. With the performers came many young, quite beautiful dancers and singers, whose presence caused news to spread as far as Nuremburg to not only the officers of the army but also to the air force and the CIA as well. As for Hitler's bedroom, I had many requests for card and crap games, so I redecorated der Führer's private lair and converted it into a casino.

The end result was that the place became a hot spot and started earning money for the first time since the end of the war. It became such an attraction that even generals were stopping by to see what I had done and asking me to re-up and make the army a career. I respectfully declined, anxiously looking forward to getting back to the States.

While running the officers' club, I discovered there were two former German soldiers who had been working there for many years. The two of them had been active Nazis during the war, which was not unusual to find, but what concerned me was that I discovered that they were active in the emerging Neo-Nazi Party. They actually had discussed it with other American officers who frequented the bar. I went to my superiors and told them of my concern. My superiors told me it would be difficult to do anything about it. The desire to keep American-German relations on good terms meant that in order to fire any German national employee, there had to be at least two documented infractions committed, each followed by a written reprimand. There had been no officer prior to me who had been willing to take the time and effort to do that.

I began a month-and-a-half-long campaign to watch the two of them, which entailed keeping copious records of the bar they were tending and money that they collected for drinks and dinners. It wasn't long before I discovered that they were skimming money from both. I wrote up a report with all the evidence and submitted it to Nuremberg headquarters. They said they would enter it into the employees' files. I gave each of them a warning, as required, both in writing and verbally. They were both upset and shocked that I was on their case. I think, however, that they didn't think I had the time to continue the tedious task of keeping tabs on them. But I did, often working hours after everything closed down, checking the amounts of liquor that had been poured from every open bottle at the bar, and controlling the inventory of liquor, wine, and food ordered to see what had been billed to customers. Sure enough, I again found systematic shortages in places that they probably thought would never be discovered. I had enough evidence to submit the second notice to headquarters, and that, too, was entered into their files. I again sent the two written reprimands.

Within days, I received the go-ahead to fire them. I confronted them one at a time. I said to the first, "Herr Rudy, you have been working here almost since the end of the war. You had a position of trust and an obligation not to cheat and steal from this operation. You violated that trust and obligation not once, but twice under my watch, and therefore you are hereby fired. You are to leave the premises immediately."

At first, his face registered utter surprise; then, as I finished telling him he was fired, he turned red with anger. He said, "You can't do this. I will complain to the authorities."

I replied, "Herr Rudy, not only can I do this, I have done it and followed the regulations 100 percent. You are finished working for an American establishment in Germany ever again. Good-bye."

My confrontation with the other employee, Herr Gerhard, was similar. He also seemed shocked at first and then quickly switched to anger.

I was happy that they were finally fired, and I was also glad that they both knew full well that I was Jewish.

If they'd had any doubts as to whether I was Jewish, that had been dispelled almost a year earlier when I was at the officers' club one evening with some friends, having dinner. I overheard a chief warrant officer by the name of Haley, a helicopter pilot that I was actually scheduled to be on duty with the next day, tell six other men from my platoon, "That guy is such a prick; his mother is probably a Jew."

Both Herr Rudy and Herr Gerhard were nearby as I got up and walked over to him and said, "I am a Jew, and don't ever say that again."

He responded with a sneer and said, "Jew boy, what are you going to do about it?"

I punched him in the face, and he immediately fell to the ground. Without another word, I walked away as his friends came to his aid.

The following morning when I reported to helicopter duty, there was CWO Haley with a visibly bruised nose and eye. He didn't say a word. When his copilot arrived, my troops and I loaded up in the back with our weapons. We were due to patrol the border area by air and make sure there were no incursions. If an emergency occurred, the helicopter would land, and my troops and I would disembark and surround the problem area. As we lifted off, I made sure all my men had buckled up their safety belts. It was a clear day, and visibility was excellent. We could see far into East Germany and all along the border area.

After about an hour, seeing nothing of concern, we were ordered back to our home base. As we neared the landing strip, instead of decreasing altitude, CWO Haley began climbing higher. I was beginning to wonder why when suddenly the engine went dead. We dropped like a lead weight, and all our stomachs were suddenly in our throats. Some men threw up. Each one of us thought we were about to crash. It lasted for seconds but seemed like an eternity. Finally, all of a sudden, the motor came back on with a deafening roar, and our sudden fall slowed down until it appeared the pilot had control of the helicopter again. When it was over, I heard Haley over my headphones laughing and saying, "That will teach the bastard a lesson." I was furious.

When we landed, Haley was quick to leave while I checked on my men. They were badly shaken up but seemed okay. The copilot remained and said, "Look, I'm sorry he had a bug up his ass, but that was a maneuver that good pilots learn how to do in case the engine really stops working." He explained that when a helicopter drops quickly, air flows up and turns the rotors, providing lift so that, hopefully, a soft landing can be achieved. He then explained how the engine had to be turned off and on to practice the maneuver. He said, "With a good pilot like we had today, the outcome is fairly assured."

I responded testily, "I have no doubt that Haley is an excellent pilot with many years of experience, but taking retribution for our fight last night out on my troops was unprofessional and broke just about every rule in the book."

As confirmation of that fact, the two of us found ourselves standing at attention in front of our top commanding officer, Major McMann, the next day. Major McMann was a legendary war hero who had fought in the Pacific during World War II. A man's man, everyone respected and liked him. He said, "I have received a few reports about what went on at the officers' club the other night and what happened on your flight yesterday. As far as what happened yesterday, that is the last time I will allow anything like that to happen on my watch again. Haley, I am transferring you out of here with a disciplinary reprimand on your record. Hadar, from now on, save your fighting for when it really will be needed against the enemy. Dismissed."

After that, Major McMann and I got along very well.

A month or so later, I was stationed on the border with my platoon. Each platoon was rotated every six weeks, staying in an old farmhouse from where patrols were sent out 24-7. It had a small kitchen and mess hall, a place to secure firearms, and a couple of barns to do maintenance on our equipment. We kept the place as neat as possible, but with troops constantly coming and going on patrols, it was not exactly a showplace for military neatness. I was more concerned about making sure my troops were well fed and rested so they could do their job when on patrol.

One early morning, I received a radio call from the supreme commander's headquarters saying the commander was flying in by helicopter to visit our post and inspect it. They didn't name him but just said he was the top officer for all NATO troops in Northern Europe. ETA: five hours. Talk about a fire drill! I rounded up all the troops I had available that weren't on patrol, and we began cleaning the place as fast as possible. I immediately called Major McMann and told him what was happening. He dropped everything and came up as fast as he could. He arrived about three hours later. As we walked through the place, we each knew that this was not going to go well. The place was too far gone to be cleaned up that fast for the top inspection we were about to have.

We did the best we could, and a couple of hours later, I got the call on the radio from the helicopter carrying the top officer saying they were on the way in for the landing and would touch down in fifteen minutes. I had our tanks, personnel carrier, jeeps, and mortar carrier moved to provide a small landing space for the helicopter. I stationed one of my men on the landing space to guide the helicopter in. I hurriedly dressed in my freshly pressed fatigues, dusted off my boots, and waited with Major McMann next to the landing strip. As the helicopter gently lowered to the ground, kicking up a huge amount of dust, I thought, *There goes my nicely pressed uniform and polished boots. This is going from bad to worse.* Holding on to our hats, Major McMann and I, side by side, approached the door of the helicopter as it completed its landing, turned off its engine and lowered the ramp. Out stepped an army officer with a chest full of ribbons that covered the whole side of his uniform. When I saw his face, I was in shock and said loud enough for Major McMann to hear, "Oh my gosh, that's my uncle!"

Major McMann said, "What, that's your uncle?"

I nodded, and he put his hand behind my back and whispered, "Get up there and greet him now. You just saved our asses."

I quickly went up to my uncle and, saluting, said, "Uncle Lou!"—not exactly your usual military discipline for greeting one of the top US Army officers in Germany.

He smiled, saluted back, and said, "Lieutenant, I am so glad to see you."

He was my mother's brother and my favorite uncle. He had been the youngest full colonel in World War II and had been in the first invasion of North Africa at the start of the US participation in the war. It was where the most brutal battles with the highest casualty rates occurred in the entire war. The legendary German Field Marshall Erwin Rommel captured Uncle Lou, along with General Patton's son-in-law. Lou had had the foresight to put "NRP"—meaning "no religious preference"—on his dog tags, or otherwise, as a Jew, he probably would not have survived being captured. Later, Uncle Lou and General Patton's son-in-law escaped together in a wheelbarrow, ultimately working their way back to Allied lines.

Uncle Lou had later served in the Korean War and was highly decorated for both conflicts. I, of course, knew he was in Germany. I had visited him quietly at his headquarters in Heidelberg, but I'd never told anyone about him, as I didn't want anyone to think I was trying to pull rank to curry favor with my superior officers.

After the surprise wore off, my uncle said he knew I was there and that was why he planned the visit. I escorted him around with Major McMann close behind us. As Shakespeare wrote, "Silence speaks faint praise," for my uncle said little. He didn't have to. Major McMann and I both knew the place was far from being ready for an inspection. We retired to the mess hall where I had coffee and some snacks served. Then, for over an hour, I listened as my uncle and Major McMann traded war stories. When he left, my uncle broke military protocol by giving me a hug and saying, "Good work, Richard. I am proud of you." We saluted again, and off he flew.

Major McMann put his arm on my shoulder as we walked back to the farmhouse and said, "This is one of the biggest surprises I've ever had, but it was a pleasure meeting your uncle. He is one hell of a guy."

During the penultimate month of my tour of duty, I had a month of time off saved up. I threw some camping equipment I borrowed from the quartermaster onto the roof rack of my Volkswagen Beetle and headed out on the autobahn for points west. In thirty days, I drove from Germany north to Denmark, then back to the mainland, and south all through the Netherlands, France, Switzerland, and Italy.

It was a great time to be a GI in Europe. The dollar was strong, and the echo of World War II and the liberating Americans still reverberated loud and clear across the Continent. I was greeted warmly almost everywhere I went.

On the first leg of my trip to Denmark, I was up for over twenty-four hours, and after taking the ferry from Germany to Denmark, I still had a couple hours' drive to get to Copenhagen. I was dangerously nodding off while driving, so at that point, I turned off the highway onto a dirt road leading to a farmhouse. I knocked on the front door, and when a pleasant-looking Danish man opened the door, I greeted him in German.

He smiled and immediately said, "*Guten Tag*, you are an American soldier, *ja?*"

That was my moniker wherever I went in Europe. At 6'3", with a crew cut that most US soldiers sported in those days, I guess it wasn't too hard to tell. Speaking to him in German, I said, "Yes, I am an American soldier, and I am on leave taking a vacation here in Denmark. I am heading to Copenhagen but have been awake for over twenty-four hours. Is there a place near here where I can get some coffee and freshen up before I continue driving? I am falling asleep at the wheel of my car."

He smiled and said, "Certainly, welcome, come in; you can rest here." With that he called his wife, both of whom looked to be in their late fifties, with gray hair and ready smiles. That along with a twinkle in their eyes made me feel very welcomed indeed. I was able to take a shower, and they gave me a room where I could sleep for a few hours. I awoke to the smell of fresh coffee being brewed and muffins being baked in the oven. After a delightful snack, I then offered to pay them for their trouble. They adamantly refused, so I went to my car and pulled out a carton of cigarettes and a bottle of schnapps (whiskey, in this case, American bourbon). American cigarettes and whiskey were better than money in those days, as they were very expensive. For my trip, I had loaded up a supply of each and was happy it was so well received on the first leg of my trip.

After visiting Copenhagen, I eventually made my way to Paris and drove right to the center of the Left Bank. I found a little pension, and as soon as I entered the door to the reception desk, I saw the owner standing behind a rather beat-up and worn counter. On top of it, among some cards, newspapers, and maps, was a sign that read, "Monsieur Jacques Henri, Propriétaire de l'Hôtel." Monsieur Henri had a pencil-thin mustache, straight brown hair barely covering the top of his head, and a small-boned, angular, and fragile-looking physique. He greeted me, smiling. *"Bonjour, soldat américain."*

I might as well have been wearing my uniform instead of a T-shirt and a pair of jeans, but I appreciated the welcome that was so common wherever I traveled on that trip. Monsieur Henri showed me a small room three flights up with a shared bathroom on each floor at a very reasonable price, at that time less than five dollars. I couldn't leave all my stuff that I had jammed into the little Volkswagen parked on the street all night, so I had to carry everything up three flights to the room, where afterward I barely had enough leeway to get to the bed. It was a long drive that day, so not wanting to go too far away, I asked Monsieur Henri if he could recommend a restaurant nearby.

He said, "You can eat right here. My wife and I make wonderful dinners for our guests. We serve it at 8:00 p.m., so please come down a little earlier for some cocktails."

At about seven forty-five, I came down, and Monsieur Henri

greeted me and introduced me to his wife, Madame Henri, a woman slightly shorter than her husband but far plumper, with a ready smile that, from the permanent creases on the sides of her mouth and wrinkles around the corners of her eyes, you could tell was probably there all the time. They showed me to a charming, small candlelit table. Monsieur Henri suggested I have a red burgundy wine with my dinner, which was chateaubriand. What followed was, until this day, one of the most delicious meals I have ever had. They served it with perfectly cooked *pommes de terre* (potatoes), *haricots verts* (green beans), *salade verte* (green salad), and a *tarte aux pommes* (home-baked apple pastry). A glass of port was the grand finale. After I finished, I thanked them both profusely and asked for the check. They refused, and Monsieur Henri said, "We just want to show our appreciation for all that you American soldiers did for us."

I was embarrassed and said, "Thank you ever so much, but I was too young to do anything in that war; a lot of my relatives did but not me personally."

He held up his hand as if to stop me and said, "No, no, you are here now keeping peace. We are thankful for that."

I realized it would be rude for me to continue to object, so I thanked them again and went to sleep that night knowing that this had been an evening I would never forget.

My favorite place, though, was Italy. The people were even friendlier there than any other country in Europe. By the time I arrived there, it was wonderfully warm, and the scenery was spectacular. I drove to Rome before heading back north again.

While in Rome, I was standing in Saint Peter's Square, looking up at all the sights, when a very short man approached me, carrying a rack of souvenirs. He asked me if I wanted to buy one: a picture of the Pope, a crucifix supposedly blessed by the Pope, and so on. He spoke little English, and I refused.

He kept following me, apparently knowing I was an American GI and probably had more money than most of the tourists there that day. I kept saying no to him, but he was tireless and kept following me, offering me his religious articles. Finally, getting very annoyed,

I turned to him and said, "Look, I'm not interested in buying any of that; I'm Jewish."

His eyes lit up in surprise, and he burst into a big smile. "So am I! Come. I take you to the Jewish neighborhood, and we have a good Jewish meal."

So off we went to what were the remnants of the Jewish ghetto in Rome, one of the largest in all of Europe at the time. I met his family, and we had a meal at a kosher restaurant that was both filling and quite delicious—if a bit rich. The *schmaltz* (chicken fat) brought back fond memories of my grandmother's cooking.

After Rome, it was time to head north, back to my home base, to begin packing for my return to the United States.

Rome fell behind, and the road took me past hilly farms and olive groves. I could smell the fresh, rich earth of fields turned fallow for the winter. At the time, it was nothing more than the idle daydream of a GI who didn't own a pot to piss in, but I would look at those farms, remember my early childhood times on my relative's farm, then recall those drives into the Pennsylvania countryside, and start to think, *Gee, this would be a nice way to live ...*

CHAPTER 11

RAFFAELLO

The day we bought and traveled to Ceppeto, there to greet Mica and me, along with the broker, was Raffaello, who had by then been looking after Ceppeto for over fifteen years. He was still coming every day to take care of the house and keep the grounds in reasonable shape all through the months the sale was up in the air. The owners had already moved most of their belongings out of the house, but it certainly wasn't ready for us to move in. Even if it was, we had nothing in Italy with which to move in.

It was late; we were tired, cold, and hungry, but happy. The broker with us suggested we could get a room in Lupaia, a tiny village only a quarter mile away, where rooms were available in what had formerly been a medieval castle. We checked into a cozy turret room with a kitchenette and were directed to the local town, Radda, about five miles away, where we could buy groceries. We stocked up on a few days' worth of supplies and then returned to our room for a quick meal, after which we fell into a deep sleep.

The next morning, we awoke to the sound of a rooster announcing the sunrise. He was actually a little premature, as it was still dark outside. The old thick walls of the castle had kept the room stone cold. Still jet-lagged, we both struggled for a few minutes to remember where we were. Then we looked at each other and smiled. "So this is country living in Italy," I said, shivering, "We better get going, or our limbs are going to rebel and refuse to move." We got up and dressed while hopping around, trying to get warm. Then we downed two cups of hot coffee and bolted for our car, turning the heat on full blast to try to get warm.

Warmed up enough to stop our teeth from chattering, we drove the short distance to Ceppeto and found Raffaello waiting for us. We took a leisurely tour around the house and property, and I kept getting even more excited about how wonderful I thought it all was. Pictures I had seen of the house simply didn't do it justice.

The main house had massive stone exterior walls. Raffaello explained that beginning in the 1400s, as the family grew, additions had been made to the house. I could see by the stonework where the additions had been made. Raffaello said his sister had lived there with eighteen other family members. "My older sister lived there as well, until after the war," said Raffaello. That was a big number, but what threw me was when Raffaello again pointed out how the lower floor was used just for the animals, which included cows, horses, oxen, and pigs. This in-house stabling also served to keep the residence warm in the winter months.

The same family had been living there for generations as tenant farmers. After WWII, the rising Communist Party had organized the tenant farmers, who began making demands from the owners to modernize the houses with plumbing and electricity. That, coupled with the younger generation leaving for the larger cities, drove many owners into bankruptcy, leaving a great many farms abandoned, including Ceppeto.

It was in the 1960s that the two sisters bought Ceppeto by paying the back taxes. They then completely renovated the main house, dividing it into two separate units, one for each sister's family. Italians are as passionate in their feuds as in anything else, and the one between the two families had become so strident that they couldn't even agree on when to paint the shutters. As a result, one side of the house had its shutters painted, and the other didn't.

Before we came over from the States to close on the property, Mica's brothers and their wives had stayed at Ceppeto over the Christmas and New Year holiday of 1998–1999. Even though, at the time, we were still waiting to receive the right-of-first-refusal responses, the owners had agreed to allow the holiday visit so we could determine what work needed to be done.

Mica's brothers are all mechanical types with a factory that makes washers for automobile engines. It doesn't sound like much of a business, but it's a large factory that supplies washers with exacting specifications to Fiat and a number of German car and truck manufacturers, including Volkswagen. After spending a few nights at the farm, their verdict was that all was in good shape. When I finally had a chance to make my first, quick walk-through, I agreed, but I knew a house that was last renovated close to thirty years ago would undoubtedly need work.

Raffaello escorted me through the property, much as he had done with Mica and Antonella, and I was immediately flooded with the possibilities of the place. The grounds were spectacular, but having been largely left untouched for over fifty years, they needed an enormous amount of attention. Every tree beyond the immediate area around the main house was literally being choked to death by thick vines. There were thousands of such trees; Raffaello pointed out to me oaks, chestnuts, walnuts, and lindens, as well as fruit trees of every variety including mulberry, apple, plum, fig, cherry, and olive trees. The place was a virtual cornucopia of nature's bounty.

Underneath the trees was brush so thick that the only way you could walk through was to cut your way with a machete. I knew it would be an enormous task and would require years to clear and clean up what amounted to 90 percent of the property, but once done, it would transform the farm into a picturesque park. It certainly had the woods, terraces, olive groves, and spectacular views to make it a worthy subject for that kind of overhaul.

The main house was as solid as anything I had ever seen. Made of stone with walls over three feet thick, I understood why it had endured for over six centuries. Hand-hewn beams were everywhere, still supporting huge stone walls and antique brick floors above. They reportedly endure better than steel in a fire, as steel beams will buckle in intense heat faster than a fire can consume these huge beams. I considered the raw beauty of these ancient materials truly treasures, and I was determined to preserve as much of it as I could. In fact, the more I saw of what was already there and what needed to be done—and what *could* be done—the more enthralled with the place I got.

After the tour that day, I said to Raffaello, " Mica and I really appreciate all the information you have given us on Ceppeto. We can tell this place is very special for you, and we would like you to stay on as caretaker."

We immediately saw a sigh of relief come over his face as he said with a big smile, *"Piacere."* ("It would be a pleasure.") We hadn't realized how important it was for him and could only imagine the anxiety that he'd been feeling while waiting for us to arrive to tell him one way or the other about his future at the farm. Then he told us, "I was worried I wouldn't be able to continue, because once the owners accepted your offer last October, they stopped paying me, but I just couldn't leave Ceppeto unattended. It would have turned into a mess by the time you got here. So I have been coming here every day making sure everything is okay and doing what has to be done."

That struck me as outrageous. It had been something like five months from the time we'd agreed to buy the house to the closing, and this man had diligently come out every day to maintain Ceppeto, yet the owners refused to pay him all during that time. We tried to call the former owners to discuss the matter, but they were dismissive and said it was our problem, not theirs. I couldn't accept that, so we paid him his back wages.

It turned out that it was one of the best things we could have done as new arrivals in a tiny, close-knit community like Radda. As often is the case, people in small towns have a natural suspicion of outsiders, especially foreigners, but Raffaello became our advocate, and word soon spread that we were good people. When it came time to hire contractors, we were able to get the best local talent in the area to work for us, based on Raffaello's recommendation.

We had no intention of starting any renovations that summer, because Mica and I had decided to get married while in Italy that May. For the time being, we just wanted the house furnished enough to invite friends and family for the wedding. When we saw the house briefly for the first time, it still had furnishings left by the former owners who had scheduled a moving van to take everything out the next day.

When the moving van arrived, sitting in the cab was an older man behind the wheel and an even older woman in the passenger seat. They both had to be in their late sixties and were anything but the beefy moving men I had expected to see. Although not a lot of furniture had been left behind, there was something that needed to be moved out of almost every one of the nineteen rooms. I thought to myself, *Oh my gosh, how are these two people going to move all the furniture out?* But sure enough, they did.

The woman didn't want any help and actually got annoyed when I tried. They were both unbelievably strong. Actually, between the two, the woman appeared the strongest. I cringed when I saw her carrying big pieces of furniture on her back, down steps, and hoisting it up into the truck. I finally had to stop watching and busy myself with continuing to look over the rest of the property.

When you buy a house in Italy, the previous owners move their possessions out, taking *everything*—refrigerators, washers, dryers, even the stoves. I was stunned; they were yanking hooks out of the walls, leaving holes and bits of plaster all over the floors. Light fixtures also went with them, leaving bulbs hanging by a wire. By the time they were done, Mica and I looked at what appeared to have been the scene of a close-quarters firefight and asked each other, "Where do we begin?"

We decided to head into town to get something to eat and buy cleaning supplies, and then we met Raffaello back at the house later in the afternoon. By the time we got back with all the cleaning gear, it was getting dark, so we called it a day and decided to start, hopefully with renewed energy, the next morning.

Bright and early the next day, we returned to Ceppeto where Raffaello—as usual—was waiting for us.

Having Raffaello there was helpful, but I soon found that, unlike most Italians, Raffaello did *not* have a good eye when it came to the kind of work the farmhouse needed.

In my experience, it seems to me that most Italians have a remarkable visual sense. You see it everywhere in their architecture, whether monumental works like churches and palazzos or simple farmhouses like Ceppeto. Even the plumbers, carpenters, stonemasons, and other tradesmen we've dealt with over the years have been artisans as much as contractors. They were so good at envisioning how a job should be done that they didn't even work from plans. We'd decide together what we wanted done, and they would figure out the best way to do it. General plans were supplied by a *geometra*—more of an engineer than a design architect—and he, in turn, gave them to the town for required permits.

That design gene had somehow eluded Raffaello. He was tireless, very dedicated, and always tried his best, and I've never felt anything but fortunate to have him with us. *But ...*

He still looked at Ceppeto as if it was the working farm he'd known as a youngster, over sixty years ago. He couldn't understand the vision I had to transform it into something more parklike, and, at age seventy-seven, he wasn't about to change. If I wanted to have a flower bed dug, he couldn't understand why I wanted the borders to be dug in a straight line or why I didn't want the grass to be cut so short that it would get scorched by the sun and turn brown. None of that had ever been a concern when Ceppeto was producing milk and crops and all the animals were kept in the main house, so why was it a concern now? When I had him paint some window frames, he painted outside the lines, so it became a *pugno in un occhio* (eyesore).

As we were cleaning the house, we discovered a lot of scorpions, *millepiedi* (thousand-leggers), ants, other bugs I had never seen before, and evidence of mice. I told Raffaello what we were finding and asked if he knew of an exterminator we could call.

He looked at me as if I were out of my mind. "We don't use exterminators here. For the mice, you should get a cat. If you don't like the bugs, you should live in a big city like Rome."

We opted for the cats and found two, just a few weeks old, being offered for adoption. We named them Fumo and Fiamma (Smoke and Flame), and they became an integral part of our life in Ceppeto. We never saw them actually kill any mice, but from then on, we never again had a problem with mice. As for the scorpions, they're generally small and slow moving, and you have to step on them to have them sting you. Even if they do sting you, it's only about as bad as a bee sting, so they weren't much of a problem. And, as far as the other insects were concerned, we saw less and less of them and eventually grew accustomed to seeing them only on occasion, which was nice, since neither of us wanted to move to Rome.

Raffaello was as fit and trim a seventy-seven-year-old as I had ever seen. When I met him, I was in excellent physical condition, but when it came time to walk up and down the steep hills of our property, he could outpace me with no problem. He walked with a military posture, straight back, chin up, and arms swinging casually. Up and down those hills he went, while I followed, hunched over and breathing hard as I tried to keep up with him.

Once, when he was about to celebrate his seventy-eighth birthday, we had to move three large terracotta flowerpots. Each was about three feet in diameter and about two and a half feet high. They had to weigh at least one hundred pounds each. I watched Raffaello pick one of the bulky things up and move it about fifty yards next to a wall and then do it again with a second pot; he didn't seem to be puffing much when he was done.

I naively thought, *If this old guy can move these things, it should be a snap for me.* I got my arms around the third one, steeled myself, and lifted—*oomph!* Oh, I got it moved all right, but then my back hurt for two days afterward.

I would watch him in awe as he worked on the property. He always worked at a slow but steady pace, which he could do all day long with only a ten-minute break in midmorning for a piece of fruit and some bread and cheese. Later, he returned to his nearby home for a two-hour lunch, and then he took another break late in the day for ten minutes or so for a piece of fruit, bread, and cheese. He always drank lots of water, didn't smoke, and drank one glass of wine in the evening. In the summer, he worked from seven thirty in the morning until six in the evening and sometimes even later. Those were more than eight-hour days of outdoor work, on his feet the entire time. I know of no other seventy-eight-year-old that could come close to equaling that. I don't even know that many *thirty-eight*-year-olds who could hack it!

He had been working like that since he had been a youngster growing up in Lupaia. He'd been in the Italian army during WWII and served on the island of Sardinia, which was largely spared armed conflict. After the war, he married and settled in Radda. He worked for a large vineyard in the area and soon rose to manager of the operation, a position he held until he retired and began working at Ceppeto.

Mica and I have grown extremely close to Raffaello and his family, and to this day, they consider us family. Whenever we return to Ceppeto after a long absence, his daughter, Tatiana, will always have a big pot of *ribollita* (bread and vegetable soup) on our stove, along with a freshly baked *torta* (cake), waiting for us. When we return to the States, they always want us to call to let them know we've arrived safely.

There's the family you're born into, and there's the family you choose, like my Sages. And then there's the family that chooses you, as Raffaello and his kin adopted Mica and me. And when you judge the character of the people who choose you and they are of the caliber of Raffaello and his family, such affection can only leave you humbled … as well it should.

CHAPTER 12

SI, PROMETTO

Our planned wedding date of May 28 loomed larger and closer. In those first few days at Ceppeto, we continued to live at the castle in Lupaia while we tried to patch up the house and ran around like crazy, buying what we needed in the way of furnishings to make the house minimally livable—not just for ourselves but also for our wedding guests.

We acquired many items from the antique fairs and flea markets held in Tuscan towns throughout the year. The most famous one is in Arezzo, where Roberto Benigni's Academy Award–winning movie *Life Is Beautiful/La vita è bella* (1997) was filmed. On the first weekend of each month, there is a large antique and flea market in the old town center, where you can find items ranging from expensive rarities to some excellent one-of-a-kind bargains. We started making a habit of going there every month, always returning with some fabulous antique or other that went toward giving our house a welcoming personal touch. To get the house livable in a hurry, we rushed out to buy some pieces from an Ikea in the area (yes, thankfully they're everywhere and all identical, right down to the Swedish meatballs). However, outside that, we were intent on preserving the character of Ceppeto and its surrounding property so that, for the most part, it would capture the spirit and look of a six-hundred-year-old farm.

Besides Arezzo, we also traveled to other towns for their antique and flea markets. At the time, Italian antiques were overlooked in favor of French antiques, so excellent bargains were to be had, and we were able to acquire a number of special items. Antique brass wall sconces that only needed to be wired for lights were a particularly good buy. Antique wooden chairs, which just needed a little refurbishing, were another. One of my favorites was an antique work bench with a wooden vise, made without any nails in the old post-and-beam manner with wooden pegs. We had a local artisan treat it, sand some of the rough patches, and then varnish it. It is like a piece of art and has a prominent place in our kitchen. We also found antique crystal chandeliers still using candles as well as various-sized dressers and night tables. Last—but not least—were old lamps with beautiful globes for holding kerosene. We had them wired and had lampshades made for them. They are exquisite.

We found that the Italian antique furniture in Lucca had a French influence, due to Napoleon's rule over Lucca and the installation of his sister Elisa as the Grand Duchess of Tuscany with her residence in Lucca, whereas the antiques we saw in Arezzo were more baroque in design, heavily influenced by the culture of Southern Italy.

It seems that no matter where you travel in Italy, you come into contact with layers of history. Centuries—even millennia—of history are etched in the piazzas and stone facades of the buildings of the myriad towns and villages of the Italian countryside, many too small to be formally noted in any book. In Lupaia, for example, we slept in a medieval castle, walked along paths the ancient Romans had used, and strolled over ground where the still-more-distant Etruscans had once thrived. Even now, there are reminders of the last generation's life during the first part of the twentieth century, when life had been lived pretty much as it had been since the beginning of the nineteenth century, particularly on the old farms where the ox-drawn plows can still be seen. There are old door locks with huge keys, hinges, and door handles forged by hand, and there are the old tools that we still have at Ceppeto—hammers, scythes, sickles, screwdrivers, ladders, brooms, wheelbarrows, rakes, barrels, hand railings—all items of everyday life painstakingly forged by blacksmiths and carpenters, a few of whom are still active today in the area. We found an antique artillery cart from the First World War on our property, complete with ironclad wheels and frame. The wood bed was pretty much rotted out, so we had a local carpenter refurbish it. It is a beauty.

I remember a story about the Coliseum in Rome: it is said that during the most decadent days of the Roman Empire, you could squeeze a handful of dirt from the arena, and because of the years of gladiatorial butchery, it would ooze blood. Italy—like no other country I have ever visited—has history in every fistful of earth, and you can almost feel it drip through your fingers when you squeeze it. It's there in the great, bustling cities like Rome, Florence, Milan, Venice, and Siena ... and even in a tiny village of thirty-two people like Lupaia.

The planned wedding was to be a civil ceremony performed at the city hall of Radda by the mayor. Now, granted, I'd assumed this would be a bit more complicated than your usual I-now-pronounce-you-husband-and-wife-now-get-outta-here deal. I was a US citizen, Mica was Italian, and we'd both been previously married ... lots of paperwork involved. A *lot* of paperwork.

But even with that in mind, I was still amazed at how nothing ate up the prenuptials clock like the Italian bureaucracy, with which I found myself dealing for the first (and, sadly, hardly the last) time.

The Italian bureaucracy dates back almost two centuries to the time when Napoleon ruled over most of Italy. The Italians have perfected bureaucratic machination to an art. While this expertise has the added social benefit of providing an enormous number of Italian citizens with government employment, in practice it has the patience-testing, teeth-grinding consequence of taking forever to get even the simplest of tasks accomplished. I am also convinced that a hidden agenda of this incredibly bloated and time-consuming bureaucracy is to subsidize the otherwise outdated and outmoded rubber stamp business. Let me explain.

Remember the stationery stores of not so long ago where you could order special rubber stamps for business or personal use? There used to be office desks with lots of different rubber stamps, all neatly hanging from a merry-go-round of a rack next to inkpads of black, red, and sometimes green ink in flat tin boxes. These have all but disappeared in the States but not in Italy. For most documents that need stamping, you have to go to the post office and buy a stamp that can cost as much as twenty dollars. Then—in our case—you need to take that stamp to the city hall in Radda and have it affixed to your document, which is subsequently officially rubber-stamped and initialed, attesting to its legitimacy.

The city hall in Radda is in a former palace dating back to medieval times. Just walking up the steps, worn down and glassy smooth from centuries of visitors before us, is an experience. On our way to get rubber-stamped, Mica and I passed the ancient prison room with its original worm-eaten wooden door no more than five feet high, containing seven dime-sized holes for air and light, with a hand-wrought iron bolt sealing it closed from the outside. It is still used today but rarely, as there's practically no crime in Radda.

Upon entering the Office of Records, I was surprised to find a chamber with a vaulted two-story-high ceiling, jammed with huge leather-bound volumes of records, mountains of them lining the walls on sagging wooden shelves. The room reeked of the odor of ancient paper and leather. It was a treasure trove of documents containing information on every person that has ever lived in Radda, plus surveys and civil, business, and government records. I am sure a historian could piece together much of the history of Radda from this mass of documents dating back centuries.

We dealt with a woman named Nadia, and I lost count of the number of times we had to go back to her with document after document, each translated through the Italian consulate and stamped by one official after another as witness, verification of accuracy, and rewitnessed by yet more bureaucratic offices. These documents included our birth certificates, prior divorce papers, title to Ceppeto, degrees from college and proof of graduation, corporate documents concerning the company organized to own Ceppeto, passports, and letters stating we had no criminal or judicial proceedings against us now or ever. Great wars have been started and ended with less paperwork. And the stamping of documents was not just a single rubber stamp; each official we went to, including Nadia, had a drawer holding dozens of rubber stamps with different-colored ink pads. I had no idea what any of them meant, but after paying a fee for each of them, I didn't understand how the Italian government could possibly be running a deficit.

I noticed that each official had his or her own unique way of stamping the documents. Some would stamp with dramatic flair, others so fast their hands were a blur, and still others so slow we were convinced they were waiting for the ink to dry before proceeding to the next one. Of all of them, Nadia got our vote for the Academy Award for Most Dramatic Performance by a Stamping Bureaucrat.

She was a slight woman, very pleasant, always stylishly dressed, and seemed reserved. But when she opened her drawer of stamps, her lips pressed together so tightly that you could no longer see them, and with swift and efficient movements she removed and opened the different-colored ink pads, lining them all up in a precise row. Then, she took the rubber stamp attached to an ebony-colored handle that had been rubbed glossy from who knows how many years of use. With a ferociousness that startled us, she *slammed* the stamp into the ink pad and then, with even greater violence, *slammed* the stamp onto the document. Looking at her finished work, she parted her lips ever so slightly in what was just the hint of a tiny grin of satisfaction. But then she picked up the next stamp, her lips pursed in a straight line again, and she repeated the process with equal ferocity.

When she finished stamping all the documents, she almost broke into a full-fledged laugh but then quickly composed herself, returning to her usual quiet and pleasant demeanor. She turned to figuring out the amount due for all that sledgehammer stamping with a first-generation adding machine—the old mechanical kind with round number keys that required a fair bit of muscle to press and then a crank that had to be pulled for the digits to register on a paper tape. All it could do was add and subtract. If you wanted to multiply, you put in the number you wanted to multiply and then kept pulling that crank for each time you wanted to multiply it. I know grade-school kids with more computing power on their smartphones.

Each time we finished getting the documents stamped, one official or another requested *more* documents, this time translated and officially stamped with approval. Some documents, such as proof of where we lived in New York City and where my business was, required me to go to the US embassy in Florence to have them notarized. Just two weeks before the wedding date, we were ready to say, "Forget about it!" and have an informal ceremony on the twenty-eighth, making it official another time (if we were still so inclined). But at about that time, as often happens when you stop pushing so hard, things began to fall into place. We got the required papers together just as our first guests began arriving.

The last days before the wedding flew by. Mica had bought a wedding dress in New York, which she refused to allow me to see before the ceremony. The night before the wedding, she stayed with her closest girlfriend and maid of honor, Antonella, who lived nearby. The Sages and Sagettes took me out to dinner that same night, and that was when I began to get a little nervous—not because I had any doubts about the marriage. I was head over heels in love, and I knew Mica was as well. No, I was having palpitations because the wedding ceremony would be conducted in Italian, and I was worried that I wouldn't understand when it was time to say the Italian equivalent of "I do."

I kept imagining what would happen if I failed to say those two very important words when called on to do so. Would the marriage be nullified? Would Mica's family go bonkers? Would it be a big embarrassment? All of the above?

And then, provided that I hadn't completely humiliated myself during the ceremony, I also had to give a speech in Italian after the wedding. I was already sweating bullets over properly saying two words at the right time, so having to make a whole *speech*?

The best you could say about my Italian at the time was that I could only kinda speak the language. For example, there was the time I was walking some Italian guests around the grounds, and after passing a beautiful tree, I said, "*Wow, guarda quella bella fica,*" which I *thought* translated as, "Wow, look at that beautiful fig tree." But *fig tree* in Italian is *fico,* not *fica.* I soon understood what a big difference a little *a* can make when everyone burst out laughing. Mica whispered into my ear that I'd actually said, "Wow, look at that beautiful pussy."

So now you understand my concern.

The Sages—being properly sage-like—knew the proper treatment for this kind of anxiety and administered heavy doses of Chianti Classico. This age-old and proven treatment (it doesn't improve your bilingual abilities, but you do stop giving a damn) proved itself again, and I began to relax, ending the evening feeling quite good and tumbling into bed for a wonderfully lubricated deep sleep.

I anxiously peered out my window right before sunrise and saw that we were going to have a beautiful day, albeit the sky had a tint of pink. Being a sailor for many years, I knew the old adage "Red sky at morning, sailor take warning." Still, there were few clouds, so if there was going to be rain, there wouldn't be much. Besides, a sprinkle of rain was considered good luck on one's wedding day.

The wedding was scheduled for 11:30 a.m. I had arranged for Raffaello to drive me to city hall in his car. He had stopped by the farm the day before and had planted two small cypress trees—the biblical tree of life—next to each other in honor of our wedding. It is a custom in the area as part of honoring the couple getting married and also a way to contribute to the benefit of the environment.

(Don't laugh, but we named the trees Richard and Mica. I don't know what symbolism you want to take from this, but some time later, Richard the Cypress was eaten by deer and needed to be replanted. Thereafter, we put wire mesh around each tree to protect them, but with Mica the Cypress's head start of a few years on the new Richard Cypress, she remains today a full three feet taller.)

On the morning of the wedding, Raffaello, dressed in his finest suit, took time to first water the new trees and then pinned a rosebud that he had brought to the lapel of my suit. Along with Raffaello's rose, I was wearing a tie Bill Persky loaned me that he had worn at his wedding a few years earlier; Saul lent me a belt, and Joe LaRosa, a spritz of his favorite cologne. I felt as if I were carrying enough good luck charms that day to supply a squad of grooms.

In a caravan, we all slowly wound our way down the valley from Ceppeto and up the other side to Radda—five miles away—to gather in front of the city hall. Little by little, the attendees arrived, and as the time approached for the ceremony to begin, the only ones missing were Mica and her maid of honor, Antonella.

Then Mica, like a vision, suddenly appeared in her flowing white gown, a veil covering her face, walking up the slight grade of the narrow medieval street toward us. It was a weekday, and passersby stopped in their tracks at the sight of her; shopkeepers stepped out on the walkway to see her float by.

When finally she arrived at my side on city hall's portico, she first turned to her father and gave him a kiss and then turned to me and did the same. Mica's father, despite being a big and tough man—a retired Carabiniere (Italy's national military police)—had a tear in his eye. There was never a question that of all his ten children, Mica was his favorite—his *figlia preferita*. Nor did I ever doubt that he approved our union; I will never forget his words upon greeting me for the first time: "*Questo e' un uomo!*" ("This is a real man!")

Joe LaRosa was my best man, or *testimone* (witness). Joe spoke Italian fluently, so I knew I could expect a sharp elbow if I stumbled on my "I dos." Antonella was next to Mica as her maid of honor. The mayor wore a red-white-and-green *tricolore* sash with our new friend Nadia next to him. Nadia, as a gift for us, had ordered flower arrangements so that the otherwise austere city hall entrance was transformed into a charming setting.

The ceremony went flawlessly; I even understood most of it, even though a lot was being read from ancient proclamations in archaic Italian. When it came to the duties of the husband that I had to avow to uphold, I was able to proclaim "*Si, prometto*" ("Yes, I promise") at the correct moments. Then before I knew it, we were pronounced husband and wife; the ceremony was over, and the celebration began.

After the wedding, our entire entourage walked through the town and back to our cars and proceeded, with horns blaring, back to Ceppeto. My postwedding speech was well received, and, in an Italian folkloric token of good luck, it did rain—if ever so lightly—for just a few minutes. The occasion was a delightful and one-of-a-kind mixture of American, Jewish, Catholic, and Italian influences, providing as memorable a wedding as either of us could have hoped for.

Bill Persky said that all the hoopla, ending with me giving a speech first in Italian and then in English, reminded him of a bar mitzvah. Well, I suppose one rite of passage is much like another, and this particular rite didn't just seem to inaugurate the official beginning of my life with Mica and hers with mine but also the official start of our life together at Ceppeto.

I would often remember that evening, watching the sun slowly slip behind the rolling hills surrounding Ceppeto, casting a glow over the valley that slid from a warm gold to an amber red, feeling the warmth of the day gradually give way to the refreshing cool breezes of evening.

PART III

CEPPETO

CHAPTER 13

BINI

Three days after the wedding when the last of our guests had departed, I noticed a wet spot on the ceiling in the kitchen. I couldn't tell if it was a leak or just moisture accumulating there from the change in temperature. This was June, after all, and we were beginning to get the typical hot and humid summer weather.

I spoke to Raffaello about it, and he said he would call a contractor he knew in town to come up the next day to look at it. The contractor arrived, as promised, the next day. His name was Leonardo Bini, and Raffaello said he was the best contractor in the area.

When we met, he simply introduced himself as Bini (pronounced "Bee-knee"), and he inspected the damp area on the ceiling. He went upstairs to find the source of the problem and then came down and went outside. He took a pick and a shovel from his truck, proceeded to open a small hole near the wall to our kitchen, and then asked us to come out so he could show us what he'd found.

Bini is an interesting character. He is about 5'9", medium build, always ready with a quick smile. He has thinning brown hair that is always cut extra short, which camouflages his receding hairline. He is not a good-looking man per se but has piercing green eyes that are, indeed, his redeeming feature. His nose is small and curved up, and he has a broad chin and expressive eyebrows that always seem raised, as if in surprise. Summed up, he looks a lot like Stan Laurel from the old Laurel and Hardy flicks.

When Mica and I joined him, he showed us where he had uncovered a pipe in the ground with a hole in it. Pointing to the pipe, he said, "All the pipes in the house are just like this. They are all made from clay and are now so old they are starting to crack, break, and leak. I am sorry to tell you, but they all should probably be replaced."

Mica and I were stunned, and as we began asking more questions, we realized that to fix the problem, the house would have to be ripped open inside and out: walls, floors with tile, and antique brick and plastered walls. I knew at that moment we were looking at a gut renovation—something for which we had been quite unprepared.

We began the work of making plans and filing permits, hoping the work could be carried out after we left at the end of the summer and be finished before we returned the following April. I loved the house and property so much that I felt that even if I had to spend a lot more time and money to fix it up, it would be worth it.

The old real estate expression is "It's all about location, location, location." Ceppeto certainly has that; it's considered one of the best sites in all the Radda valley, atop one of the highest hills, with a panoramic vista of the entire area. We would eventually learn that it's actually considered one of the top five most beautiful vistas in all of Italy, ranked up there along with Lake Como and the Dolomites. The world-famous Italian pasta manufacturer Barilla, after scouting locations all over Italy to shoot their TV commercial, made Ceppeto their first choice. However, I rejected their offer as I didn't want the nuisance of a huge film crew possibly ruining the property with all their equipment. Still, it was flattering.

We returned to Ceppeto in March 2000, by which time the permits had been received and work begun on the pipes. We had hoped it wouldn't be long before the work was finished, but when Bini came to meet us, he was the bearer of even more bad news.

He took us on a tour throughout the house, which had been ripped apart to smithereens. Pipes were exposed, and electrical wiring hung chaotically in every direction. Stone walls that had previously been covered by plaster were now bare, and floors had been ripped up with antique bricks piled up neatly outside of the house. Bini dejectedly said, "I am really sorry to have to tell you this, but not only do the pipes for the water lines need replacing, but also we began checking the conduits for the wiring that runs everywhere buried in the walls, and they are in bad shape. Actually they are a danger the way they are now, and I strongly advise that while we have everything opened we redo both the electrical wiring and conduits. It has been almost forty years since this work was done, and they are long past their useful life."

Then he took us to the room where the heating and hot water system was located. "The furnace for your heat is fed by an underground oil tank that is leaking and should be emptied and replaced, but I would strongly urge you to convert to gas. Even though you are the next to the last farm on this road, they do have gas lines running to your house, so it would be a simple matter to change. The furnace needs replacing anyway, and gas is a lot cleaner than oil."

As if that weren't enough, he then showed us the roof from outside: "See where the center is visibly sagging? I went up on the roof to check it, and that too is probably fifty years old or more, long past its useful life." I thought Bini was going to look at me next and say, "By the way, after looking at you, I think you are also long past your useful life." He did say that the big beams were still strong as ever, which was good, but that the smaller cross beams were rotted from all the dampness caused by small leaks over many years. After slowly letting all this sink in, Mica and I looked at each other and weren't sure whether we should laugh or cry. Our friends always kidded us because it seemed that we were always renovating *something*, whether one of our homes, a boat, an apartment, or a building I owned. After each renovation was complete, I kept swearing that it was my last. Both Mica and I knew that some work had to be done on the house, but we had no idea it would turn into a complete gut renovation. To do that on a six-hundred-year-old house was not going to be the proverbial piece of cake, especially when we were new to the region, and I was essentially a foreigner—a stranger in a strange land. As my mother and grandmother would have said, "*Oy vey.*"

As bad as the news from Bini was, I knew he was correct in

everything he said; there was no need for a second opinion on that, and for me and Mica, there was no thought of not doing it. As much as we wanted to sit back and enjoy Ceppeto, we would never rest comfortably knowing that the infrastructure was lacking. We've never believed in just patching up problems; they always come back to haunt you.

Critical to making the decision to go forward with a full renovation was having Bini as the contractor. In the short time I'd dealt with him, I'd recognized that Raffaello's opinion of the man had been right on the button.

On the strength of nothing more than my word and my handshake, I'd been able to build my business starting with just an idea—no money and never borrowing a penny—into a company worth a hundred million dollars (which, in the mid-1980s, was a damned respectable number). That was the way I preferred to do business, and that was how Bini conducted his. No lawyer could draw up a contract stronger in its obligations than Bini's promise, sealed by his calloused hand.

As it turned out, Bini was everything I thought he would be and more. I only wish I had a contractor in the States that was as good as he was. Besides his honesty and superb ability, he was a joy to work with.

We found that his most unwittingly comical moments were during August when it got boiling hot. To stay cool, Bini donned a pair of plaid Bermuda shorts, a tank top, white socks, and a pair of battered construction boots. I forgot to mention that Bini has a slightly duck-like walk, so seeing him march toward you in this outfit with his skinny, ivory-white legs, his belly pushed out in front of him, and his arms loosely flailing by his sides, is a remarkable sight. As he nears you, his eyebrows go up, and a big grin flashes, telegraphing the "*Buon giorno*" he always says upon meeting. You just can't help but smile and say to yourself, with admiration, "Here's a man without a pretense in the world. He is what he is and is as comfortable in his own skin as anyone I've ever met. Bravo, Bini!"

When I first met Bini and spoke to him in my best Italian, he looked at me with his nose wrinkled up as if he had smelled something bad. I wondered if maybe I shouldn't do a quick underarm check, but then I slowly caught on that the nose wrinkle was because he couldn't understand a damned thing I was saying, and, with his strong Tuscan accent, I could hardly understand *him*!

I did the only practical thing I could think of: "*Mica! Vieni subito per favore.*" ("Mica! Come here right away please.")

As time went on, my Italian improved enough for me to no longer get the wrinkled nose, and I got used to Bini's local accent, which had its own peculiarities.

In spite of his slight build, Bini always has his stomach protruding over his belt. It is not fat but comes from him being totally relaxed; it's like a Buddha belly. Bini breathes from his stomach just as a baby does. It is unusual to find many adults who breathe like that or, for that matter, even a child past infancy. Most Westerners begin breathing shallower and shallower as they grow up and encounter tension, until by adulthood most are so unconsciously tense they breathe in only to the top of their chest. It takes years of practice to undo that ingrained response to tension and begin breathing naturally and more healthfully from the stomach. Bini is the first adult I have ever met who breathes this way naturally; that's how calm and relaxed he is.

In a business that is often in one crisis after the other, Bini is unflappable. He's a joy to be around because he's competent and confident in what he's doing, and yet he never lets his pride get in the way of reason. We refer to him as the "Factotum," for he does everything. If we need a kitchen carved from solid rock or an iron bridge built to support a two-foot-thick wall or something as minor as fixing a fallen curtain rod, Bini is right there, doing the job without hesitation and with a smile.

Leonardo Bini was born in Radda and married a woman from Panzano, about eight miles from Ceppeto. He has two sons, both of whom came to work for him when they came of age. He is an exemplary father, and although he hunts, he is a pacifist, as are his two sons, who will be serving their military duty in the ambulance service instead of the army.

Bini's father was a shepherd, tending to flocks in the pastures near Radda. When Bini was in his early teens, his father had an accident and broke his leg. He was unable to return to work, and, with no other source of income, Bini left school and began working.

He started as an apprentice for a *muratore* (stonemason) and proved himself a fast learner. It wasn't long before he started his own company, primarily as a subcontractor specializing in stonemasonry. He worked on many jobs where the project was either renovating an old house or building one from scratch. After several more years, he had learned enough about building to start his own general contracting business: *Leonardo Bini, Impresa Edile* (construction contractor), which he proudly rubber-stamps on top of his invoices. Bini built himself into a one-stop *edile,* handling the whole range of building trades: electrical, plumbing, carpentry, plastering, and painting. He gradually bought his own equipment for hauling materials, excavating, and grading. He not only had the means but also established himself as a top-quality, reliable, and honest contractor. Frankly—and here I speak from years of construction experience—these are rare qualities in that business, anywhere in the world.

His only evidence of a lack of a formal education is calculating numbers; as surprising as that may be for a contractor, he compensates for it by either asking you to do the computation or getting back to you with them.

Shortly after the euro replaced the lira as the national currency, there was chaos all over Italy, trying to calculate the conversion rate. Keep in mind we're talking about switching from a currency that had had very few coins and banknotes denominated in the thousands of lire. Unsurprisingly, the conversion was difficult for many Italians. Silvio Berlusconi, then prime minister of Italy, sent every household a free calculator to help people figure it out. The banks did the same for their customers.

For Bini in particular, the currency change was a big problem. One day, I gave him 1,000 euros for miscellaneous items he had bought for us. At the time, that was worth about $800. He looked at the bills, mostly 100 euro notes and, with a puzzled expression, asked, "How much is one thousand euros?" When we told him it was worth two million lire, he was surprised and even *more* confused. With time, however, he, along with everyone else, adapted.

Despite Bini's difficulty with currency and simple math, when it came time for him to calculate the amount of materials he needed for a project, he suddenly became a savant and was able to figure out in his head exactly what he needed to order.

The renovations for Ceppeto would start by our discussing the idea for a design. Bini then would check with an engineer in case it involved a structural element. Once we agreed on it, he would just *do* it—no drawings, no plans.

Once we started redoing the entire infrastructure, there were constant surprises and design decisions that had to be made. Mica and I were there every day, watching what was being done and making adjustments as the work progressed. Every step of the way, Bini flawlessly calculated the amount of materials needed so there was never a delay because of a shortage.

By local law, you could not change the outer appearance of structures by altering, for example, the windows or doors. Permission had to be granted for any renovations before starting and, when finished, had to receive final approval. This was controlled by a government agency called the Belle Arti, not unlike the Landmarks Commission in New York City. As difficult as the Belle Arti can be at times, it is an important reason why Italy has preserved its historic beauty better than most other countries in the world. I am thankful for it.

Interiors, however, are a different story; there, the concern is structural. Parts of the main house at Ceppeto are six hundred years old. It was built from large stones that were native to the immediate area when the land was first being cleared and cultivated. The three-foot-thick walls act as support for the upper floors (they also happen to be excellent insulators for keeping heat in during winter and hot air out during summer; air-conditioning is rarely used or needed in houses like these).

During the six-hundred-year history of the house, sections had been added to accommodate the tenant farmer's growing family and the animals. There is no basement in the house, as it is built on top of a huge, naturally formed stone slab that provides an excellent, solid base for the house. When you look at the stonework on the outside of the house, you can see where the additions were made over the centuries and where there used to be doors and windows. Many of those three-foot-thick support walls that were originally outside walls are now inside the house.

When we decided to redo the kitchen and make it larger by knocking down a portion of a supporting wall to combine two rooms into one large eat-in kitchen, Bini's solution to the support issue was to build an iron bridge spanning the opened space to provide the needed support for the floors above. Once we knew we had a way to combine the two rooms, we hired a well-known firm in Florence that specialized in kitchens to design and install it. They presented a beautiful set of blueprints to Bini, with full color renderings of the proposed kitchen; along with removing the wall and support bridge being installed, they asked him to demolish the old kitchen, level the floor between the two rooms, run wiring, and put in electrical outlets and tubing for plumbing in specific locations. Mind you, all this was to be done while preserving the rustic nature of the original house and materials we had found there, something that the local workers really appreciated.

There are two basic types of homes on farms in this area. Those like ours are *colonica*, or colonial, which is a farmhouse lived in by tenant farmers. The other kind is a *baronale*, which, as the name implies, is suited for nobility or the owner of the land. These latter have none of the rustic characteristics of the colonial houses, inside or out. Most of their stonework is covered with plaster or stucco, flooring is usually covered with carpets or tile, and the layouts are very formal. We'd been told stories of foreign buyers renovating the interiors of *coloniche* houses so they looked like brand-new *baronale*-type homes, losing all their rustic character in the process.

Not that there isn't a gray area in between. Original farmhouses had no interior bathrooms, and kitchens were places to cook in open fireplaces; under those circumstances, a little tinkering is understandable. But to quote one of the workers, "These farmhouses have their own unique charm that we learned to appreciate growing up in this area. Trying to make it into a supermodern *baronale* home is like trying to make a duck look like a peacock. You can pin all sorts of beautiful feathers on it, but it is still going to look like a duck, and a ridiculous one at that."

After getting the project started, we returned to the States and were back in Italy when the work was halfway to completion. When we met Bini on site, we asked him to show us the Florence outfit's plans, so we could review the work he had done. He sheepishly pulled them out from the bottom of a pile of rubble saying, "Here they are, but I never used them."

Yet everything was in place and done exactly to specifications for the hookups for the sink, stove, lights, switches, and other appliances as well as the cabinetry. I asked how he could work like that, and he said that he had met with the design firm a couple of times and they had showed him what they wanted. That was all he needed.

As the work on the house was drawing to a close, we began to focus on the exterior and the grounds. We renovated the pool, installed an irrigation system, drained and repaired a large pond used for supplying water for the irrigation system, installed a well, transformed the original large garage into a guesthouse, and built a new garage. We put in a new driveway and replanted trees and flowers. It was a complete makeover, while still preserving the wonderful Tuscan character of the property. During the process, Bini became a good friend and has continued to do projects for us, right up until this writing.

Bini came to me a year ago with a sad face and asked, "Don't you love Ceppeto anymore?"

I didn't understand what he was talking about, until he said he'd been wondering why we'd returned to the States a couple of months earlier than usual. I assured him that I still loved Ceppeto and that

I simply had business to take care of in New York. I added that with every year that passed, we appreciated more and more the fabulous work he had done there.

His eyebrows raised up, as they were wont to do, and a big grin lit up his face as he shook my hand and said, "*Sono molto contento di sentirle dire cosi', voglio solo che Lei e La Signora siate felice.*" ("I am very happy to hear you say that, and I want only that you and the missus are still happy here.")

From working with Bini and his crew almost every day we were in Italy, we got to know them all quite well. Most were young. Oliviero, an excellent stonemason, along with Pietro, an older married man who had immigrated from Albania over twenty years earlier and whose wife would later work for us, were real artisans. They repaired the interior stone walls and repointed areas of the outside wall and patio. We had daily conversations, which certainly helped my Italian, but they were always as interested in learning about America as I was interested in learning about their lives in Italy.

Massimigliano and Gianni were the other two workers. Massimigliano married the local blacksmith's daughter, and Gianni married the daughter of the owner of the local hardware store. Unlike many members of the younger generation, there was a good chance they would all stay in the area. The number of eligible young people in the area was growing ever smaller, so intramarriages between distant cousins were becoming more frequent. It seemed to us that practically everyone we were meeting in Radda and Lupaia was somehow related to one another. It was one giant family tree with lots of intertwined branches.

When Oliviero—a stocky and always smiling young man with thick, curly black hair who reminded me of John Belushi—got married, Mica and I were invited to the wedding. It was quite an event, held at the Santa Maria Novella church, which dated back to the eleventh century and which Bini had restored several years earlier. He and his crew were the organizers of the event.

The church had a beautiful antique organ with bellows that had to be pumped by hand. Massimigliano and Gianni were given that task, so whenever music was being played, they would pump away on a mechanism that looked like an old railroad handcar. They were dressed in suits and ties, and it was a very hot June day; it didn't take long before they were drenched with sweat. When it came time for the bells to ring, Bini and Pietro each held a rope leading from the bell tower into the main chapel where the ceremony was taking place. The two of them pulled and tugged, trying to create some sort of tune. They too were soon sweating profusely.

When it came time for the priest to conduct the ceremony, apparently the wine was missing, so after a few minutes of looking for it around the altar, Bini saved the day by fetching a bottle from God knows where. I don't know anything about the Catholic Mass or prayers Catholics say for a wedding ceremony, but the priest certainly looked as if he'd been heavily dipping into the sacramental wine before he'd gotten there, which perhaps explains why it was missing. He began slurring his words and teetering a bit from side to side. No one seemed to care much, and after the couple was declared man and wife, all happily filed out of the church, throwing rice onto Oliviero and his new bride.

CHAPTER 14

THE CASTLE

Once Bini began the renovation of the farmhouse, we moved into an apartment in the castle in Lupaia, right next to where we stayed the day I saw Ceppeto for the first time. Our apartment was in a tower of the old castle and had circular walls with narrow winding steps leading to the upper floor. By coincidence, it was where Raffaello was born and where he had lived in the 1920s and '30s.

Our castle apartment had been completely modernized and was only a ten-minute walk from Ceppeto. Living there during the summer gave us a chance to experience what life was like living in this tiny medieval village of thirty-two people.

Lupaia is considered one of the most picturesque and best-preserved villages of its period, dating back to the 1100s. When Lupaia had been a defensive castle and part of the Chianti League, it had a moat around an outside wall and drawbridges. The moat and bridges are long gone, but inside, the character of the original castle is much the same.

Originally, for defensive purposes, all the rooms and what are now individual apartments were connected so that when under siege, the defenders could race from one part of the castle to the other without having to expose themselves to the attackers. The connecting doors, though long unused, are still there. They are, however, head-bangingly low—proof of how much shorter people were in those days.

In the center of the village, there is a small piazza where the main feature is a fountain with a constant flow of fresh water. The availability of fresh water was a primary reason the castle had been built there in the eleventh century, along with its position on the crest of a mountain ridge two thousand feet above sea level, affording it a spectacular—and tactically advantageous—panoramic view of the valley and surrounding area. Ceppeto has that same ridge and view, less than a half mile away.

While we stayed there, I noticed that the piazza was the central meeting place for all the villagers. Every evening, they gathered round on benches and chairs, chatting together. The group was mostly older people, predominantly women who were widows. The fountain was still used for washing pots and pans and had been, at one time in the not-too-distant past, where laundry had been done. A stone basin that caught the water had been worn smooth from centuries of scrubbing clothes along its sides.

The summer we stayed there was brutally hot, and everyone kept his or her windows open. There was no air-conditioning there since, like Ceppeto, the thick stone walls usually keep the heat out and cool air inside. Typically, there was a refreshing breeze at night that makes for comfortable sleeping, but the castle was in an enclosed area, and the breezes were often blocked from entering, making it much hotter than Ceppeto.

The most difficult thing for us to get used to in such a tiny village was the noise. During the day, rather than use a telephone—even if a resident had one—to call a neighbor, people would poke their heads out of the windows of their apartments or take a strategic position in the street and scream the intended recipient's name. Everyone in Lupaia had amazing lungs, and their voices sounded as if they were bellowing into a megaphone. Most of the time it was the women who would be calling one another, some so tiny in stature I wondered where all that volume was coming from!

Loud was normal. Even conversations between people sitting right next to each other were always at high volume, as if the participants wanted to be sure all thirty-two people living in the village (well, thirty-four with Mica and me) could hear what was being said.

There were no secrets in Lupaia or, for that matter, in the much bigger town of Radda, where a little over two hundred people live within the old medieval walls. No secrets ... but plenty of gossip.

To hear the latest gossip was the reason most everyone turned out after dinner and took their places in the tiny piazza. I do not know how the secrets were found out, but it was as if there was a Big Brother watching everyone. If you wanted to do something quietly, discreetly, or hidden from everybody, you just didn't do it in Lupaia or Radda. The CIA and KGB could both learn a thing or two about how to discover secrets there.

If there weren't any juicy stories to tell, the piazza crowd was equally content just to talk and listen about who was sick or under a doctor's care, who went to town that day to buy what, or who had a visitor and what the visitor was like, along with the weather forecast and anything amusing they could think of that would cause outbursts of laughter.

In the hot and humid evenings when it was difficult to sleep, people talked noisily in the piazza until the wee hours of the morning. A couple in their nineties—actually the wife was in her late nineties, and the husband was over one hundred—lived opposite us. The two would get dressed up every day no matter what the weather was, he looking very natty with a jacket and bow tie and cane and she with a flowery-patterned, very dated dress and bonnet. Side by side, they would slowly make their way to the piazza, only about fifty yards away, sit there in the morning sun, partake in some conversations, and after an hour or so, return to their apartment.

The husband was hard of hearing, so in the evening, he had the habit of turning up the volume of his radio until it was blaring. On one particularly scorching evening when it was impossible to sleep, his radio was blaring until late in the evening. After putting up with it as long as she could, Mica got up and went to the couple's apartment. The front door was open, and the man was alone in a chair fast asleep with the radio on at full blast. Mica quietly entered, turned off the radio, and left. The man never even twitched. When Mica returned and told me what she had done, I asked, "If he didn't even move, did you check to see if was still alive?"

Mica laughed and said, "Oh, come on! I could hear him snoring." Allaying any doubts, the next day we saw them taking their daily stroll, dressed to the nines as always.

Most evenings after working all day at Ceppeto, we returned to Lupaia and, after dinner, took a little walk to the piazza just to say hello to everyone. We were always greeted warmly and with some excitement at our being newcomers. This gave the locals the opportunity to repeat some of their stories, so old and told so many times that no one else wanted to listen to them. I used the opportunity to ask them questions about what it had been like to live there when they had been young.

Tina and Fabio, along with their daughters, Maria and Gina, ran a *bottega* in town and were the first people we'd met when we'd closed on the house. We had since become good friends and even had them cater our wedding. During one of these sessions out in the piazza, Tina told me she hadn't lived in Lupaia her whole life, as so many of the others had. I asked her where she was born and grew up, and she said, "Oh, a long way from here." I was curious and pressed her for the name of the town or village, and she said, "It doesn't have a name, but do you know where the back road from Lupaia to Panzano is?" I told her that I did, and she said it was halfway along that road. That was no more than a mile and half from Lupaia, but, for her, that was far away.

In 1966, a wealthy businessman, Piero Stenosa, bought two-thirds of the village of Lupaia and nine hundred acres of the surrounding land, including a number of farmhouses and vineyards. In 1970, he gave his property to his daughter, Elisabetta, as a wedding present when she married Martino Furbone. They are largely responsible for preserving the village as it is today and deserve a lot of credit for doing such a terrific job. They have planted cypress trees on the sides of the long road leading up from the bottom of the valley to the top where Lupaia sits, making it one of the more beautiful roads in the area.

There were, at one time, three churches in the village. Today, there is only one still operating as a church. Once or twice a month, a priest or friar comes and performs mass. The other two churches have been converted into wineries by the Stenosa-Furbones who, along with all the other buildings they own in Lupaia, have one of the largest wineries in Italy, all of it underground so as not to disturb the appearance of the village.

Besides all the good things the Stenosa-Furbones have done, there is unfortunately a dark side. As often happens when children are given too much too soon, rather than learning how to appreciate what they have, the Furbones seem to have a sense of entitlement, which is why the Stenosa-Furbone couple is not very popular. A number of contractors we've hired at Ceppeto have told us they refuse to work for the Furbones because of the problems contractors have had when dealing with them.

While we were living in the castle, the whole town ran out of water, which is quite amazing for such a small village. We noticed enormous amounts of water being used to clean the huge two-story-high stainless steel vats used for fermenting wine, which was undoubtedly the main reason for the shortage. Most of the inhabitants of Lupaia lived in small apartments and used minimal water themselves. When I asked one of them if he thought this was fair, he shrugged and said, "When you are a big fish in the pond, you get to eat the little ones."

We felt the consequences of this when, in order to get water, we had to drive to a fresh spring in the woods about a mile away to fill bottles of drinking water for ourselves. When taking a shower wasn't possible, the best we could manage was a sponge bath with the drinking water, which was hardly satisfying after a hard day's work at Ceppeto in very hot weather.

I had only two occasions to meet Elisabetta and Martino Stenosa-Furbone. While living in the castle, I needed to have a FedEx package sent to me. The only address I knew to use was Richard Hadar, Castello di Lupaia, Siena, Italy. About a week later, I still hadn't received the package and had the sender track it. They advised me that it had been delivered to Castello di Lupaia and signed for at the reception desk. That was the Furbone-Stenosa office.

When I went to the office, I spoke to the receptionist, a

pleasant-looking young woman, and asked her if they'd received a package for me.

The receptionist, smiling, said, "I do not know, but I will be happy to check, just one moment please." She then went into an office and a minute or so later came back. This time she wasn't smiling and looked worried; an older woman who had a serious frown and was far from attractive preceded her. Without altering her frown, the older woman said, "My name is Elisabetta Stenosa-Furbone. I am the owner of the Castello di Lupaia. May I ask what right you have to use my address for your FedEx packages?"

This was the first unpleasant confrontation I'd had in Italy, and I was quite taken aback. I responded as courteously as I could: "I am renting the apartment in Lupaia and gave FedEx the same address I used when I rented an apartment here in 1999. I didn't think it would be a problem since there are only thirty-two people living here, but if I am mistaken, I apologize. I meant no harm."

This had absolutely no effect on her, and her frown continued, as if she hadn't heard a word I'd said. She then said, "That apartment you are now renting is not owned by me; it is owned by the *Grechis*." She put emphasis on the name *Grechi* as if they were her archenemies. I only wished at that moment my Italian were better, since I could only think in English, *Oops! Obviously a cardinal sin in your kingdom. I am happy to know your dungeons are no longer in use.* If I could have gotten that thought out in Italian, it would not have made a difference, because before I even finished thinking it, she turned and went back into her office, only to emerge a moment later with my FedEx package. She said, "Here. And next time use the correct address." Then she abruptly returned to her office.

The receptionist stood frozen in her place, her face beet red from embarrassment. She meekly and in almost a whisper said, "I am so sorry for this, but I'm glad you got your package."

I whispered also and said, "Is she always like that?" The receptionist just nodded her head, smiled, and shrugged her shoulders.

As I turned to leave, I saw a portrait hanging on the wall behind the reception desk with a plaque underneath stating *Elisabetta*

Stenosa—Proprietaria (owner). I was not sure what happened to her husband, Martino Furbone, but I knew I wouldn't want to ever change places with that man. It seemed to me that he had made a Faustian pact in marrying that woman.

But then I happened to meet Martino and felt whatever bedeviled fate he'd made for himself he deserved.

This occasion came about because Mica and I were also renovating a small hut that was in ruins below the main Ceppeto house next to our olive grove. It had originally been used for storing feed for the animals, but we were converting it into a guesthouse (later, it became our small winery).

Martino apparently seemed to think that he and Elisabetta were the king and queen of Lupaia, not just the owners of most of it, and had rule over even the areas for which they didn't hold deeds. To carry out this unofficial self-proclaimed reign, Martino would regularly go to the town architect to read the filings submitted by property owners for all renovations and building plans in the area contiguous to his landed estate. It was during one of these forays that he found our filing for the guesthouse, and he immediately took exception, claiming that since it was visible from the main road leading to "his" village, he therefore had the right to object. The nature of Martino's objection was that he believed we were going to rent out the guesthouse and, therefore, that it would be a nuisance.

When I heard this, I called Martino and, having never met him, asked if I could make an appointment to see him. He agreed, and I went to his house early on a Saturday morning.

His house was in Lupaia, behind one of the churches that now houses one of his wineries. It was in the style of a *baronale* villa. Instead of the exposed stones typical of the farmhouses, the exterior of his villa had stucco painted a pale yellow, covering the stones. The entrance was a large courtyard surrounded on three sides by the main rooms of the house, the open end facing the valley.

Martino Furbone was, I must say, very cordial. At the time, he was probably in his late fifties or early sixties, slightly built, and about 5'9" with short-cropped gray hair, a healthy tan, and an ever-ready diplomat's white-toothed smile. He was fashionably attired Italian style, with Gucci loafers, no socks, white slacks without a wrinkle in sight, a loose-fitting silk shirt unbuttoned at the top, and a sweater draped over his shoulders.

We met alone on his veranda in front of the courtyard and exchanged pleasantries. He claimed that his English was minimal, so we spoke Italian.

After a few minutes of conversation, I removed an envelope from my briefcase, saying, "Martino, I understand you expressed concern that we may be renting the little hut we are renovating down by our olive grove to tourists. First of all, I have no idea why what I do at Ceppeto is of any interest to you. But just to make it clear, I am in the real estate business in New York City." I then showed him a photograph taken at night from our residence in Manhattan and said, "This picture was taken from our apartment on the forty-seventh floor. Do you know Manhattan, Martino?"

"*Si, certo.*" ("Yes, sure I do.")

"Then I am sure you recognize this building." I pointed to the Citicorp Center building, which could clearly be seen in the photo. "I'm a principal owner of that building, which has 1.2 million square feet of office and retail space and is fully rented, averaging over sixty dollars per square foot." I then showed him an article from the July issue of *Crain's,* a real estate publication, with the headline, "Citicorp Building 100% Rented." I pointed to where I had underlined "co-owned by Richard Hadar."

Martino took a moment to look at the article. When he looked up, he was clearly embarrassed, as he understood where I was going and how wrong he had been.

I said, "Do you really think I would be interested in renting perhaps four hundred square feet of a small hut to make a little extra money? I can assure you, Martino, I'm not here to make money. I'm here to spend it, and I intend to make Ceppeto as beautiful as possible. I hope you can appreciate that, and I hope that we share the same objective in keeping this entire valley as beautiful as we can."

Martino, still blushing, quickly regained his composure and, with that diplomat's smile, said, "Of course, I'm not concerned about what you do. I think my inquiry was completely misunderstood, and I am happy to hear of your interest in restoring Ceppeto." He then added, "I would like to invite you and your wife to our big celebration in August."

I knew about his annual party, with hundreds of invited guests, and I thanked him, saying that we'd already made plans for that evening.

At that moment, Elisabetta came in with, apparently, a guest of theirs. Martino, evidently not knowing of my previous encounter with his wife, introduced me. She acted as if she had never seen me before and was quite pleasant. She introduced me to the man at her side, who was also from New York City.

Martino told him I was in the real estate business, and the man asked what kinds of buildings I owned.

I mentioned the Citicorp Building, Studio 54, and a few others, including a development site next to the Puck Building.

He said, "Oh, I know that building on Lafayette Street. That's where David Bowie and Iman moved and also Ian Schraeger and Patrick McEnroe."

"Why, yes it is," I said. I then turned to Martino and his wife, whom I call the *Fabissana Faccia* (a mix of Yiddish and Italian meaning "sour face") and their guest, said my good-byes, and left.

It is not usually my style to brag or even talk about my business, but I was delighted to do it this time.

CHAPTER 15

LEARNING TO LIVE
LIFE ITALIAN STYLE

Those early days at Ceppeto were an education in rural living. Did you know that cuckoo birds cuckoo day and night, nonstop, when they're looking for a mate? We learned this because one of the damned things ensconced himself on the property and didn't stop cuckooing for close to two months. That poor guy had to have been the ugliest cuckoo bird that ever lived to take that long to land a partner. As if that wasn't enough, when the partner lays eggs, they have the audacity to use other birds' nests. Talk about chutzpah!

We also learned that there are male and female cypress trees—those tall, majestic evergreens that so beautifully punctuate the Tuscan landscape. The male trees—and I'm not making any of this up—are tall, slim, and straight. The female trees are curvier and broader at the base.

Then there are the venomous vipers. Luckily they will only bite if stepped on or, even worse, sat on (perish the thought!). Mica found a baby viper under the doormat at our front door, hardly bigger than a worm but still dangerous. Apparently, when the female gives birth, she climbs up a tree or some other high place so when the babies are born, they're dropped beneath her, far enough away that they can't bite her. If they bite her, she dies. We assumed the mother viper in this case had climbed up into our grape arbor, but all attempts to find her by hitting the arbor with a long—*very* long—stick were unsuccessful. We never saw any traces of her or any more babies after that first one. She must have retreated to a more peaceful abode in the woods.

Then there are nonvenomous snakes, the garden variety that are quite big. I saw one at least three feet long and several inches round. Everyone waits with anticipation for the warm summer temperatures to arrive, and the sure sign that time is close is when these snakes start showing up. They leave their nesting places to come out and start getting warm, and when they do, invariably warm weather is just a few days away.

Then we have the cicadas. They make a loud noise similar to crickets as they sit up in the trees. I learned to silence them by using a long pole to hit some of the branches in their tree until they stopped. After doing this a few times, they became trained, so if they started making noise, all I had to do was walk outside with a stick in my hand, and they immediately stopped.

Lastly, we developed a problem with our neighbor Rosa's rooster. You see, a neighbor of ours, Ennis, who raises bees, also has some hunting dogs. One of his dogs got into the chicken coop and killed one of Rosa's hens, after which the rooster started getting up at all hours of the night cock-a-doodle-doo-ing. I guess he was in mourning. However, when we heard Ennis's dog also goes after roosters, I have to admit we didn't think that would be such a bad idea.

And then that damned cuckoo bird came back. Apparently, his relationship didn't work out, so he resumed his perch, cuckooing almost twenty-four hours a day. It had been a short romance, sadly, but at least there were no children involved.

We did have hope that a beautiful pheasant that had been coming right up to the house would be a good spousal candidate for the cuckoo bird. Alas, that didn't work out either.

It took me some time to learn to navigate the Italian road system. Generally, Italian roads have plenty of signage, but they tend to overdo it and often make errors placing them. As an example, when driving in Milan, the center of the city is a veritable maze of curving and inevitable "Wrong Way" one-way streets. Rather than trying to use a map, which doesn't show one-way streets, I tried following signs to the Autostrada (Turnpike). The first time I attempted this, everything went well, until we arrived at a fork in the road: three streets all heading off in different directions. There was a sign on *each* street with an arrow indicating it was the way to get to the Autostrada. I guess the mentality was that since all roads led to Rome, it didn't make a difference which street you took (making the point: the one we took *did* take us to the Autostrada).

Another fact: Italian road signs only post arrows pointing in two directions—left or right—but these can also mean go straight ahead. They rarely use an arrow pointing up to indicate go straight. When you come to an intersection, you have to decide if the arrow pointed left or right actually means turn left, turn right, or go straight.

Then there are the signs that are simply *wrong*. One sign in Panzano indicates that Florence is twenty-five kilometers away, and then the next one *after* you leave Panzano as you get closer to Florence says, "Florence, 30 Kilometers." There's a sign on the way to Greve from Florence indicating you should turn left to get to Greve when you should turn right—no big deal, if you don't mind ending up back in Florence. Then, outside of Greve, there's a stop sign that suddenly appears on the highway for no apparent reason. It's like seeing a typical hexagonal stop sign pop up on a turnpike as you whiz by at sixty miles per hour. (Imagine trying to teach your children how to drive on such roads: "Daddy, I thought you said to always stop at stop signs." "Shuddup, kid; on this road, it stands for 'Step on Pedal.'")

In the summer of 2002, we decided to buy a Jeep. It had occurred to us that a 4x4 would be a lot more practical—and fun—for exploring some of the back roads in the area that were too difficult for our station wagon to navigate.

The Jeep was shipped to the Chrysler dealer in Siena, who called to let us know when it arrived. When we got to the dealer to sign some papers for the plates, we were told they'd need another week to get the vehicle ready for us to pick up.

"I don't understand how it could take so long to prepare a car," I said. "May I see exactly what you're doing?"

He took us into their garage, and there was our Jeep—all in pieces. It had been shipped in a box and had to be assembled.

I looked at the dealer and asked, "Are batteries included?"

There are no barbers in Lupaia and only one in Radda: Maurizio. Maurizio is more or less an institution in Radda. Like so many people here, he is related either directly or by marriage to practically everybody. Every time I mention a name to him, he says, "Ah, yes, he's my cousin/brother-in-law/nephew" or something. For this reason, you have to be careful of what you say, not only because he's related to everyone but also because his chair in his little shop is a center for a lot of gossip among the men in Radda.

When I first started going to him, Maurizio had been cutting hair for probably thirty-five years, and I doubt the routine for any of his customers has ever changed. You climb up in the chair, you get a bedsheet wrapped around you, and Maurizio asks, "So how do you like it cut today?" You explain with words and finger pointing and holding up clumps of hair as to how you want your hair cut.

I always say, "Not too short, trim the top a little, leave the back long, and just trim the sides a little. Don't cut the sideburns too short."

The haircut only takes about ten minutes, which gives us enough time to discuss the weather and happenings in Radda. When he is all finished, he dusts me off with a brush and proudly holds up a mirror so I can see the finished product.

It is always cut short all over: top, sides, back, and sideburns. In fact, I am not sure why he doesn't just use an electric shaver. His idea of short is to shave off all the hair, just as they did when I was in the army. Leaving it long means cutting it just short enough so it still looks like you have hair. No matter what I tell him, he cuts my hair short all over every time. I bet if I told him, "Don't cut my hair this time; just comb it," he would cut it short.

All the men in Radda have the exact same haircut, maybe some a little longer than others but not by much. It is sort of a prescribed uniform. If you want to be considered a resident of Radda, you have to have your hair cut by Maurizio.

I still can't get over the fact I haven't been able to find a good barber in Italy. No one believes me when I say that Italy doesn't have good barbers anymore. I find that exasperatingly ironic since I grew up getting haircuts from Italian barbers. Italian barbershops were where I heard Italian opera for the first time and learned to recognize Enrico Caruso's arias. The barbers always sang along, and I never heard an Italian barber with a bad voice. Through the years, I remember I was always able to tell them how I wanted my hair cut. Granted, they weren't like the "stylists" of today who charge hundreds more than the two bits (for any youngsters out there, that's twenty-five cents) that I paid back then, but they would follow my requests and do a very good job. Here in Italy, it is a completely different story.

As a test, one day, when Mica and I were in Siena, we passed a fashionable-looking hair salon—mind you, a *salon,* not a barbershop. It had pictures plastered all over the windows of fabulous-looking men and women with great haircuts and hairstyles. I needed a haircut, so we decided to give it a try. If I got a good haircut, it would be worth the trip to Siena every now and then for an alternative to Maurizio.

I sat down in the chair, and as he covered my shirt with a wrap, I explained how I wanted my hair cut: long in the back, not too short on the sides, and a little off the top. Mica was next to me when I told this to the barber (excuse me, I should say "stylist"). As Mica turned to sit down, she picked up a magazine, and the "stylist" began on the back of my head. I heard several fast snips of the scissors, and then Mica said, "No, no, that's too short, stop!"

Too late. He had cut off such huge pieces of hair that the only way he could make it look balanced was—you guessed it—short all over.

The last week of August was the second and most important running of the Palio—the bareback horse race they have in the Piazza del Campo twice a year—in Siena.

Each entry represents one of seventeen neighborhoods in Siena, each called a *contrada,* with its own mascot emblazoned on its own unique flag. Mica and I had been there the previous year with the Sages, and Saul, Joe, Bill, and I had decided to adopt the *bruco* (caterpillar) *contrada* as a mascot for our office in New York. Its flag had a design with three caterpillars, representing Saul, Bill, and me, plus a rose, representing Joe LaRosa. Unfortunately, the *bruco* hadn't even placed anywhere in the money for the fourth year in a row. The losing streak would extend until 2003 when it finally won the race at 51:1 odds.

Betting on these races is a big deal in Siena. The biggest historic bet was made between Ludovico Sforza and Cesare Borgia in 1498 for a castle of the winner's choice in the loser's province. Ludovico won the bet, but Cesare had him poisoned to avoid having to cough up a castle.

We became friends with a couple, Giorgio and Vittoria Scolto, who grew up and continue to live in Siena in the neighborhood called *tartaruga* (turtle), so we got a firsthand look at how life is conducted in the *contrada*. The Palio is only one event of many throughout the year, all of which heighten the friendly but serious rivalry between each neighborhood.

But it is the pageantry that precedes and follows each race that is unique. Each neighborhood represents itself with its own distinctive banner, costumes, and colors dating back hundreds of years. Every Sunday from Easter until the end of summer, there is a parade through the heart of Siena for one of the neighborhoods, which is led by a drum and bugle corps, followed by a group of all ages waving their distinctive flags in unison and singing their neighborhood anthem, after which comes a full marching band and then a group of neighborhood dignitaries, each wearing their colorful sashes.

The week before the Palio, about thirty horses are brought by their owners to the Piazza del Campo, which is where the race is run on the day of the Palio. The moment they enter the piazza, the horses become the property of the Comune di Siena. A panel consisting of the mayor, several deputies, and veterinarians then judges them, along with local horse experts, who all sit at a long table set up in the piazza. From the group of thirty or so horses, the panel chooses seventeen to participate in the race. The numbers of each of the seventeen horses are placed into a bingo-type mixer at the end of the table, controlled by youngsters. At the other end of the table is another mixer with seventeen numbers in it representing each of the *contradas*. A number is drawn from the pool of horses and then matched to a number drawn from the pool of *contradas*. This all happens under the eyes of thousands of people, and as each *contrada* is assigned a horse, the crowd goes wild with excitement. At the point the match is made, that horse goes from being the property of Siena to the property of the *contrada* to which it is assigned, where a stable, a vet, a trainer, and a rider are all waiting. The week following the selection, the horses are trained in the Piazza del Campo, and the night before the race, they're brought to the church in the *contrada* where they enter for a final blessing.

Each *contrada* is a tightly knit community with its own churches, social affairs, and community organizations in which involvement begins in childhood. They each run neighborhood programs for local youth (soccer, basketball, etc.), and they have programs to deal with the problems young people encounter while growing up. They also run social programs for all ages that are small enough that no one in the neighborhood gets lost in the shuffle. What makes it all so unique is the pride and celebration of a wider culture, which is brought down to a small social unit where all feel included. In today's world of disenfranchisement, what passes for connection is who "likes" your status on your Facebook page. Instead, in Siena it is quite the opposite. The social connection in Siena is a fascinating phenomenon that has been the subject of sociological research for years. The involvement of the community, the outpouring of emotion, the sense of fairness ... it's all remarkable and has enabled the Sienese to live in a confined area for centuries with a minimum of internal dissension.

We were supposed to go to the prerace ceremonies but decided not to when we realized that there'd be thousands of people packed into the Piazza del Campo. We later learned that during the race one of the horses fell, and because no one is allowed to stop, it was trampled so badly that it later died.

Sometime afterward, we had dinner with Mario and Gina Massini at their vacation home outside Siena. They had been introduced to us by Giorgio and Vittoria Scolto. In the city, they live in the *contrada* that has the *bruco* as its mascot. From them, we got a completely different take on the Palio. Neither of them liked going to the race. According to them, it had become a major betting event, which wasn't so bad in itself, but as a result, the horses were being drugged with syringes that were literally hidden up the handlers' sleeves, oftentimes right after they were tested and while they were being led into the piazza. It wasn't unusual for riders to be thrown from their horses as a result of being hit by the whips of adversaries. More often than not, however, the horses were the ones injured, and in many cases, as happened that year, they had to be destroyed. For our hosts, the race had become too corrupt and brutal to watch. As a visiting friend said to us, "The Kentucky Derby it's not."

What troubled Mica and I even more, however, was an incident that happened to the Massinis just a couple of months earlier. Their home, where we were having dinner, was robbed. Cash and jewelry were taken, and some damage was done to the house as the robbers searched for valuables. What surprised us, however, was that they didn't even call the Carabinieri, the Italian equivalent of our police force.

I asked Mario why, and he said, "You know, Richard, our families have lived here for many, many generations, and we are now seeing a gradual but relentless change in Italy caused by an enormous influx of immigrants. Now, I am not xenophobic. I think, handled properly, immigration can be healthy, but Italy is doing it all wrong. They are allowing hundreds of thousands of illegal immigrants to enter the country with little effort to stop the flow. When the number got so large for the illegal ones, they extended amnesty to them. That only encouraged more to enter. It has overwhelmed every system designed to provide social services to our citizens. We are not like America, a whole country built on welcoming immigrants; this is relatively new for us. As frequently happens with large groups of immigrants, there is a criminal element among them. It is largely those groups that are committing a lot of these petty crimes. This was not the first time we've been robbed. The first time we called the Carabinieri, and they never showed up. They called us back a day later and asked if we would come into their office between 9:00 a.m. and 5:00 p.m. to file a complaint. We did, but nothing ever happened. This last robbery, we knew it would be useless to call them, so we have done nothing. We are just doing something we never had to do before, which is lock all our windows and doors, even if we are just going out for a short walk. In Siena, we are no longer comfortable taking walks in the city after dark. Many of the wives of friends fear walking alone on the streets at any time as a few of them have been followed and harassed by young immigrant men. Have you ever read anything by Oriana Fallaci?"

Mica and I both answered yes. Actually, Mica and I both were very familiar with her books, which were worldwide best sellers but controversial. Oriana Fallaci was a journalist who had interviewed leaders from countries all over the world, on both sides of wars and revolutions that were being fought. She was particularly outspoken about the threat of the Muslim influx into Europe and claimed that with the uncontrolled immigration and birthrate of Muslims into Europe, in particular Italy, they would soon form the majority of the population and destroy the culture. She railed against the "inept" politicians who were catering to them for their votes and not for the good of the citizens. Fallaci claimed that Europe would soon be called "Eurabia."

I was fascinated with Mario's comments, primarily because this was the first time I had heard firsthand any contrarian opinion as to what the serious issues were facing Italians. I, in particular, much more than Mica, who had grown up in Italy, tended to romanticize life in Italy—almost with blinders on. I saw only the good things, partly because we lived in a rural area that was isolated from the issues caused by immigration, at least until now. I found this troubling because it was the first crack in my perception of Italy as a place for the ideal, good life. As Mario continued, I began to think more about this.

Mario said, "Then you know what her dire predictions are for Italy. When I first read her books and articles, I didn't agree with her conclusions, but now I see the changes happening and think she is entirely correct. Unfortunately, no one in Italy or Europe is doing anything about it. As a group, the Muslim immigrants have only been here for a relatively short time, and rather than try to assimilate into our culture, they are trying to change it—and in some cases, they have been successful. First, they objected to our church bells ringing so often as it interfered with their prayers five times a day. Then they complained about the crucifixes displayed on public school walls. These have been part of our culture for centuries and accepted by every other religious group that has made Italy their home. It is as if they hit the ground complaining and trying to tear down our culture rather than getting to work and contributing something to our country. Richard and Mica, what worries me and Gina is what we are leaving behind us for our children and grandchildren. From what I have seen lately, it is very troubling, and there are no leaders in sight that seem to have the backbone to change it."

Mica and I sat in silence for a few moments as we let some of what Mario had just said sink in. Mica was the first to speak. "I happen to be a big fan of Oriana Fallaci, and I think she is saying exactly what has to be said. There is a reason her books have been translated into dozens of languages and are best sellers all over the world. I left Italy almost twenty years ago because of some of the problems she talks about, but it was never as terrible as it seems to be now. The answers are there, but being Italian and knowing how Italians think, I am not sure there is the will to do what has to be done to get the ship righted, as they say."

Mario said, "Sadly I agree with you, but I am hoping there are enough like-minded people around that will try. I know Gina and I will."

We ended the evening on a much lighter note. After a delicious dinner, we said our good-byes and drove back to Ceppeto, about a half hour away. Neither of us said a word, until I finally broke the silence and said, "Damn, Mario was absolutely right. What a splash of cold water on my face. I really have to wake up and realize that, as much as I love Ceppeto and Italy, we are not isolated from the world's problems." How unfortunately right I was soon to be.

CHAPTER 16
SEPTEMBER 11, 2001

I remember September 11 as a beautiful summer's day. It was the kind of clear-skied, perfect day that made me think, *This is why I came here; this is why this place exists.*

The Chianti hills rolled out from the villa, a brilliant late-summer green here and there speckled with golden *ginestra* (forsythia) blossoms. Some of the hills and fields were patterned into farms and vineyards, and the hilltops across from us were crested by the low silhouettes of small villages that looked as natural a part of the terrain as did the woodlands and vineyards.

In the same way that one might sit in a museum and stare at a landscape painting for an hour, absorbed in its beauty and yet always finding something new to appreciate in a previously skimmed-over corner of the frame, on such a day one could sit outside our home, a glass of wine in hand, and spend a good part of the day just *looking.*

And that's what our friends from New York were doing. It was midafternoon, about three o'clock, and I had just come out of the shower and was in the upstairs bedroom getting dressed. I could hear them through the open window, relaxing in lounge chairs, chatting with Mica. There was Bill and Joanna Persky, as well as Joe LaRosa and Liane Revzin. Back in New York, hardly a week went by that at least some of us Sages didn't get together for a lunch, a dinner, a show … something, anything. They were the people whose visits we looked forward to during the six months that we'd taken to spending in Italy each year.

They had flown in just a few days before, to ostensibly celebrate Bill's birthday on September 9, although if it hadn't been Bill's birthday, we would have undoubtedly found some other pretext to get together. In honor of Bill's birthday, we had planned to go into Florence that evening for dinner at the famous Michelin-starred Enoteca Pinchiorri, one of the best restaurants in Italy and perhaps all of Europe.

The phone rang, and I picked up the bedroom extension. It was Mica's mother. She was very excited, the Italian spilling out of her mouth like a machine gun. "Look at the television," she said. "There was an accident with the twins."

My immediate thought was that something had happened to Mica's twin brothers, although I couldn't figure out what that had to do with the TV. I stuck my head out the window and called Mica to come up right away, telling her that there had been an accident. When Mica came upstairs and took the phone, still not knowing what the connection to the TV was, I flipped on the bedroom set.

We usually didn't spend much time watching TV while in Italy, so we never bothered with a cable hookup. I was surprised then to see CNN on the air, since the channel was normally only available on a subscription basis. But they had evidently opened up the signals to the regular broadcasters. In fact, CNN was on every channel.

CNN anchor Aaron Brown was reporting from on top of a building in New York City, saying that a plane had hit one of the World Trade Center Towers. Just then, Mica—still on the phone with her mother—turned to me and said, "Oh my gosh, a plane hit the Towers, the Twin Towers."

I don't remember if I got the idea from some speculating they were doing on TV, but I got the notion that what had probably happened was that a private plane had gone off course and hit one of the Towers accidentally. I remembered that something like that had happened many years ago to the Empire State Building.

I put my head out the window again and called down to the group that a plane had hit the Twin Towers, and they all made the same assumption about it probably having been a small plane. They all came up, and we sat around the TV, watching the story unfold.

As we watched the news, the truth sickeningly set in.

And the rest you know.

Of course, we canceled dinner. For hours, we just sat and watched, growing more and more depressed, as the news grew worse and worse. None of us could contact our families and friends back in the States: there was no phone or e-mail service into New York City.

Through the window, I heard someone crying out on the road that led up to our house. It was Maria from Lupaia. She had walked from Lupaia to our house sobbing, "*Non ci credo, non ci credo.*" ("I don't believe it.") She asked if we had relatives in New York and if they were okay. At that point, we could only guess—and hope—that they were.

Joe LaRosa, who is quite the photographer, thought to take a picture of us standing around the TV, watching the tragedy play out. The looks on our faces sum it up: disbelief, devastation … just like everyone else who was glued to his or her TV that day. But as horrible as it all was, I took some comfort that Bill and Joanna and Joe and Liane were there with us at Ceppeto. It was one thing to feel stranded and helpless while our homeland was attacked, but it would have been even worse to have faced the day alone.

The following morning, we decided to go to Radda. As we headed there, we could hear church bells ringing in all the little villages in the area in commemoration of what had happened in New York City the previous day. In Radda, one familiar face after another came up to us, commiserating, extending sympathies, visibly concerned not just for us but also for all the people back in the States.

It seemed to me the way someone would feel when a parent becomes sick: this strong person, whom you had the utmost confidence in and upon whom you could always rely, was now weak and in need of aid. The United States had been akin to a patriarchal figure to Italy since the end of WWII, always there to help in times of need and also to protect from enemies, and yet it was now severely suffering, injured and damaged. This was the way our Italian neighbors felt: as if they were watching a parent dying.

For the next week, there were all sorts of commemorative ceremonies, and every afternoon the church bells rang in honor of the dead. While visiting nearby Volterra, we saw banners in Italian proclaiming "Italians are Americans" and "Italians are New Yorkers."

It reminded me—on a grand scale—of the way people react to death. A loved one dies, and you say, "Oh damn! I never told him the way I felt! I wish I'd told him this; I wish I'd told him that." That was the kind of feeling that seemed to be coming out everywhere we looked.

As soon as air traffic in the States resumed, Bill and Joanna and Joe and Liane flew home. Mica and I took a few days to close up the house and managed to get seats on a flight about ten days after the attacks. Raffaello, our caretaker, had us over to his house for a farewell dinner with his family.

He had his grandson there, maybe eleven or twelve years old, who was going on about the people who had attacked the United States. "These guys don't know what they messed with," he said. "They're in for it now!" And even if he was just a kid, it seemed to be the sentiment wherever we were in Italy at the time. The sense of unity and affection for the United States was absolutely heartwarming.

When it was time to leave, Raffaello—and this was a mark of how close we'd all become since we'd bought Ceppeto—began crying. He begged us not to leave, frightened for our safety. But there had never been a question of our going back, even for Mica. We may have had two homes, but New York was *home*. And our home had been hurt; our place was there.

I assured him it was probably the safest time to fly. He and his wife, Marina, insisted we call them as soon as we arrived in New York, which we promised we would do.

When Mica and I arrived at the Milan airport, I saw I was more right than I'd known. All around the airport—in fact, at every major entry point in or out of the country—all sorts of heavily armed Italian soldiers were visible. On our Delta flight, we were given plastic forks and spoons for our meals—no knives, not even plastic ones.

When we flew into New York from Europe, we usually came in during the afternoon. As we made the approach to Kennedy Airport, we could see the Manhattan skyline. As many times as I'd made the trip across the Atlantic, I'd always had a great feeling—a real sense of "Welcome home, Richard!"—on seeing the familiar, iconic silhouette of the city. But this time, seeing that void where the Towers had stood … only sadness. It was, I knew, a hole that would never truly be filled.

For the first few days after we'd come back, like everyone else, we asked ourselves, *What can we do? How can we help?*

But the days turned to weeks, the weeks into months, and the great wound the country had suffered scabbed over. Some kind of rough normalcy returned, and we came to look forward to going back to Ceppeto. In the same way that, on 9/11, there had never been a question that we needed to get back to the States, there had also been no question that, eventually, we'd be going back to what has sometimes seemed a little island of sanity and peace and friendship in a world that regularly wants to go crazy.

PART IV

REBUILDING EDEN

CHAPTER 17

PASQUALE'S RETURN

When we returned to Ceppeto in March of the following year—2002—we set about looking for local full-time help who were legal for both the house and the grounds. We tried three different workers since Pasquale left the year before, and with each disappointment, it became all the more clear what we needed, but there simply was no one around who could do the job as well as Pasquale by a wide margin.

We first tried a legal immigrant, who was from Albania but didn't speak Italian (instead, he spoke German as he had been working for a German family for many years). I was able to piece together my German from my years in the army and communicated reasonably well with him, but his work ethic was terrible. To put it another way, he was just plain lazy. The final straw was when he began asking Mica to make him coffee in the mornings. When I found this out, I told him to go get a job in a coffee bar.

Then we tried a young Italian man, who was very nice and had experience in farming. It turned out that all he could do was drive a tractor, so that is all he did. He drove our tractor here, there, and everywhere but got little else done. So he too was soon gone.

Not giving up and needing someone more than ever as Raffaello wasn't able, by himself, to keep up with all that had to be done, we hired a local Italian man who claimed to have gardening experience. That experience must have been in a tiny backyard, because grass literally grew under him, he worked so slowly. I began cutting the acres of grass with the tractor and tending to the lawn around the house. It didn't take long to realize our Italian gardener wasn't going to be able to do the job, and after a couple of weeks, he was gone. Ceppeto was becoming a place of ex-employees faster than we were growing tomatoes in our garden.

Meanwhile, Pasquale had been calling us almost monthly since he left the year before. It made no difference if we were in Italy or New York, he kept calling us, hoping that we would change our minds and agree to let him come and work for us. From the conversations I had with him back then I figured out that he must have been really struggling. In our later more-candid conversations, I learned that after he had arrived back in the south of Italy, he had been able to find some work as it was the harvest season then. But after that was over, there had been no more work to be found. He'd soon run out of money and had been getting by on stale bread and foraging for food in the woods. His experiences surviving in the forests of Albania and Greece had saved him once again.

When he called us shortly after the last Italian gardener left and asked if he could come to work, I finally said to myself, "To hell with it," and told him, "Okay, come on up, and we'll figure something out."

I was very concerned about hiring an illegal immigrant, but I also knew the work we wanted to get done wasn't going to happen otherwise. Almost to the day that Pasquale had started heading north, a new law was passed in Italy giving amnesty to illegal immigrants as long as they had an Italian sponsor and could prove that they had a place to live and a paying job. So it seemed that for Pasquale and us, the stars had all favorably aligned.

The date was June 5, 2002. I was waiting on the platform at the Florence train station when Pasquale arrived; he was at the door of the train, looking even shorter than his 5'5" and every bit the startled immigrant. If it weren't for his mustache, I would have thought him to be a young boy with his battered and worn suitcase that contained all of his worldly possessions and was held together by rope.

He jumped off the train, and as soon as he saw me, he came

running over and threw his arms around me, kissed my hand, and said, "*Grazie, grazie, Capo.*" From that day forward I was *Capo* (Boss) to Pasquale.

Once we got Pasquale settled at Ceppeto, I then started to have him and Raffaello work together again. Raffaello is a proud man and wasn't happy about being phased out, albeit he was now eighty years old. We told him it would be another year before we started the transition, and in the meantime, he would continue full-time working with Pasquale, showing him how to take care of the property.

The tension this created was understandable and gave me the opportunity to observe one of Pasquale's many admirable innate qualities, namely, that of tactfully handling and defusing confrontational situations. In this case, he deferred to Raffaello's position as having seniority over him and, in a joking manner, disarmed him so much that Raffaello practically had no choice but to end up liking Pasquale.

As Pasquale worked alongside Raffaello, he always showed him the utmost deference. He said to me, "*Capo*, Raffaello is old now, enough old to be like a father; me must show him respect he deserves." On the chores that I wanted done, Pasquale would insist on doing all the heavy work while letting Raffaello do the lighter tasks. This still didn't particularly move Raffaello, and he continued to treat Pasquale in a gruff manner, which fazed Pasquale not at all.

Pasquale later told me that growing up in Albania, he was always taught that you must show respect to an older person, especially the very old. If an older person came into the room, you were to stand up, go over, bow, and kiss his or her hand. I have since read that this is part of Albanian culture.

After a few months of working together, Pasquale began calling Raffaello *Babbo* (Dad), a name that has stuck ever since. He continued to joke all day long with *Babbo*, suggesting that he marry Pasquale's widowed mother, even though Raffaello was happily married. "*Babbo*, you young and strong," Pasquale would joke. "Why not you two women make happy instead only one?" Eventually, the slightest of smiles would spread on Raffaello's face but still no words of encouragement from him.

Mind you, being funny in a language that isn't your primary one is no easy task. Yet Pasquale was able to do just that by using his broken Italian and with an expert manner of playing charades for words he didn't know. He did this so fast that when he couldn't find a word in Italian, he would make it up with such speed that it never slowed the conversation down. It was often quite humorous.

As an example, he didn't know the word for chicken, so when it came time to say *pollo* in Italian, he just flapped his arms at his side and said "cluck cluck." No mistaking what he meant. If the grass or flowers needed watering, instead of using the Italian word *annaffiare*, he would throw his head back, open his mouth, and raise his arm up, as if he were pouring water down his throat while making the sound "gluck gluck." When he said "zin zin" while rubbing his fingers together in the shame-on-you motion, he meant a match. In Italy, putting your finger near the corner of your eye and pulling down means *furbo*, "con man," but for Pasquale it meant "I see what has to be done."

His combination of charades and Sid Caesar style of making up words that sound Italian but meant nothing by themselves was innovative and hysterical. But when you combined all of that with his facial expressions, body movements, and gestures, you'd swear he was speaking fluent Italian. For the most part, he made himself understood and did it all without the slightest hesitation or embarrassment.

As an example, Pasquale came to me one morning before Raffaello had arrived and said, "*Capo*, me no shnori last night"—he put his head on his hands and made a snoring sound—"because my brain no stop thinkin." He shook his head back and forth as if indicating no while saying "tsk tsk," and then he made a face spit on the ground. At that point, I figured out he was trying to tell me that he couldn't sleep the night before because he couldn't stop thinking about something that he didn't like. Pasquale, undeterred, went on: "Man who came here." He put his hand on his chest and patted his heart while shaking his head in disgust, and then he said, "Like this," as he pointed to some dirt. So at that point I understood that a man had come to Ceppeto yesterday and that Pasquale, for some reason, thought he was bad and had a heart like dirt. I knew the man he was referring to: someone I had called to move some cypress trees that were growing in the wrong spot as a result of repositioning the driveway. When the man had arrived, Pasquale had been working nearby. The man's breath smelled of alcohol, he had a cigarette dangling from his mouth, and every now and then he turned and spat on the ground. I knew instantly that this guy was not someone I would hire and made short shrift of our meeting. I hadn't told Pasquale my decision, so he thought that I was going to hire him. It was nice to have my decision confirmed by the ever-vigilant Pasquale and to realize how much he cared for Ceppeto and us. In the meantime, I began to be able to translate "Pasqualese" almost as well as I was doing with my Italian.

What is interesting about this whole mode of communication is how at ease Pasquale was with it and how fast his mind worked to figure out how to express what he wanted to say. In working with Pasquale so much, I soon found that I was learning *his* cockamamie vocabulary, instead of him learning Italian. Mica soon referred to our conversations as being in "Ceppetoese." The only thing missing from this new hybrid language, according to Mica, was some of my Yiddish.

CHAPTER 18
PASQUALE BEGINS LIFE ANEW AT CEPPETO

That first spring and summer at Ceppeto in 2002, I was struck by the beauty of the Chianti countryside, the mix of woodlands and the wildflower-dappled fields with terraced farmland and vineyards, the explosive colors of the flowers and shrubs, and the venerable grace of the centuries-old villages and towns. It didn't take long for me to see that Pasquale felt the same way—albeit, he expressed it quite differently. Everything about Chianti was the antithesis of the homeland he'd left behind, which was colorless, begrimed, dysphoric. Pasquale fell in love with Ceppeto, as I had.

We made great progress in the morning meetings I held before work started each day. In what became a ritual, I would meet him in front of the house to discuss what had been done the day before and what had to be done that day. These little confabs had started when Raffaello was here working by himself and continued after Pasquale joined us. Because sound carries up to the bedrooms, Mica and I insisted that there be no noise that could disturb anyone sleeping until I arrived.

Raffaello began the morning by leaving on our kitchen windowsill a freshly baked loaf of bread that he had bought at the *forno* (oven) in Radda. There is nothing as delicious as a slice of hot Tuscan bread right out of the oven with a sprinkle of olive oil to start the day. Then, while patiently waiting for me, Raffaello would start sweeping the *lastricato* (paving stones on our patio) outside the kitchen with a broom he made from the branches of *ginestre* bushes that grow wild on our property. The *ginestre* are similar to the American yellow flowering forsythia. When Pasquale joined us, he would quietly work on weeding the gardens around the house.

As Mica and I awakened, we would hear through our open bedroom window the rhythmic swoosh of Raffaello's broom across the *lastricato*, the morning chorus of *fringuelli* (songbirds) chirping in a variety of octaves and musical patterns, and the early wind gently rustling the leaves in the trees as if they too were just waking up. Raffaello's broom was like the baton of a conductor leading a virtual symphony for us to enjoyably start a new day. It is one of the most exquisite virtues of living here, away from the cacophony of sounds of a big city. Here in Ceppeto, it is so quiet that people stop to look up when an occasional plane flies overhead. Our friends and family who visit us here have often said they wish they could bottle the air and silence to bring back home.

When Pasquale began joining us at these morning meetings, the fun began, because it wasn't enough to just tell Pasquale what I wanted done. To his credit, he wanted to be sure he understood my instructions completely. We would move to an open spot on the ground, and just like in the days when we played sandlot football and drew the plays in the dirt during the huddle, Pasquale did likewise with a stick. Because he was also short on Italian words, this was the time when we learned Ceppetoese. During these conversations, Raffaello just listened and became speechless since what went back and forth between me and Pasquale didn't seem much like Italian to him.

This Ceppetoese was a language for just Pasquale and me. The two people that I mostly spoke with in Italian were Mica and Pasquale. Raffaello was not very talkative, except if you asked him about the history of the area, but how many times can you do that? So it was only natural that my Italian became infected with Pasquale's iterations (and I have no idea what influence I had upon his Italian). As we each adapted to the other's interpretation and (mis)pronunciation of Italian, making mistakes all over the place with no one to correct either of us, it got to the point that I was the only one who could communicate with Pasquale.

Here is just one example:

Pasquale: "*Capo, la si urine domand mi contoll con negoz a Radda se han lat da moo moo. Ha bisogn qualcos tu forz uove cluck cluck?*" ("*Capo*, the Signora asked me to go to the store in Radda and if there is milk, she wants two liters. Do you need anything, perhaps eggs?")

The proper way to have said that in Italian would be: "*Capo, la Signora mi ha domandato di andare al negozio a Radda, e se c'e del latte, ne vuole due litri. Ha bisogno di altro, forse uova?*"

In addition to the ill-gotten pronunciation, injected in Pasquale's language are "moo moo" (cow) and "cluck cluck" (chicken) referred to as eggs from chickens.

Practically every word in the Italian language ends with a vowel, and Pasquale drops the vowels on most of his words. In a language where, with few exceptions, every single letter is pronounced, Pasquale's pronunciation can drive an Italian speaker *pazzo* (crazy).

After the morning huddle, I acted as interpreter between Raffaello and Pasquale until I was sure they both understood the chores for the day. As they walked away to start work, I heard only Pasquale chattering, with Raffaello presumably listening. In any event, the work never failed to get done, so whatever language was being spoken, it seemed to function successfully.

CHAPTER 19

THE EARLY YEARS

In 2002, I wrote to our friends back home:

> We have had Pasquale, the gardener from last year, for a couple of months now, and he has single-handedly whipped the place into fabulous shape. Mica and I have never seen anyone work like he does.
>
> He starts around 7:00 a.m. and continues until dark at around 9:00 p.m. When I tell him to stop, he says, "*Capo*, what Pasquale can do? Me love work! Me like work; me no like do nothing. When me work, Pasquale more happy." So we let him work. Without exaggeration, he does as much work as three men combined. When he walks, he walks fast and sometimes jogs.
>
> I saw him the other day walking up the hill from the olive grove carrying a bunch of equipment on his shoulder, pushing a lawn mower with his free hand, and whistling as happily as one could be. I get out of breath just walking up that damned hill empty-handed. The guy should be the subject of a scientific study.

By August of 2002, Pasquale's Italian had improved considerably, and we began communicating a lot better. I wrote the following to our friends:

> There are fewer made-up words that sound Italian but aren't. Instead, he has developed phrases, some of which are priceless.
>
> For example, we have seven olive trees planted along the top of a long wall crossing the lawn in front of the house. One died, and Mica wanted to transplant a large flowering bush to replace it. Upon hearing this, Pasquale looked up at the sky for a moment in deep thought, raised his eyebrows while extending his palms up in front of him, and, shrugging his shoulders, said, "Excuse me, Signora, but when you got seven sheep, why you want put a goat in the middle of them?"
>
> He treats the grass and plants like living creatures. He doesn't just water them: "Capo, today Pasquale *give* water to the grass and flowers." "The plants need food," which means fertilizer. When he describes someone as mean or bad, like his old mafioso boss, Renato, he says, "That man has a black heart." If you think about them for a second, they all make oddly logical sense.
>
> His descriptions of people and expressions are also novel combined with the fact he has an uncanny ability to read people by just looking at their faces. It is like a sixth sense for him, and over the years I can't remember one instance in which he was wrong in his initial assessment of a person. He said to me, "Pasquale look at face and me tell right away, the kind of person they is. Good, bad, nice, mean, can be trusted or no." Here are a few of his "right on" takes on people we know who he has met:

"She is fuzzy and nice on outside like some fruit, but inside she is bitter and mean."

"She is friendly with everyone. But she doesn't know when everyone you meet is your friend, you really don't have friends."

"He is like a dog. No values. Drinks and does drugs. Pasquale know he is my friend, but when he came and wanted to live with me, me said, 'What do you think, my house is a barrack for dogs?'"

"Eduardo, is my best friend. He is a Carabinieri; he from Rome. He has heart of gold. Me can trust him. He is a good person with strong mind."

"Bini is good man. Very honest, always. Wants what is best for his customers, not just for himself. Me trust him."

"He looks in two directions always when he speaks. Past you, and as if he has a mirror and looks at himself. Never cares to see you or cares a damn about you, only himself. No, no, can't trust him."

"She is nice but has a *cervello* [brain] that is *morbido* [soft]."

"Me feel sorry for him; his brain is confused. He tries but can't do things right."

In summary, "Humans are not nice. Animals are better. 99 percent of people are problem; 1 percent are good. No time for the 99 percent. The 1 percent are hard to find."

Because of all the rain we had been having, I had turned off the irrigation system. I didn't say anything to Pasquale, nor did I think he would notice since the grass was lush and green. The next morning, he came to me and said, "*Capo*, what's wrong with the irrigation? No water last night."

"Pasquale, how can you tell? The grass looks great to me."

"*Capo*, Pasquale can feel it when the grass needs water. When it needs water, me get sick just like the grass."

Late one summer morning, Mica and I took a wonderful walk down into the valley. The vines in the vineyards were laden with bunches of deep, violet-colored grapes. The fruit trees were all filled with pears, apples, and figs. The flowers were just passing their peak and resplendent in all their colors. The fresh fragrance of everything combined was intoxicating—as much for us as it seemed for the bees buzzing excitingly around the flowers and for the birds fluttering and chirping above, occasionally diving into a tree or vine to peck at the fruit and extract their delicious nectar, as if they all knew this was the elixir of life and time was nearing when it would all end with the fall harvest in just a few weeks. It was already difficult to remember that only a few months ago, everything had been devoid of foliage. I remember thinking, *It's like looking in the mirror every day; we see no changes, but, boy, do they sneak up on you! And when you finally recognize the fact that you are aging, there is a tendency to begin hurrying, realizing that there is an end coming and it is coming faster than you would like.*

After another year had passed, we continued to learn about the perils of country living, which were never more evident than when Rumba—Mica's black cat—decided that hunting *lucertole* (lizards) was too tame. So one day, while Mica was reading, comfortably stretched out on the couch in the living room, Rumba brought her a viper, a very venomous snake, and plunked it down on the floor right beneath her. Mica screamed, and Rumba, apparently sensing her gift was unappreciated, picked up the viper and carried it back outside.

I was upstairs, and by the time I got downstairs, Pasquale had arrived, grabbed the viper by the neck with his bare hands, and immediately killed it. It was about ten inches long and not pretty. I didn't even want to think what would've happened it if had bitten Mica or Pasquale. We have an emergency kit here for snakebites, but, nevertheless, a bite from a viper can be dangerous and requires the person to be rushed to the hospital. Pasquale, yet again, showed his fearlessness and quick reaction. I came to understand more and more how he had survived living in the woods in Greece and also how he had survived the difficult life he'd led before we met him.

It's not very consoling, but I'm told if you're wearing clothing, it's difficult for the viper's bite to penetrate through and pierce the skin. If it had bitten Rumba, however, she would've died within twenty minutes. But apparently, cats are faster than vipers and can ward off their attacks—as can Pasquale.

At certain times of the year, especially after a lot of rain, vipers come out to get away from the dampness and warm themselves in the sun. That year we had seen more of them than ever before. They hide in some strange places. That same summer, near Milan, a viper had somehow gotten into a store where the owner chased it but was unable to kill it or get it out of his place. It disappeared and later came out of his computer. That experience would have convinced me to go back to writing with paper and pen.

In Rumba's case, I thought she would have known better. Only a few weeks before, she had come running up to Mica with a giant *lucertola* (lizard) clinging to her neck. Yes, there are little *lucertole*, and then there are *big lucertole*, about ten inches long and husky. For some reason, Rumba thought one of these big ones would be easy pickin's like the little ones, only this time the big guy fought back, grabbed her by the neck, and wouldn't let go. Raffaello was there and swatted it off, and it ran away. Rumba *seemed* as if she'd learned her lesson as she ran meekly back into the house, but apparently whatever lesson she'd learned was short-lived, as she was soon back out chasing down *lucertole*, big and small.

I think she knew she had nine lives and was consequently burning her candle from both ends.

A couple of years after arriving, I began trying to learn how to prune olive trees. It's considered something of an art, but I was determined to learn so that the following spring I could start pruning our trees myself. We'd had Raffaello prune them two years earlier, but he'd cut them down to the point that they looked like twigs stuck in the ground. We were very upset and told him to go easy on the cutting, but no matter what we said, he still continued cutting the life out of the trees.

The landscaper we use told us that this was the way the older *contadini* (farmers) had trimmed the olive trees for centuries and that it's hard to get them to change their ways. There was a more modern way of doing it, which maintained the beauty of the tree, but it was next to impossible to convince Raffaello that it was correct. Consequently, I decided to prune them on my own.

In the process of reading up on olive trees, I became fascinated with the whole subject. They're really quite remarkable. They are evergreens, and what makes them so unusual and durable is their root system, which can survive almost any catastrophe. Even if the trunk of an olive tree is destroyed, when properly cared for, new sprouts can grow from the same roots.

The average olive tree's lifespan is similar to that of humans: about eighty years. During their early years up through their teens, they don't produce much fruit, but their late teens into their early forties are their most productive period, and then they slow down until they stop producing fruit and die. All through their productive life, they alternate between producing a lot one year and resting the next. Once they stop producing, the old trunk can be cut away and new sprouts can be grown from the same root ball, which is why there have been stories of olive trees living for hundreds of years, with some believing the very olive trees Christ walked among on the Mount of Olives before being captured and crucified are still living today.

The use of olive oil is fascinating as well. It's well known that it reduces bad cholesterol and improves good cholesterol. Some varieties, such as those found in Chianti, have natural ibuprofen that reduces inflammation. At one time in the Mediterranean area olive oil was considered as precious as petroleum is today. It was used for light, as it was the eternal oil celebrated on Hanukkah for miraculously lasting eight days when the container was practically empty. The wood is treasured also. Because the trees are too small to harvest wood profitably, the wood, which has beautiful grains, is used sparingly for making bowls and small wooden utensils. For many cultures olive trees are considered the tree of life and are cherished. Suffice it to say that it has been a lot of fun to learn about the history of olives and to try my hand at becoming an olive grower.

Nature has a wonderful way of keeping you informed on the change of seasons. We know autumn is here when our geraniums, roses, and hydrangeas are no longer flowering, and the red, blue, purple, and pink flowers start fading. Then the vines in the vineyards begin showing their orange and yellow fall colors. The days begin growing noticeably shorter as the sun heads farther south to begin a new spring and summer for that part of the world. The days become brisk and sunny, with some of the most spectacular sunsets we have seen anywhere. The afterglow creates rose-tinted skies, which make everything look like an impressionist painting. It's a painter's paradise.

The seasonal workers start to arrive at the vineyards in mid-September to begin harvesting the grapes. They'll first select only those bunches that are ripe and leave the others to ripen for another week or so depending on the weather. The grapes are all harvested by mid-October.

This is when the olives on our trees start getting fatter by the day. It is always a surprise to me because up to the last few weeks before the harvest, they usually look pretty scrawny, but suddenly, like a mad dash to the finish line, they fatten up, and we invariably end up having a plentiful harvest by November. Even though we only bottle the extra virgin olive oil, or first cold pressing, we always end up with more than we could ever possibly consume. Most of it is given away to our friends and family.

In September 2002, Mica and I went to Portofino. Wow! It was fantastic! We fell in love with it. It's on the Mediterranean coast, just below Genoa. High rocky hills covered with a painter's palette of various shades and textures of evergreen trees descend to protect three sides of the tiny port. Every now and then, there's a piece of the hill carved out for some of the most exquisite homes and gardens we've seen anywhere. We stayed in one such place called the Hotel Splendido, which, if anything, was an understatement.

At the time, Prime Minister Berlusconi had a house there that he rented from a *contessa* who refused to sell it to him and understandably so; it has to be one of the most beautiful residences in the world. It sits atop an evergreen-covered promontory that is at least one hundred feet above the water. It's right along the main road that goes to the center of Portofino, but it is so high and naturally protected by solid rock that it affords all the privacy and security anyone could want.

Portofino itself is very small. The port holds no more than a few dozen boats, from forty-footers on up to over one-hundred-feet mega-yachts. There are a lot of small one- and two-man fishing boats painted different colors that are moored all over the harbor, which is surrounded by three- and four-story walk-up narrow houses also painted in a variety of colors, all of which gives you the impression that you're surrounded by a rainbow. There are interesting shops on the ground floors and a number of restaurants and bars scattered about with outdoor seating. No cars are permitted by the port, which makes it all the more pristine. And at that time of year, there were practically no tourists. It was truly heavenly.

We met a friend of Mica's from Genoa for dinner. We ate the most delicious *gamberoni* (giant shrimp but really more like baby lobsters) I've ever had. The shells were cracked and cooked in a garlic butter sauce so that the meat inside was marinated through and through. What a taste! When we sat down, the waiters—without so much as a question—tied cloth bibs around our necks. Everyone in the restaurant had one, and after eating a giant dish of *gamberoni* dripping in butter with our hands, I could understand the need for them. I wouldn't have objected to donning a pair of mechanic's overalls. It was a real eating frenzy, like that famous eating scene in the movie *Tom Jones*.

As September turned to October, Pasquale continued to transform Ceppeto into a parklike atmosphere. He started clearing the underbrush in the woods that covered much of the forty acres of land. It was a monumental task; brush had been growing there for over fifty years and was so thick that you couldn't even walk through it. This was a project that would take years to complete, but Pasquale worked as if he intended to finish it next month. His only diversion from work seemed to be watching TV on a small set we had given him.

Pasquale and I were walking on the road outside our property. It's a dirt road that leads to Lupaia. On this particular day it had recently rained, so the road was muddy and filled with puddles. Suddenly, a cross-country motorbike came roaring by. The cyclist was dressed in racing gear with a helmet and outfit all ablaze with logos from different companies feigning sponsorship. His boots and bike were covered with mud.

As he sped by in a deafening roar, Pasquale looked at the driver—a man perhaps in his thirties—as if he were studying some strange alien from another planet. After the bike passed, Pasquale said to me, "Why he do that? Why he driving in this mud?"

A good question, and though I told Pasquale I agreed with the absurdity of it all, I also realized that Pasquale had no concept of recreation or hobbies, just work.

He also couldn't understand why Mica painted. He asked, "Why La Signora paint much?" as if she were painting the walls inside her studio instead of creating works on canvasses. His completely ingenuous manner made me realize that he didn't comprehend the idea of art for art's sake and the fun and enjoyment of it.

I suspect this is true of many first-generation workers struggling to make their way up the economic ladder. Art and pastimes are things that, hopefully, will be something Pasquale's children have the luxury of appreciating and enjoying. But having said this, I will say that Pasquale does have a good eye, and when he works, he does so neatly and with a vision. The gardens are trimmed and manicured, and he has turned the soil around all the trees on our lawn and in the olive grove in a perfect circle. That requires a certain aesthetic that he seems to have come by naturally. In his own instinctive way, this man, with no concept of art for the sake of art itself, is really something of an artist himself.

Besides taking care of the property that was already cultivated, he was still clearing overgrown brush and cutting down vines, some as thick as a tree trunk, that were choking practically every tree, as well as reclaiming the miles of dry stone walls that had collapsed.

I enjoyed watching Raffaello work at restoring the stone walls. Watching him work was like watching a sculptor. He would select just the right size stone and then use a special hammer to chisel away at it so it was shaped just right to fit snugly into the wall and hold the other rocks around it in place. While he did this, Pasquale was always at his side, lifting and moving the heavy rocks that had fallen out of the walls. It took over two years to redo all the stone walls, but after a year, Pasquale was almost as good at it as Raffaello, and certainly to this day he has been able to maintain them beautifully.

Maintaining the walls is a constant chore because there are a lot of *cinghiali* (wild boars) that roam our property. With their powerful snouts they dig up the soil and are able to push down the large heavy rocks of the walls as they dig for roots, the staple of their diet. *Cinghiali* are hunted during the winter months after all the harvests are finished, and hunting them is strongly upheld by the hunters, even though the hunters are occasionally challenged by animal rights groups. The hunters have an unbridled right, by law, to hunt on private property as long as they stay a few hundred yards away from dwellings. *Cinghiali* can do major damage to crops, lawns, and vegetation, so it is considered a good thing to have their number reduced every year.

This was a difficult position for us to adopt after seeing them travel in tight-knit family groups, with the father in the lead, the newborns—usually at least four—in the middle, followed by the mother. They look menacing, but as long as they don't feel threatened, they are peaceful, although I never would want to get one angry. The larger ones weigh in at over three hundred pounds. I have come face-to-face with them on a few occasions, and when they turned to look at me, I felt a cold chill run down my spine. I chased one off our front lawn once after having grabbed a camera to take a picture of it. It ran into the woods next to the lawn, and I could hear it stomping around and making their distinctive sound, a mix between an oink and a howl. It can be loud enough to be heard echoing across the valley. Just as I got to the edge of the wood line, this three-hundred-pound hulk with its tusks looking better suited for an elephant jumped out of the woods right at me. I immediately clicked the camera, and thank heavens the flash went off and spooked it. (I think it was a male, but I wasn't sure.) The picture just shows a huge, dark, furry mound hightailing it into the woods.

CHAPTER 20

TRANSITIONS

As the first year of having Pasquale and Raffaello working at Ceppeto came to a close, I looked back in admiration at Pasquale's displays of diplomacy, his humor, and his desire to learn. I had, from his earliest days with Renato, always admired his work ethic. However, I'd wondered, when I'd brought him on full-time, if that was just a tactic on his part to impress me to get me to hire him and if his diligence would continue after he'd been engaged to work at Ceppeto. But we soon found that dedication to his work was as much a part of him as any of his other traits.

And to all his qualities, I came to add loyalty.

Once the Italians instituted an amnesty program, which allowed us to sponsor Pasquale, we did the same for Edita, our Peruvian housekeeper, who was also an illegal alien.

As sponsors, we had to go to the considerable expense of hiring a lawyer to file all the necessary documents, which, in typical Italian bureaucratic fashion, were voluminous. We needed to provide Pasquale's and Edita's passports, prior residences, proof of where they lived in their native country, driver's licenses if any, date they entered Italy illegally, and where they were living. Because Mica was an Italian citizen, she became their sponsor, and she too had to provide her passport and documents proving ownership of our house at Ceppeto. We were required to provide a place for them to live and ensure they were properly fed and paid, according to a rate schedule established by the unions for the level of work they did. We decided the prescribed wages were too low, and so we paid each of them substantially more.

During this time, we had Pasquale move into our guesthouse with its own kitchenette and private bath. In addition to the wages we paid we had to pay federal taxes, workers' compensation, and medical insurance, plus an additional percentage of their salary to the unions.

Then, government officials conducted interviews and made background checks. Anyone with any kind of criminal background was deported. In addition, we had a surprise visit from the town police to inspect the living quarters for Pasquale and Edita. When Pasquale saw the police car entering the property, he quickly ran into the woods below the main house in absolute terror. As an illegal immigrant, his biggest fear was being stopped by the police and deported. He had no idea what other reason the police could have for coming to Ceppeto.

It was of concern for us as well. I thought, *Have Pasquale or Edita done something wrong to make the authorities want to check either of them?* The policeman's name was Officer Bene, which in Italian means "well" or "good." We only hoped it would be the case for Pasquale and Edita. He was completely decked out in what looked to me like a dress, blue-black, perfectly fitted uniform with epaulets bordered in gold and matching braids hanging down from his left shoulder. His well-tailored coat had a shiny black patent leather belt around the waist. The one thing I noticed about the police and the Carabinieri was that they dressed impeccably well. It was as if they were walking advertisements for Italian men's fashion. Giorgio Armani couldn't have dressed them in better-looking outfits. They didn't look as if they were ready for action but rather for a parade or some ceremonial function. By comparison the police we have in New York dress as if they are ready for action, whether in the form of a bank robber, speedster, or crowd control.

Our fashionable guest, Officer Bene, was businesslike and told us, "I am here as part of the process of checking on the two illegal immigrants that you are sponsoring for amnesty and work permits.

May I see the documents that you have filed so far and where the applicants you are sponsoring will be staying?"

Mica, who is always meticulously well organized, quickly got the folders she had for Pasquale and Edita. She showed him all the documents that we had filed under the new amnesty rules, which were all in order. Then we showed him the guesthouse where Pasquale slept and cooked for himself as well as the room with private bath inside our home that Edita used. Throughout the entire process, he gave no hint as to what he was thinking or whether everything was in order.

Mica and I were nervous because we weren't sure if there would be problems. We already knew that a number of applicants had been deported because their records revealed they had prior convictions, even though they were for minor offenses. We really didn't know if either Pasquale or Edita had any issues that could cause them to be deported. The fact that Pasquale was now hiding out somewhere in the woods didn't bode well, and we both began to wonder whether he had been concealing some prior incident. Mica and I exchanged glances without saying a word, but each of us knew the other was worried and was thinking the worst. Finally, after what seemed like an interminable period of time during which Mica and I were trying to hold our breath, Officer Bene said, "I believe I have all that I need at this time. Thank you both for your cooperation. The authorities will be in touch with you once all the information they have has been reviewed."

Mica asked, "Any idea when that will be?"

"No," he said, "I just know the number of applicants has been overwhelming for the authorities. My job is just to report my findings, and than my part is finished. *Arrivedirci.*"

Bene adjusted his shiny black belt with a look of satisfaction as if he thought he had just done a good job and smartly marched off to his car with a stride that looked as if he were marching in a parade. When we saw him drive away, we finally breathed a sigh of relief.

Edita was in the next room of the house, working while all this was going on, but we had no idea where Pasquale was, so I immediately went to find him. I looked everywhere, but there was no trace of him.

I began to think he had run off somewhere into the huge forest that surrounded our property and was hiding the same way he had when he'd been trying to cross the Albanian border into Greece.

I could not find him anywhere, even after calling him until I got hoarse. After almost two hours, I finally gave up. It was now starting to get dark. Mica and I both worried that—thinking he was about to be deported—he would do something stupid and get in trouble.

The sun was just about to set when, out of nowhere, Pasquale appeared at our door. His face was crestfallen; he was obviously thinking that all was finished for him. Why else would the police come looking for him? We explained to him what had happened and that part of the whole process of becoming a legal, documented immigrant were these background checks. There would be more in the days to come, and we told him not to worry, that we were confident all would be okay. He was so relieved and kissed both our hands and thanked us over and over again. He returned to his guest room, and I am sure he slept well that night.

The process of getting the legal documentation was a long, drawn-out affair. In that first week alone after the amnesty legislation was passed, 750,000 illegal aliens applied for work permits, creating havoc with the ill-prepared Immigration Department. Finally, after months of waiting, Pasquale and Edita received their permits for staying, after which either could have left Ceppeto immediately.

Pasquale stayed.

Edita didn't.

She surprised us by announcing that she was pregnant, and then she took a maternity leave. She had hidden this fact and thought that once she had obtained her permit, we would have to pay for her maternity leave, but we were told that because she had only worked for us a few months, we didn't have to pay. Three months after she had the baby, she returned to work, which she had a right to do, but she obviously didn't want to work and was so bad on the job that we had no choice but to fire her—which is exactly what she wanted to happen.

She immediately went to the union, and we were sued for payment of all her back wages while she'd been on maternity leave, as well as severance pay and a Christmas bonus. We ended up paying rather than be dragged through the notoriously slow judicial system in Italy where the average case takes ten years to resolve.

The unions are primarily far left, including the Communist Party, and are in favor of immigration without restrictions since the law requires workers join the union. Once immigrants join, they can be counted on to vote for the far-left parties, which are strong in Italy. The far-left parties and unions are strong supporters of the entire social welfare system in Italy that is today bankrupting the country. It is just one of the political dilemmas the country is facing. With over twenty political parties, most of them left of center, getting a majority in Parliament and a sustainable government in power has been next to impossible. Since WWII, there have been over fifty different leaders in Italy, each one falling after being unable to stitch together a lasting ruling coalition.

I can tell you how one Italian, Mica, felt about Edita. Mica was beside herself over how this *vacca* (cow) could be such an ingrate: "How could I possibly have been so stupid to think that this *vacca* was anything else but a phony trying to milk the system?"

Trying to calm her down and add a little levity to the situation, I said, "Mica, you just said Edita was a *vacca*—a cow—and now you say she was trying to *milk* the system. Cows don't do the milking; people are the ones who milk the cows."

"Don't try to be cute," Mica snapped back at me. "I am an Italian citizen. I was born here, and I get infuriated to see how immigrants like Edita worm their way into the country, pretending to want to work, but really all they want to do is sponge off our generous social system that showers them with benefits, especially when they have a baby. She is a *cretina* [stupid idiot]." That is only a few of about a hundred choice words Mica had for the *vacca*, all of which I heard several times a day for about a week. Things eventually calmed down as we accepted the fact "we wuz robbed."

I assured Mica, "This wasn't the first nor will it be the last time, whether here in Italy or back home in the States. It comes with the territory where there will always be people wanting to take advantage of you and the system. Sorry, my love, we just have to live with it."

The fact was that Mica was justified, as an Italian citizen, to be upset. There is an underground information system of sorts that teaches illegal immigrants like Edita how to milk the Italian social system. Italy has not adjusted appropriately and, instead, is confronted with an ever-growing number of illegal immigrants coming here not only to find work but also to take advantage of the system. When an immigrant becomes documented and has children who are minors that cannot work, the government pays them a monthly stipend. If they lose their job, housing allowance and stipends are given to them. I have no issue with there being a social safety net, but these benefits are attracting hundreds of thousands of illegal immigrants a year to Italy and putting a devastating burden on the social resources that Italian citizens pay for most of their working lives. The system encourages larger families, and so with the shrinking birthrate of Italian citizens and high birthrate of immigrant families, the Italian population will soon be a minority in its own country. Adding to the difficulties is that a large percentage of the immigrants refuse to assimilate and accept the Italian culture, and a large majority want the Italian cultural system to change in order to accommodate their beliefs (as I previously mentioned in chapter 15).

This destroys the positive sentiment that Italians have for immigrants, to the detriment of the many, like Pasquale, who come here to improve their lives by hard work. But even in the town near Ceppeto where Pasquale eventually began living after bringing his family to Italy, there is an office in his community (where mostly Albanians settled) whose sole purpose is to help immigrants obtain all the social benefits possible.

I found out that Pasquale had arranged to have the government pay him $250 a month because after his family arrived, he had two children under the age of eighteen living with him but not working. His wife didn't speak Italian and couldn't work either, so somehow they qualified to get the monthly payment.

I found out about this because we suddenly started being billed by the state for the monthly stipend. I asked Pasquale about it, and he told me, "*Capo, va bene paga lo Stato.*" ("It is okay; the government pays.")

It was one of the few times I ever reprimanded Pasquale. I asked him, "Where do you think the government gets the money to pay you?" He didn't know, and I showed him our monthly bill for his salary and other expenses we paid for him. He was shocked to see we paid an additional 60 percent on top of what he received and now even more because of the $250 we were being billed for.

I told him, "Pasquale, I am sorry, but I am already paying you a salary far in excess of what the union calls for, and I have to insist that either you live on that or I will cut your salary by the $250 a month I am being forced to pay the government."

He immediately understood and said, "*Capo*, me sorry, you right; me know never you pay for that. Pasquale give up that money right away." To Pasquale's credit, once he understood what the issue was, he was eager to change things for the better. I also had to remind myself that Pasquale was raised in a suffocating Communist regime with few incentives to be self-sufficient, and as meager and often fruitless as it was, the first place its citizens turned to in need was the government. When Pasquale's family arrived in Italy and found the government so accommodating, out of habit they saw nothing wrong with accepting all they could get.

To show him more of the benefits of capitalism, we gave him a bonus every year that rewarded him for his hard work and made him realize more than ever that that was the way to increase your income, rather than looking for a freebie from *Lo Stato*. It was perhaps his first lesson in capitalism.

The transition for many immigrants to Italian life wasn't easy, nor was it easy for Italians to suddenly have to deal with millions of immigrants arriving and spreading out into almost every area of the country. There were inevitable clashes.

Some of the illegal Muslim immigrants had marched, demanding more rights for such things as trash removal in their ghetto-like communities that they themselves had refused to keep clean and orderly. The Muslims and supportive leftist parties sided with them on that issue and others that our friend Mario Massini told us about, such as the church bells ringing during their prayers and crucifixes being displayed in the schools. Thus in some communities, church bells stopped ringing as often, and crucifixes were removed from the schools, much to the chagrin of many Italians.

Pasquale is one bright ray of hope here. He's a Muslim from Albania working for a Jew from the United States and has an exemplary value system from which others would be well served to learn. He treats Raffaello with the utmost respect and complete deference, ensuring that Raffaello maintain his position as the custodian when, in fact, Pasquale has all but taken over those duties here at Ceppeto. With Pasquale, there is no ego; he just wants to get the job done, and there's nothing he takes on that isn't completed to perfection. He takes great pride in his work and takes care of Ceppeto as if he is guarding it with his life, which is no exaggeration.

Someone in Lupaia once asked if he was afraid of confronting an intruder, and he answered, "Me grow up on my own from age of seven years. Pasquale learned good how to take care of myself. No man scares me as long as he has two arms and two legs. If man has four arms, Pasquale probably be scared."

Furthermore, if anyone sets foot on the property, he's on them in a flash and, in a firm but polite manner, sees they get the clear message: "It would be a good idea for you to turn around and leave here at once." He has often said to me, "Anyone try to trespass here and hurt Ceppeto have to kill me first," and he means it.

When Pasquale came to work and live here, Raffaello instinctively looked down on him as an Albanian Muslim coming in to take over his job. Faced with that kind of prejudiced attitude, Pasquale could have reacted in any number of different ways, including being equally hostile to Raffaello. Instead, Pasquale slowly won over Raffaello— as he did with almost every other Italian. Today, everyone knows Pasquale because he is not afraid of making his presence known and does it in a way that makes people both laugh and respect him. There is no one that we know of who doesn't like and admire Pasquale, but most importantly for Pasquale, they also show him respect.

As Pasquale took over most of the work at Ceppeto, we, as planned, began phasing out Raffaello and put him in charge of our newly planted vineyard. Raffaello had been the manager of one of the largest vineyards in Chianti before he retired and became the custodian for Ceppeto, so we were comfortable having him take over that job. It made him feel good that he still had something to do that was not work intensive. He began coming a few hours a couple of days a week.

Raffaello continued to tend to the vineyard for the first few years, but we never got a harvest that we could process into drinkable wine. Raffaello and Pasquale working together on the vineyard caused the first serious verbal argument between them.

Apparently, Pasquale was working on Sundays, his day off, for who he said was a "gnome." After much animated conversation, I figured out, in Pasquale's concocted faux Italian lexicon that "gnome" meant an expert in cultivating grapes and making wine.

According to the "gnome," the leaves at the base of each new grapevine should be trimmed. When Pasquale suggested this to Raffaello, Raffaello went ballistic. I imagine he thought his work was being criticized. All I heard was Raffaello yelling, "I've been growing grapes all my life! Don't *you* tell me how to do it!"

I couldn't recall hearing Raffaello yell before, so, concerned, I ran toward the commotion. As soon as I arrived, I saw that Raffaello had apparently thrown down a rake he had been using and was glaring at Pasquale just a few feet in front of him. I was hoping the situation wouldn't come to blows and realized that there was little chance of that when Pasquale told Raffaello, "*Scusi*, Babbo, Pasquale hope you still marry my mother, so I become your son."

That was the last word. Raffaello picked up the rake and marched off right past me in one direction, while Pasquale shrugged his shoulders and went off in another direction to do his work, whistling as happily as could be. The tiff didn't last long, thanks to Pasquale's indefatigable sense of humor, and they were soon working together amicably as if nothing had happened.

That always seemed to be the way at Ceppeto.

CHAPTER 21

LA VITA A CEPPETO

In April of 2003, we returned to Ceppeto and had an uneventful flight over from New York except for our *bidone* (trash can). We were never happy with the trash cans available in Italy for our kitchen. We have no space under our counters for a trash can, and the ones that are left out don't have a lot of capacity and are unsightly. We found just the one we wanted on sale in New York and bought it to bring with us. Before we left for Italy, I bought special boxes, tape, and packing supplies to wrap it and make sure it wouldn't get damaged on the trip over. The final package was so long that with all our other bags (a total of six checked bags plus the trash can) we had to order an SUV to take us to the airport.

When we arrived at the check-in counter, they refused to take our trash can because there was a ban on shipping anything in cardboard boxes. We had time before boarding, so they suggested we go to an airport luggage shop and buy a duffel bag for it. Off we went, pushing two carts filled with our luggage as we looked for a big enough bag, finding one for the bargain price of ninety-five dollars (it would have cost a third of that in New York City). We transferred the trash can to the duffel bag, filled in the name tag on it, zipped it up, and raced back to the check-in counter, only to be told now we had to pay extra for the seventh bag (the limit was six). Putting aside the fact that I would have appreciated being told this at the outset, we again had to race off, pushing our two carts of luggage to a cashier where there was a line waiting to pay for overweight and extra luggage. Although we always arrive at the airport close to two hours before flight time, we were beginning to feel stressed, as all this was taking a lot of time and we still needed to check in and get through security. Arriving at the cashier, we had to fork over a ninety-dollar fee.

We finally were able to check in and boarded shortly after. Upon our arrival at the Milan airport in Italy, we met the car service, which informed us they had to bring two cars because they didn't have a car big enough to carry seven bags, including our body-sized trash can stuffed in a duffel bag.

For those bean counters in the audience, we paid $50 for the trash can, $15 for packing supplies, an extra $40 for the SUV, $95 for the duffel bag, $90 to the airline for the extra bag, and $50 in Milan for the extra car, for a total of $340.

We made it to Mica's hometown of Biella, where I picked up my car, which I'd left there over the winter, and began transferring— or I should say cramming—all the luggage into it. Although the car was a station wagon, I still had to work at getting everything to fit inside. To make a little more room, I took the stuffing out of the trash can bag only to notice for the first time that this beautiful, perfectly designed trash can had been ... *Made in Italy.*

When we arrived at Ceppeto, Fumo (our fat cat) hadn't missed a beat. We got the usual fabulous welcome, with him following us wherever we went, just like a dog. He had gotten into a couple of fights over the winter with some wild cats and had a couple of ugly scars, but he was on the mend. Fumo was the ultimate pacifist, hating to fight, and was so trusting and friendly he kept getting himself into trouble. While we were on a walk, he stopped and watched as a *topolino* (mouse) ran around his paws. He then chased after it, only to play with it. After a few moments, he just continued on his walk, totally uninterested in the little creature. So much for the ultimate mousetrap.

We had summerlike weather all that week. The birds had migrated back to Ceppeto and began their daily concert around five fifteen in the morning, just before sunrise.

It always started with the sopranos singing, probably the *rondini* (swallows) ever so softly: just loud enough for me to come out of my deep sleep and open one eye. Then, as I lay there gathering my thoughts, I began to hear the rhythmic coo-cooing of the cuckoo bird, and then a full chorus of *uccelli* (birds), sounding like tenors and mezzo-sopranos, joined in as the dawn gave way to the full daylight, with the staccato of the rooster announcing that it was time for everyone to awaken. If there was a breeze, as was usually the case, the rustling leaves sounded like tambourines, completing the symphony. As the sun filled the room with light, the foxes began yapping, and then the dogs in the valley started barking, as if in applause for a wonderful performance.

Yes, Ceppeto was paradise.

By 2003, when the Iraq War had been ongoing, Italy as a whole seemed to be evenly divided on the issue. The Communists and left-of-center parties were against the war, with those in favor forming a slight majority. The *pacifisti* (pacifists) were more vocal and had demonstrations every chance they got, which was a lot, because most were able to get a lot of time off from work while the government still paid them all sorts of benefits. Most were young and had a poor recollection of history, particularly the events leading up to WWII and afterward, when America poured money through the Marshall Plan into Europe to rebuild it, including Italy. Italy went from being a third world country with only two million cars when I first visited it as a GI in 1963 to the seventh largest economy in the world, with over forty million cars by 2003.

We were struck by the number of peace flags outside many homes, apartments, and offices, colored in a rainbow design with the word *Pace* (Peace) in white letters across it. Some had the old dove's foot for peace from the Vietnam War era. Whether the country was evenly divided was hard to say, but there were certainly a lot of people who were very much against the war, and the anger toward America had become palpable. For example, when we spoke to our neighbors, it didn't take long before they told us they felt America was wrong to go into Iraq. Going after Bin Laden and al-Qaeda was one thing, but invading Iraq was another and uncalled for. To emphasize their point they permanently hung a peace flag in front of their house so we couldn't miss it whenever we came and went from Ceppeto. Since we were the only ones who ever went by their house, there was no question it was a message for us alone.

For the first time, we began hearing from our Italian acquaintances that America was acting too aggressively and arrogantly and creating problems in the world rather than fixing them. Berlusconi was a supporter of the war and had sent Italian troops to fight there, but in the area where we lived, that was unpopular. In casual conversations people would complain about President Bush and then ask us, "Did you vote for Bush? He doesn't seem like a good president to us." We felt that was a personal question, and it made Mica and me feel uncomfortable. We simply answered, "We never discuss who we vote for," and that always abruptly ended the conversation. Having witnessed an outpouring of love for America less than two years ago, after the 9/11 tragedy, this demonstration of anger against the United States was a difficult adjustment for us to make.

The older people with memories of World War II, however, were all in favor of the Iraq War. They still believed in America, but our concern was that that trust seemed to be evaporating quickly.

When Raffaello was ready to retire, we turned the reins of the vineyard and the rest of the property over to Pasquale. We called on Raffaello for special projects for which Pasquale needed some help, but, for the most part, it was now Pasquale's show.

To help me and Pasquale learn the proper way to grow grapes for wine, we hired a wine consultant, Bernardo Bianchi, who was the manager of a large vineyard nearby. He began teaching Pasquale how to tend to the vines, harvest, and make the wine. Pasquale was a rapt student eager to learn from a respected expert in the area. It wasn't long before Pasquale mastered the task, and since then he has taken care of the vineyard by himself, doing a great job.

Even though Raffaello was no longer working full-time with us, we still remained close to him and his entire family. They were happy to see him, for the most part, finally retire at the age of eighty-two, which is a remarkable feat when you consider that his occupations always involved physical work.

With Pasquale in charge, we continued to have our morning meetings, which not only involved work schedules but also discussions about other topics. Pasquale had a curiosity about the world and loved to watch the news and special programs about world events. He admitted he could hardly read, so TV played a big part in how he got information.

One morning, he said, "*Capo*, Pasquale saw on TV last night Saddam Hussein is being put on trial. Me don't understand; why are the Americans putting Saddam Hussein on trial?"

I replied, "First of all, the Americans captured him, but they are not trying him. The Iraqis are trying him to help satisfy the anger the families of his victims feel."

Pasquale shook his head back and forth. "No, no, that no going to ease pain. Those people dead; it is *finito* [finished]. If they good, they in heaven with God. If they no good, who cares. Saddam Hussein guilty of crime against his people. He a mean person, like Hitler. No need for trial. *Capo*, Pasquale tell you, one thing good about Communists in Albania is they kill criminals, no trial when everyone know they are guilty. Now that Americans find Hussein, just hang him. No need for trial."

In April, our computer, e-mail, fax, and telephone all shut down. To live without these connections to the outside world was, at first, charming, but it quickly wore thin and became a major pain in the neck. Living here in a somewhat isolated environment, especially compared to New York City, we realized more than ever how dependent we'd become on these things and how much we took for granted that they were always going to work.

Having a problem like this gives you insight into what it's like living here day to day. First, when something goes wrong, you have to be prepared to do without, and second, you need patience. When you start calling the appropriate people—at least, those you think are appropriate—you need *more* patience because, generally, after placing a call, you need to wait for them to call you back as no one is ever in. Presumably, they are out fixing other people's problems, taking a two- to three-hour lunch, or on some holiday (there's practically one every week). When they do call back, you then need to convince them to come right away—which, at best, means a few days. If they aren't convinced it is their problem or that it is urgent, you could be wait-listed for weeks.

In our case, I started with the phone company and got this response: "I understand the problem, and it is not a telephone company problem. Thank you for calling Telecom; I hope I have answered your question."

"No, you have not. I don't think you understand at all ... Hello, hello, are you still there?" Silence. They had hung up.

So I called the company that installed the phones. "Hello, my phones are not working, and you installed them. I need someone to come right away as I have no way of making important phone calls."

"If they are not working, where are you calling from now?"

"From a bottega nearby."

"When did you have the phones installed?"

"In 2000, why?"

"Sorry, Signor Hadar, your warranty has expired, and we no longer service home phones, just businesses. Thank you for calling, and have a nice day."

After that, I just heard a click ... end of conversation.

Then I called the computer company that had installed our system, thinking it might have been interconnected with the phone. "Sorry, Signor Hadar, I understand the problem. I assure you it is not our problem. You must call the telephone company."

"But I just called them, and they said ... Hello, are you still there?" They too had hung up.

We finally had an electrician come five days later, and although I am not sure what he did, the phones and computers started working again.

I'm not sure what is worse: the United States where you go mad getting voicemail messages and prompts to keep pushing numbers on your phone or here. Either way, it's like pulling teeth to get the job done. At least here, when things get frustrating, I can take a nice walk, breathe in some fresh air, and bask in the beauty that surrounds me.

Later that month, it was the flight-of-the-bumblebees time. We had almost forgotten the annual ritual when the honey-making bees, raised in the woods across the road from our front entrance by Ennis (who lives nearby in Lupaia), decided to change their queen—out with the old and in with the new. During this royal transition of queen bees, all the thousands of bees left their hives at the same moment and flew over Ceppeto in one big, black, menacing cloud. Seeing and hearing this monster cloud moving at tornado-like speed and sounding like a low flying B-(no pun intended)52 got us running for cover faster than we ever thought we could move. Into the house we dashed, slamming doors behind us and racing through the house, shutting windows and closing the chimney flues.

We were alerted by Pasquale, who had innocently arrived at the front gate to start work and then realized he was being followed by a swarm of bees. He called us from the call box at the gate after being stung a couple of times and then took off toward the lower pasture. Fortunately, the bees didn't follow, and he wasn't hurt.

We, in turn, quickly called Ennis to commandeer his bees. He arrived a few minutes later, decked out in his bee armor-alls with a thingamajig that emitted smoke, and was able to lead his wayward regime-changing mob back to their homeland where, through a miracle of nature, a new queen was being inaugurated. All quickly returned to normal, and we were able to come back outside, assured by Ennis we had nothing to worry about … until this time next year.

CHAPTER 22

AGRICOLA DI CHIANTI

At Ceppeto, Mica and I felt as if we had full-time jobs working for the place. It wasn't that we were doing a whole bunch of things; it just took longer to do them.

For example, we needed cash every other week to pay out-of-pocket expenses, such as gas, groceries, materials, and items for the house. Credit cards were not welcomed, partly because of the fees charged by the credit card companies. That was something quite easily resolved in the States by going to the nearest ATM or bank.

But in nearby Radda, we had to call the bank in advance and tell them how much we wanted to withdraw to make sure they had enough cash; if they didn't, they had to order it. Either way, it always took a second call for them to tell us if they did have enough cash on hand or if we had to come another day. If they had the cash, off we went to the bank.

Now understand, the bank here is very small, but it is one of only two tiny banks in this entire area. The one we don't use is only for Italian residents, so we are relegated to the other by default.

Just entering our bank is a production. Because of the many bank robberies over the years, to enter and leave the bank, you need to push a button to open a sliding round door, which allows one person to enter a round chamber about the size of a small revolving door. Only when you are inside the chamber and the door behind you is closed will the door into the bank open. To exit, the same procedure must be followed, which again allows only one person at a time to enter and leave. I assume the system works, as it seems that it would be difficult for a robber to get in and out without getting trapped inside the chamber by a teller who can stop the door from opening with the simple push of a hidden button.

Inside the bank, there is one teller, a manager (of what, I am not sure), and a woman who scurries around, laden with papers and entering numbers in a huge ledger. Invariably, there are customers waiting, and by the time it's your turn, it is not unusual to have waited a half hour or more (our record so far is fifty-eight minutes). The transactions—no matter how simple—seem to take endless time, extended by the chat each customer has with the teller. The end result? Getting cash can easily be a two-hour round-trip chore.

Major grocery shopping, which we do an average of once a week, takes four to five hours; it's an hour drive just to get to the closest big supermarket. To pick up a few items in the local tiny grocery store is an hour round-trip to Radda. Most weekends there are open markets that are fun to go to for buying fresh fruits and vegetables; those usually take half a day.

If we need to see a doctor, that's a whole other matter. *Dottore* Dell'Anna is the doctor in this area, and he spends one day a week in each little village: Monday in Gaiole, Tuesday in Lecchi, Wednesday in Siccele, Thursday in Radda, and Friday in San Sano. There are no appointments; you just go there and wait your turn.

We have had occasion to see *Dottore* Dell'Anna a few times, and he is an excellent physician. He's a trained surgeon who probably sees and treats more stuff as a country doctor than he ever would in a big city filled with specialists. If you need more than what he can provide, he'll direct you to the right specialist, usually at the hospital in Siena or Florence. He uses a laptop computer to keep track of all his patients and does a top-notch job. The few times we have seen him, he has opened his file and had everything about us recorded there.

His fees are reasonable. For Italian citizens and people on pensions, the government pays. For nonresidents, the fee is between twenty-five and fifty dollars. Once, when my back went out, he came to the house and gave me an injection and then left a supply for Mica to give me. For that, he charged fifty dollars.

The last time I went to see him was to get a prescription. That day, his office hours were in Lecchi, which is tucked away on a high hill between here and Siena. It's about the size of Lupaia but much more remote. It has all the same charm and then some, with a long winding road providing you with magnificent views of the surrounding countryside as you climb up to the town. The town center has a tiny grocery store, a restaurant, and a post office, which is where the doctor sees his patients.

Because there are no appointments, inevitably there are people already waiting, no matter how early you arrive. In this case, we got there a half hour before the doctor was to arrive, and there were already a dozen people sitting outside the office.

We settled in for the long wait, chatting with a few of the people there, most of whom were elderly. When the doctor pulled up in his chartreuse-colored Volkswagen Beetle, everyone applauded.

Dottore Dell'Anna is a slightly built man, about 5'7", in his early fifties, with brownish hair, fair skin, and light-colored eyes. He seems younger than he is. He doesn't look Italian, although he is from the south, as are many of the professional people in the area.

The post office was closed, so the doctor unlocked the door to the two-room building. One room served as the waiting room with a couple of benches, and the other—where the post office operated for just a few hours a day (there's apparently not much mail in Lecchi)— acted as his office. When we went into the waiting room, we realized that only three people were there to see the doctor; the rest were there simply because they had nothing else to do. It's sort of a social get-together whenever the doctor comes to town.

After about fifty minutes it was our turn. We entered the small office, where the doctor sat at a desk with his laptop computer. As always, he said warmly with a big smile, "*Buon giorno*, sit down please," and gestured with his hand to the only chair in the room besides the one he was sitting on. Mica sat down, and I remained standing.

There was a small safe in the corner, probably for whatever stamps or money the post office needed to store safely, although I seriously doubted there was any threat of theft in little Lecchi. Against the wall opposite the doctor's desk and behind the single chair was a table, probably used for sorting mail but now apparently to be used as an examining table. It was about five feet long, obviously meant for his short patients and not for an over six-footer like me, especially because it looked ready to collapse. I noticed a couple of paperback books propping up two of the legs to keep the table level. Light came from a bulb hanging from the ceiling.

I said, "This is the first time we have seen your office in Lecchi. Very elegant."

Dottore Dell'Anna, who has a good sense of humor, laughed and said, "Well, at least the surrounding countryside is beautiful."

Mica said, "Yes, it is. We really enjoyed the ride here, and we see you have a lot of fans that just want to see you to say hello."

Laughing, he said, "I am not so sure they want to see me as much as my green Volkswagen Beetle. It is a novelty for them."

We think *Dottore* Dell'Anna enjoys seeing us, as it gives him a chance to laugh. He wrote the prescription we needed, and we chatted for about ten minutes. That was it.

In any event, for a visit to the doctor we have to figure waiting time will be an hour, so depending on where he is on the days we need to see him, it can take up to three to four hours round-trip. It's perhaps not that different from some New York doctors, who are notoriously overbooked and behind schedule, but at least here we get a chance to have a pleasant visit with the doctor and see some nice scenery going and coming.

There are other reasons why it takes so much time to get things done here. Each town has one day a week, besides Sunday, when they are closed. The problem is that every town is different. On Wednesdays, for example, the stores are closed in Radda; in Castelina, it's Tuesdays, and in Panzano, Mondays. Complicating the situation further is that the hours stores are open are all different. Most close around twelve thirty in the afternoon and reopen anywhere between two and four thirty in the afternoon. You can go crazy trying to keep track of who is open where and when.

Last week, I made two appointments in Siena: one to bring our cat in to get treated for an ear infection and the other at the car agency to get a headlight fixed. I was told that the car agency opened after lunch and that I could wait for the headlight to get fixed as it wouldn't take a long time. I got there at two thirty, only to find out that they were closed until three. By the time I got the car fixed, it was four thirty. I then went to the vet with our cat and didn't arrive back home until seven.

On a recent trip to Greve to buy pet food, I found the store closed when I arrived and had to return the next day. Each way was about a forty-minute drive. When I did return, the owner, with whom I had become friendly, said, "You may want to consider buying a dog because there is a new law in Italy that allows you to deduct the cost of upkeep for dogs as they're considered useful for the home as watchdogs."

I replied, "What about cats, are they eligible?"

He laughed and said, "Sorry, cats are not eligible. I have yet to see one that would qualify as a *watchcat*."

"Well," I said, "you and those lawmakers have obviously not seen the likes of our cats, Two-Ton Fumo and Big Puffy Fiamma. I don't think there's a thief in town that could withstand an onslaught from these two critters."

He chuckled and said, "Please bring photos of them the next time you come. I want to hang them on our wall, and if you want, I'll get a sign made for you that says Beware of Guard Cats."

"That's a deal. Get the sign made, and I'll bring some pictures for you."

Three weeks later I did exactly that. He now has pictures of our cats in his shop over a Beware of Guard Cats sign. He gave me a sign as a gift and told me he is selling them like hotcakes.

Getting back to the routine, it forces us to slow down and develop that innately inhuman trait called *patience*, which here is not only a virtue but also a *requirement*. The pace is as different as can be compared to frenetic New York. We quickly learned to carry a book with us or to sit and meditate because we never know how long the wait will be. It usually takes us a few weeks after our arrival here to slow down our interior clocks, stop rolling our eyes in disbelief, and realize it is the slower pace of living that helps make this place as magical as it is.

One thing we have learned is that it's not easy being a farmer. One year in early May, the temperature dropped to freezing, and the ensuing frost did a lot of damage. As if that wasn't enough, we were hit with a hailstorm. It lasted only a few minutes, but in that short time, the ground was covered with hailstones the size of large marbles. We had a hard plastic PVC-type pool cover that was fairly strong, yet holes were punched right through it by the hail. Between the frost and the hail, we lost that year's production of grapes, olives, figs, lemons, pears, cherries, apples, apricots, and plums. Our perennial flowers and blossoming bushes, hydrangeas, oleanders, and roses have been damaged before as well. There are ample stories in this region of similar hailstorms literally wiping out entire crops in a matter of minutes, a setback that could take years from which to recover. Fortunately, this isn't our livelihood, but if it were, we would surely be in trouble.

We became a government-registered, card-carrying, and official *Agricola* (farm) *di Chianti*, entitled to all the benefits of a working farm. If it was our livelihood, we could probably apply for government subsidies. We limit ourselves to buying our farm supplies—such as seed, fertilizers, tools, and all the paraphernalia for growing, making, and bottling wine and olive oil—at the Agricola Consortium where you can buy just about anything a working farm needs, from the smallest hand tool to large tractors, all at special discounted prices for its members, usually at least 20 percent.

As members, we are also eligible to enter contests for growing the biggest tomato, zucchini, *melanzane* (eggplant), chicken, pig, cow, or whatever. And then there are the tractor-pulling contests. At any other time, it's all fun being a farmer in Chianti, but these two freak acts of nature made us realize how difficult farming can be.

Being in the farmer mode, we built a *pollaio* (henhouse) that can hold up to fifteen chickens. It is a mansion by hen standards. Our contractor, Bini, had a steel frame fabricated for it with solid walls and roof that are waterproof and protective during inclement weather. It is in a completely fenced-in area to keep the foxes and wolves out, but with a lot of space for the chickens to roam about freely. The idea, of course, is to have fresh eggs every day. We started off with six hens, and we'll decide how many to add later. I am not sure how long it'll be a thrill to collect fresh eggs every day, but I'm hoping it will last for at least a few dozen. I have a visceral feeling this venture will be like my vegetable garden in the Hamptons on Long Island in New York, where I had a summer house for many years. I planted a vegetable garden, and after I calculated all the costs involved—getting the soil ready, vegetable seeds planted, irrigation for watering, and a tall fence around it to keep the deer, rabbits, and other hungry critters out—it ended up costing me five dollars a string bean. If this venture ends up costing me five dollars per egg, I'll consider myself lucky.

CHAPTER 23

THE ALBANIAN TANK

Pasquale loves to talk, always bursting with things he wants to say. We continued to meet outside our kitchen in the shade of a grape arbor. That was where we had most of our meals during the warm summer months. He usually started with what he was planning to do that day on the grounds. "*Capo,* weather good for next week, so me begin cut grass in fields by cantina next to olive grove. Grass is this high." And he would show me on his leg how high it was. "Me need use big mower for fields. Pasquale bought yesterday enough gas. After me use Weedwacker along walls. Pasquale needs one day for that. Tomorrow, me start on trails through woods down to river. La Signora likes walk there, so me want to cut grass and fill in holes *cinghiale* [wild boar] make looking for roots to eat. They also pushed big rocks down from walls. Me don't want La Signora trip and fall, so me clean up and make smooth to walk." He continued, "It may rain on Wednesday, so me working in garage. Me bought some varnish and sandpaper. Will sand and varnish outdoors furniture. Big tractor and Jeep need lubricated and have old oil changed. A good day to do. On Thursday and Friday me mow big lawn, redo dirt around flowers and trim bushes. First hour each day, me clean pool. If no rain, me bought product for vineyard and spray vines early before sun get too hot." Then he added, "*Cinghiale* broke five fence posts and wires by vineyard, so me made fence posts from big tree branches fallen down and me use to fix."

I marveled at how it was not only what he wanted to do but how and in what sequence he planned to do it, with a timetable to boot. His planning was meticulous and took into account every eventuality as well as what he'd need to get the job done. Many of those items—like fence posts or ladders—were made from trees on the property, another thing that Raffaello taught Pasquale how to make in the time-honored historic fashion.

Pasquale continued, "*Capo*, Pasquale planted *orto* [vegetable garden] and make extra lines of okra, because me know you like. Me plant tomatoes, lettuce, zucchini, fava beans, string beans, onions, corn and watermelon."

I said, "Watermelon?"

Pasquale laughed and said, "Yes, me love and think me try to see if me can grow. You told Pasquale you too like. Me also plant in two sections so you have vegetables all summer and fall also."

Mica and I love okra, and it's popular in Albania but not prevalent in Italy, so Pasquale grew those from seeds a friend brought from Albania, and then, after the first season, saved some seeds—as he did for all the vegetables—to plant for the next season.

We were fortunate in that we had a good start. The land had many fruit and nut trees, berries of all types, and, of course, grapevines. The vine over our grape arbor produces an American concord grape that we make into marmalade every year. It's located right outside our kitchen, and we enjoy eating under the shade it provides during the summer months. Ceppeto had been a self-sufficient farm, and we are enjoying the fruits of the centuries of work it took to make it so. All we're missing from the original farm are the animals: cows, oxen, pigs, and horses. They also grew their own wheat, but we mowed those fields, so they are now grass. But the glue that has held all this together is the constant attention Pasquale pays to every little detail. The discussion that day is just a small sampling of the myriad of projects he does as routine. He works the land at Ceppeto twelve months a year from sunrise to sunset every day except Sunday and holidays. For him, it is a labor of love.

At this time, in 2003, after working out the plans for the day and generally for the next week, our discussions moved to world and local events. With those discussions, I learned, bit by bit, about Pasquale's past. I also began asking him more about his background because I was curious about how he developed his work ethic and sense of morality, which I was finding remarkable given what I already knew of his difficult past and the suffering he'd endured.

A major news event of the day was the ongoing legal procedure against Slobodan Milošević, the Yugoslavian president, who was being tried at The Hague for crimes against humanity. He had, among other charges, been accused of ethnic cleansing, in which he'd ordered the killing of Albanian Muslims in Kosovo as a way of reducing their population.

As the trial of Milošević unfolded, so did Pasquale's memories. For most of that month, he came in each morning relating bits and pieces of his bitter past under the Communist regime in Albania. Throughout his ordeal, he somehow never gave up hope. His plight reminds me of the travails of Phillip Carey in W. Somerset Maugham's *Of Human Bondage*, where, as bleak as the circumstances that Phillip found himself in were—starving, out of work, with no money, even contemplating suicide—he came through it by believing things would get better in the future.

Pasquale told me, "At time me quit Renato and left you at Ceppeto, me gone back south and thank God for money you me gave. It saved me. Pasquale no never forgot that. Me find some work that hoped come into steady job, but farms in south no hiring anyone. No go good there, and at end of year, me almost out of money. Me worry on my family in Albania more than me. Speak to wife a little times. She tell me they no go well also. Very difficult. Pasquale lived in small shed on the last farm me work. The owner let me stay in exchange me helping him do little jobs, but he no pay me money. Me unload trucks for him and carry things from here to there. No work more than couple hours every week. But me knew how to live on nothing. Me did in Greece. Me able find food in woods; me knew what good to eat. And owner of farm give me leftover food he had from time to time. The truth, *Capo*, Pasquale almost ready give up hope of things going better. That why me calling you every month. You my only hope. Always me think one day soon arrive you hire Pasquale."

Yes, Pasquale, like Phillip, was starving but somehow did not give up. He always believed that there would be a place for him someday at Ceppeto, and it was that belief that kept him going.

Pasquale has never forgotten those experiences, and to be given a steady job with pay generous enough to be able to send money home to his family in Albania accounted for his enduring loyalty.

He considers Ceppeto his responsibility; he takes every task very seriously and is determined to do each task the best way possible. It is his badge of honor to do that, and his gratification is the compliments we give him for work well done as well as the accolades from all the people in the area that have seen the amazing transformation Pasquale has single-handedly accomplished at Ceppeto.

I know this may sound like bragging, but the truth is that no one comes to Ceppeto—workers, deliverymen, contractors, visitors— without saying how it is one of the most beautifully kept farms they have ever seen. It has developed a reputation for being truly a *paradise,* thanks to Pasquale's hard work.

Our morning meetings first revealed how much Pasquale appreciated the opportunity to work as well as have a boss who did not take advantage of him and who treated him with respect.

When Mica's mother, who lives in northern Italy between Turin and Milan, came to visit us and met Pasquale for the first time, she offered him a cup of coffee one morning. He took it and told me, "*Capo,* mother of La Signora is wonderful person. She offered Pasquale coffee. No one ever me offered coffee free in life of me. It me made very happy. Pasquale, never forget." That such a little act of kindness was a monumental event in Pasquale's life is very telling. He still repeats that event today with the same emotion as if he is telling it for the first time.

He, in turn, treats Mica's mother with the utmost respect and checks in with her by phone at least once every two weeks to see how she's doing. She is now in her mideighties, and when she has the slightest ailment, he will call her every week to check in on her.

Once, Mica was taking a morning walk through the property along the miles of private paths through woods and along a babbling brook. She approached an area where she could hear Pasquale speaking on his cell phone, but she was not able to see him. As she got closer, she realized he was talking to her mother and making sure all was well with her. He is more in touch with her than any of Mica's six brothers.

As Pasquale steadily assumed more and more of the responsibility he'd formerly shared with Raffaello, he showed a unique ability to reason and to make decisions based on his own life experiences. If he didn't understand how something worked, he talked to me about it and told me what his thoughts and ideas were until he could figure it out.

About a year after Pasquale took over Raffaello's position, after he'd received a few raises, Pasquale was finally in a position to buy his first car. In his early days with us, he would walk the five miles across the valley to the next town on Sundays, his day off. He would dress as well as he could in clean clothes and march off, obviously feeling good that his plight in life was changing for the better. He recently remarked that in all the times he'd walked to and from the next town—Radda—no one had ever stopped to offer him a ride. Now he could afford to buy a used car. He was so proud to be able to drive that he began disappearing early Sunday without us trying to force him to take some time off. To this day, when Pasquale drives from Ceppeto to Radda and back, if he sees a person walking, he will always stop and offer them a ride.

He did just that in 2010 when he saw an elderly man walking along the side of the road toward Radda. Pasquale stopped and offered the man a ride. It turned out we knew the man and had been to his house for lunch a few years earlier. His name is Nicolo Grillo, and he's a retired cruise ship captain. He's a charming man, speaks many languages fluently, and lives in a beautiful villa on the side of the road not far from where Pasquale saw him. He'd been heading to Radda about a mile and half away to buy a newspaper. He had some heart problems and was not in the best of health. Pasquale realized this immediately and offered to bring him the newspaper in the mornings on his way to Ceppeto. He always stopped in Radda to buy fresh baked bread for us at the local bakery, as well as to have coffee at the Radda café, so it was no problem for him. Since that day in 2010, Pasquale has brought Nicolo Grillo a newspaper every day, leaving it at the door of his house, and he has never asked to be reimbursed.

"*Capo*, it a little *regalo* [gift] from me. The Signor is elderly man. He not well. Not good he walking along the road. Worse when weather makes bad. It dangerous. *Capo*, getting old and sick is *peccato* [shame]. We always must try help olders. For me it is *niente* [nothing]."

Shortly after Pasquale purchased his car, he received his documentation so that he could soon rent an apartment and have his wife and children come to Italy. These were monumental achievements for Pasquale, and he couldn't have felt more pleased to have attained the success that he'd only dreamed about just a few years earlier, when he didn't even have enough food to eat. His daily diet then often consisted of stale bread soaked in boiling water, some fruit and berries he found in the woods, and, if he was lucky, some vegetables, pasta, and, on a good day, some chicken.

After Pasquale received his work permit and legal documentation to stay and work in Italy, he took a week off to return home to Albania and see his family for the first time in several years. He couldn't have been happier. He returned to Albania like a hero. He had money in his pocket and a car, and he was going to be able to bring his family over in a year or so to live with him in Italy. In the meantime, he was free to go back and forth to visit. He called us from Albania one morning to tell us, "*Vi amo tutti e due.*" ("I love you guys.")

As Pasquale began experiencing some economic freedom and success, I wouldn't have been surprised if he'd slacked off and his work habits and loyalty diminished. Instead, they only grew stronger.

He loved having the authority to run Ceppeto and deal with contractors when we weren't there. He made it a point that no contractor was allowed on the property when we weren't there, unless he was with them. While with them, he paid rapt attention to what they were doing, asking them questions so he understood how they were fixing whatever they were repairing. The contractors, all native Italians, at first looked down upon Pasquale as a simple laborer. In their own way, they were prejudiced in thinking that Albanians are not good workers. Over time, Pasquale, with a firm manner and that persistent sense of humor of his, disarmed the most stoic of the contractors and won them over. When they began to see the amount and the high quality of the work he did and how he was transforming Ceppeto into a park as much as a farm, they began to respect him, as did most of the area residents as well.

But, just as importantly for Pasquale, he was letting the contractors teach him—without their realizing it—how to do the work we were paying them to do. The result is that today Pasquale can do almost any repair, except the rare extreme complicated ones that require special tools or know-how, such as electrical and some heating system problems.

Instead of this level of accomplishment going to his head, he is thankful to us for having had the confidence in him to entrust him with these responsibilities. As his reputation for being such a stellar worker grew, so did job offers from other farms and contractors in the area, all of which he refused to even discuss.

What I think those making the offers don't understand is that Ceppeto isn't just the place where Pasquale works. It's even more than a home to him. He has put in years and immeasurable sweat into this place. Anywhere you look, you see where his hand has been at work. Ceppeto is a part of him, and he is a part of Ceppeto.

Once Pasquale had a car, a few months after he returned from Albania, he asked if he could have a weekend off to go to Foggia, in the south of Italy (about a six-hour drive), to visit some friends. Despite his insistence on returning to work by Saturday, we told him to leave on Thursday and come back on Monday so that he could have the entire weekend there. His compromise was to come back on Sunday.

But that Sunday evening, Pasquale did not return, and we could not reach him by phone, as he was out of range. After staying up until eleven thirty at night waiting for him, I began to worry. I did, finally, fall asleep, but awoke at five thirty in the morning and saw that he was still not back. I began thinking the worst. But then at seven, the buzzer at our gate rang.

Pasquale had, in fact, returned Sunday night after hitting a lot of traffic and driving for almost eight hours. Not wanting to disturb us, he'd slept in his car outside the property on Sunday night until the next morning at seven when he rang the buzzer to open the gate and start work.

CHAPTER 24

CEPPETO YEAR BY YEAR

It was not always perfect living in Italy, such as in the summer of 2003, when Italy had the worst heat spell on record for the last two hundred years. It was ideal summer vacation weather, as long as you stayed put, but it was oppressively hot in the cities, as much as 105 degrees. Most of Italy was suffering a severe drought; it hadn't rained in over a month. In the north, you could walk across the River Po, which should have been at least twenty feet deep, as well as the Tevere in Rome. There was not enough water to cool the electrical generators, so there were controlled blackouts in most major cities.

As the heat wave persisted that summer, the death toll rose alarmingly. In France, estimates were as high as ten thousand. In Italy, they claimed there were 20 percent more deaths that summer than the year before. Air-conditioning is not popular in most parts of Europe and certainly is not a luxury older people on pensions can afford. In the older homes, it's difficult to retrofit air-conditioning into them, and until that summer, in those older homes the thick stone walls acted like natural insulators, so air-conditioning was not a necessity. Certainly, that summer's heat wave had all the hallmarks of the effects of global warming. Scientists were predicting that, unless this pattern was altered in the next fifty years, most of Europe would be a desert.

Thankfully for us at Ceppeto, we have three sources of water, which have held us in good stead the entire time we have been here during these droughts and heat waves. First, we have our own well, which provides all the water for our personal uses. Second, we have a large reserve of fresh water in our lake that is hooked up to our water system if we need it. Third, we also keep in reserve three large underground cisterns that hold enough water to last months. We do have water provided by the community but never use it. It wouldn't help much, as they frequently run out of water, even in the best of times, and have to truck it in.

I remember how the drought and heat wave that summer ended.

Mica's wrist started hurting, which had become as accurate a barometer as any, and sure enough, the next day it rained. And what a rain: it lasted for almost eight hours. People were cheering and clapping and running around all excited.

It was a beautiful rain, starting off slowly and making us think that it was yet another teaser from Mother Nature. But then the sky was blanketed with dark, menacing clouds, some as low as treetop height. The wind picked up speed, and it seemed as if it would accelerate to gale force just as the rain started coming down in torrents. Thunder and lightning were everywhere.

We got out our flashlights and candles and disconnected all our phones, computers, and appliances in anticipation of a miniblackout (which happens with regularity here whenever there's a thunderstorm). We opened a bottle of wine and sat sipping it as we stared out the window at the rain. It was a delicious sight, and, in an instant, the heat wave was zapped. The temperature dropped, and when we went to bed, we fell asleep with a refreshing breeze blowing through our open window and the sound of raindrops on our roof.

A leftover reminder of World War II still lingers in the area. Recently, a new house was being built right outside the walls of Radda where a previous house had stood for centuries until the Germans blew it up as they retreated from the Allies, perhaps because it stood next to the road on which the Allies were advancing. At any rate, before building could start, the old foundation and grounds around it had to be searched for unexploded bombs. Apparently, only harmless fragments were found. I hadn't realized it, but there's a government agency that still inspects new building sites to ensure that no undetonated bombs from WWII are buried there.

At the end of our yearly stay, we had what became, after a few years, a standing ritual to close up the house and bid farewell to our Italian friends. During our stay, I drove to Panzano every Sunday morning to get my standing order of the best grilled chicken in the world. It was only fitting that on my last trip each season, I always took extra time to say my good-byes to the grilled-chicken family booth: Marco, the son; his two sisters, Viviana and Maria; and the mother, whom we just call Ma. Unfortunately, the father and founder of the business died a few years after we arrived in Italy, but the family was determined to honor his legacy, and they continued on, raising and cooking those fabulous-tasting chickens.

At the same time, I always say good-bye to Dario, the butcher who throws anyone who asks for chicken out of his store, and Piero Vegni, the real estate broker we like so much and to whom we are forever grateful for having helped us buy Ceppeto.

The week leading up to our departure, we always get the house ready to close up, moving all the lawn furniture and lemon plants inside and packing our bags. Every year it's always hard to say good-bye to Fumo, who still thinks he's a dog and never fails to come galloping, wagging his tail, whenever we call him.

After we leave, we always miss the two cats. Fumo has developed a habit of following us around the property, although he often plops down and rolls on his back with his legs in the air, faking total exhaustion in the hopes that I'll carry him up the hill. Stupid me; it usually works. By the time I arrive at the top, I always end up ready to roll on *my* back with my legs up in the air. Fiamma, who is as cute as a button and very much a precocious seductress, is also missed.

Pasquale is always more upset at our leaving than we are. I know that when we are gone he misses our morning huddles where we now discuss the day's projects for only two minutes and spend the rest of the time catching up on local news or gossip. At our last meeting in 2003 Pasquale said, "*Capo*, me know what need done while you gone.

Don't worry; me have everything ready by time you back. Pasquale continue cutting dead limbs from all trees in woods and will ask Babbo help me harvest grapes and olives as soon they ready. By way, you remember Albanian, Salvatore? He work here for Bini."

I did remember him. He was an excellent *muratore* (mason) and did a great job on the stone walls inside the house. "What happened?" I asked Pasquale.

"Well, he and two other Albanians, they all go drink together. They are friends and go out drink in Radda after get pay. They drink too much and argue about girlfriend. Friend begin punch other friend who grab knife and stab him in back."

I was surprised. "Was it Salvatore?"

"No, no, it was other two. Salvatore no make trouble ever, but they all probably take drink too much."

This was the first serious incident that had ever happened in the time we had been there, and I asked, "Where are they all now?"

"They all arrest by police, but Salvatore let go. The one that was stabbed, he go to hospital and is okay. The one who stab him tell police, 'Not my fault, he back into knife me hold to keep him away.'"

That defense may have flown in Albania but not here; he's now in jail awaiting trial. The victim lives in the area and is now fully recovered.

So the outside world and all its problems are coming to town. Sadly, there is no getting away from the world's craziness as there's just too much of it and too many people spreading it to every nook and cranny.

In 2004, before we returned to Ceppeto, we decided to hire a cook/housekeeper from New York to come over and work at the farm. The woman we hired had excellent references, so we thought she would work out great. We fixed up the studio that Mica had been working in, which was really a private guesthouse, installing a computer line and cable for TV. We told her we were isolated, and since she didn't drive, she would have to be comfortable taking public transportation on her days off. She was fine with that and was excited about the opportunity.

When she arrived with four large suitcases of matching designer luggage, I knew we were headed for trouble. The first day, my suspicion was confirmed when Mica asked her to dice a few onions and garlic cloves. An hour and half later, she was still dicing and getting more on the floor than in the containers. It got worse from there.

She was obviously unqualified, and even though she had received good recommendations from what were supposedly previous employers, I suspect they were either phony or just not being truthful. From the moment she arrived, she was more interested in finding out how to get to Florence and Siena than in working.

Pasquale summed it up accurately: "Pasquale think she come here and be tourist not worker. *Scusi, Capo*, she from big city in America; how she ever happy here on farm where she no can go to town without you take by car? She no speaks Italian. No, no, *Capo*, *scusi*, it big mistake you hire her."

Of course he was right; three weeks after she arrived, we put her on a plane back to New York.

For five years we had been trying to get reliable household help, without finding anyone. It wasn't a matter of pay; it was just that no one wanted the job. This was an ongoing issue for us, and after a number of tries in the ensuing years, we were finally able to get the help we needed, but it only came about as the economic times became increasingly bad in Italy.

That April, when we arrived in Ceppeto, the two fat cats were waiting for us, probably out of hope we'd feed them, more than out of their having missed us. Fumo looked like a rugby ball, while Fiamma looked as if she had taken a big breath and wouldn't exhale. Not only had Pasquale kept feeding them, but he'd also been carrying Fumo up the hills because after having gone down them, our fat feline was too out of breath to walk back up.

We started them on a boot camp regimen. Forget about the South Beach Diet; this was the Ceppeto Diet where you eat a lot less and if you walk *down* a hill, you have to walk back *up* the hill. The day we started them on the diet, both Fumo and Fiamma followed me as usual as I walked the property with Pasquale. Coming up the long trail from all the way at the bottom of the property, they played every trick they could think of to get us to pick them up and carry them the rest of the way as Pasquale had over the winter. The roll-over-and-play-dead-with-all-four-paws-stuck-in-the-air maneuver almost worked until I patted them on their stomachs and they began to purr.

Then there was the one where they started limping. That almost worked until a *topolino* (mouse) crossed their path, and they bolted off after it like a pair of rockets.

The final ruse they came up with was to lie flat on the ground with their legs splayed (not hard to do when you're as round as they are) and pretend they couldn't move. *That* almost worked until I said the words they always understood: *"Hai fame?"* ("Are you hungry?") They suddenly jumped back to life, racing up the hill to the house to be fed.

The last week in April was the time to put down *concime* (fertilizer) around the olive trees and vineyard as well as to plant our *orto* (vegetable garden). Right afterward, a slow, steady rain started and continued for three days. The timing couldn't have been better, and it turned out to be a good omen as the *orto* produced the best crop of vegetables that year we'd ever had.

That kind of rain also replenished the aquifers, which were depleted during the prior year's drought, historically the worst ever. A lot of trees did not survive that drought, including an old cherry tree near the house. Many were still fighting their way back to health, as could be seen by the lack of new buds and many dead branches, which Pasquale carefully cut down that summer. His work helped bring hundreds of trees back to life and trigger their full blossoming the following year.

Pine trees were also hard hit, and to make matters worse, they were stricken by a disease. They turned brown, and dozens had to be cut down as there was little chance they would recover. It was interesting to find out that pine trees are not indigenous to Chianti; they were imported from Canada and America. When I called our landscaper to inquire as to what, if anything, we could have done about the disease, her answer was "There's nothing to do, and besides, they aren't even Italian." I hope they don't say that about me if I have a serious illness here.

But the summer that year was not lost; with all the rain, a lot of vegetation recovered. The *fiori di campo* (wildflowers of the fields) blossomed again in all the lush green fields, their bright yellows, blues, and reds weaving a tapestry of artistic grandeur as far as the eye could see, interrupted only by the geometric patterns of vineyards and the occasional olive grove. Seeing all that beauty, I thought, *If only the human race could be inspired to emulate that beauty, that symmetry, and that balance, then perhaps there would be hope for a better world.*

There's a myth in this area that Chianti was the location of the Garden of Eden. When I saw that lush vegetation, it was easy to believe. The old-timers told us that the cold and snowy winter that prior year was healthy for the flora and would help it become a great year for the olives and grapes. Sure enough, they turned out to be correct. Our 2004 olive oil and wine were some of our best.

After five years, the two cypress trees that Raffaello had planted for our wedding had grown a lot. He'd planted them near where we park the cars, and we had named them Mica and Richard. Richard, as you might remember, had fallen on bad times a couple of years prior, having been eaten by deer, so we replaced him. Now, Mica was at least ten feet high while Richard II was only about eight. Nevertheless, they were a striking couple.

After Fumo and Fiamma had been on the Ceppeto Diet for a few weeks, they both were looking about the same. However, Mica and I had both lost several pounds each. Go figure!

Fumo and Fiamma were constantly hanging around the house waiting for their mealtimes, which were once in the morning and once at around six in the evening. They were both as affectionate as ever. Fumo was constantly snuggling up to me, purring and licking me while also taking playful bites of my hand. Sometimes I thought he was not so much showing affection as he was probably trying to eat me. But we did not relent and were determined to see them svelte once again in the not-too-distant future; at the same time we hoped that neither Mica nor I would become emaciated in the process.

Later in May, we went to Biella where we celebrated Mica's sister's fiftieth birthday. She and her husband, Giovanni, had a sit-down luncheon for twenty-five people (all Bagnascos) at this little sixteenth-century restaurant outside of Biella in the foothills of the Alps. The setting was gorgeous, and the day was crystal clear, so you could see the tops of the towering Alps completely covered with sparkling snow.

The area—Piedmont—has a long history of ties to France. The local dialect is heavily mixed with French; in fact, the waiter thanked us by saying *"Merci"* instead of *"Grazie."* I now understand why Mica has no problem understanding French; virtually half the words spoken in this area, where she was raised, are French. Cavour—considered the father of the modern unified Italy in the late 1800s—came from this area. He spoke French first and used Italian as his second language.

The food was a mixture of Italian and French country cooking. Wow! Was it ever delicious! We ate a fourteen-course luncheon over a four-hour period. We had salami and hot, just-baked bread, stuffed onions, stuffed eggplant, stuffed artichoke, escargot (which the chef insisted was an Italian dish introduced to the French), ravioli, soup, veal, duck, vegetables and pureed potatoes, a cheese selection (all local varieties) the likes of which I'd never tasted, fresh mixed fruit salad, birthday cake, coffee and tea, port wine, and a thirteen-herb mixed drink fermented to help with the digestion. Just what the doctor ordered! *"Burp!* Excuse me" was about all I could say when it was over. It was a culinary workout but worth every minute of it.

Our trip from Ceppeto to Biella to get to the party was a nightmare. It was May Day, which is still a big holiday here in Italy, so the weekend traffic was horrendous. The trip took seven hours; by comparison, it took us only four hours to come back home early Sunday. The traffic on the way there was so slow that I had time to read all the overhead signs spanning the Autostrada (Turnpike), which, when you're trapped and crawling along in traffic, is about the only way you can keep your sanity.

A few years ago in Italy, they instituted a new system of giving points for driving infractions. They had overhead signs warning drivers of the infractions and corresponding points. Speeding above eighty miles per hour got you ten points; not wearing a seatbelt, two points; talking on a cell phone, five points; not turning on your headlights, two points; following the car ahead too closely, five points.

Italians are renowned for *not* obeying traffic laws. Since instituting these laws, I had seen countless drivers (me included, from time to time) openly violating these regulations, often nonchalantly doing so, while they drive by the police. Still, I've yet to see anyone violate the following rule that was flashing on a sign just outside Milan (although I have a feeling one day I will): "Driving backward on the Autostrada—ten points!"

There was a big celebration in Europe on May 2 that summer because ten new countries joined the European Union, making twenty-five countries in the EU in all. As an announcer on TV said at the conclusion of the ceremonies, "Now everyone can get back to fighting."

At the time, there was immense optimism as to how well the EU would function. Much of its success depended on the countries voluntarily cooperating with each other, something that had never been done before with any consistency. It started with the common currency, the euro, which at least in Italy turned out to be the start of severe economic conditions. The cost of living instantly sky-rocketed once the lira was replaced with the euro, and most Italians rue the day this change was made. There is now a huge backlash against the European Union, not only in Italy but also in Spain and the Netherlands as well. The feeling is that they have lost their sovereignty and that Germany holds all the power because economically they are the most powerful country in the European Union.

One day in mid-July 2004, Pasquale came to me very troubled. He told me, *"Mia cervello in giro e non ho dormito ieri sera."* ("My mind is spinning, and I couldn't sleep last night.") According to Pasquale, the contractor we'd hired to build a wooden post-and-beam fence around part of the property had a worker with him, an Italian man, who had asked Pasquale if he was married. Pasquale had answered yes, explaining his wife and children were in Albania.

The man had told Pasquale, "While you are here, you should be looking for a woman to sleep with."

Pasquale was infuriated and said to me, "Some men always looking for *donne* [women] instead working and caring for wife and children." He was upset, yet he didn't want to create a problem for me by saying what he thought of this man. He couldn't understand this man's values and felt insulted that anyone would suggest he should be unfaithful.

He's often told me people do not respect boundaries. He once said this as he drew a square in the dirt with a stick. He continued—while pointing with the stick—"*Capo*, see when person stay inside boundaries, all go well, but when step outside, there are problem. They put noses in things none of their business."

He used that example to talk about Muslims, despite being one himself. He said, "When they stay in mosques and pray, all goes good because they are inside the boundaries. But when come outside and make trouble in the world, is wrong." According to Pasquale, "Me a Muslim, but me no pray five times a day. Me eat pork, me sometime drink glass wine and beer, and when Muslim tell me no do those things, me tell him go care yourself. Pasquale take care me. *Capo*, Pasquale no hurt other unless other hurt me or family my. Pasquale do what me want, not what he want." He shrugged, saying, "If he like pray five times a day and makes feel good him, do it. For me, no, no, no." He walked back toward where he was working and was still shaking his head, saying, "No, no, no, no ..." until I slowly lost sight of him.

Pasquale is always thinking about how he can improve Ceppeto. In his mind, he has divided the entire property into sections: triangles, squares, terraces, areas defined by certain trees, the pond, the paths, and so on. For each section, he has a plan: when to carry it out and how much time he will spend each day on a certain section, making sure to divide his time in a way that allows him, in a week's period, to work in every section. He knows when he'll cut the grass and how many times he'll do it in each section over the next six months. He knows when he'll dig up around every tree, when to cut the vines and weeds around each tree and plant. He has scheduled days and times he'll spend in the vegetable garden, caring for the chickens, doing maintenance on the tractors and lawn mowers, tending to the vineyard, cleaning the pool, watering the flowers, and on and on ad infinitum. All of this is in his head because he can't write that well. When he changes one thing, he can tick off the repercussions that alteration will have on the grand plan in all the other sections of the property, and he can make the necessary adjustments. I love seeing how his mind works and how he sees the big picture but is still mindful of the details. After building several businesses from the ground up, I can tell you that if Pasquale had been better educated, he could have been a big success at virtually anything he tried.

There are approximately twenty acres of grass to cut that, for the most part, can't be cut with a mower but only with a *decespugliatore* (what we call a Weedwacker) because there are so many trees, stumps, and rocks. In the summer, it is truly a Sisyphean task, for no sooner does Pasquale finish working his way through the grounds when the grass needs cutting again.

I suggested to him that perhaps we should hire another worker a few times a month to help him, but he didn't even want to discuss it: "*Capo*, no worry; Pasquale do all by me. No hire me help. For me, no need."

One week, I walked every day to the area Pasquale was working. On Wednesday, I found him on one of the lower terraces. I was amazed at how much he'd accomplished since the previous day. I complimented him, and he said, "Don't worry, *Capo*; Pasquale finish all by me. You no need anyone else. Me know *Dio*, the big *capo*, me watch always, so me never stop working. Me go fast, *Capo*; no you never worry about Pasquale. Me know I'm always under the eyes of big *capo*. Pasquale no disappoint him or you ever."

I call Pasquale *il nostro carro armato* (our tank). To him, work is like playing golf: he's always trying to improve his score. For him, that means seeing how much he can accomplish each day. And, like every good golfer, a lot goes into strategizing how best to play the game.

Mica says, "If everyone in Italy worked like Pasquale—especially politicians—there wouldn't be a deficit, and the country would be in great shape, instead of constantly being on the cusp of collapse."

In August 2005 we realized a little bit of Americana had arrived. Believe it or not, one of the hottest imports in this area became American mailboxes—the kind used out in the country with the pull-down door in the front, a little metal red flag that lifts up to signal mail has been delivered, and "US Mail" embossed on the side.

The post office manager, Luciano, suggested we get an "American" mailbox because when it rains, the mail doesn't get wet as it does in the "Italian" mailboxes. When we went to the local hardware store to buy one, they told us they couldn't keep them in stock and we'd have to wait for the next delivery to come in. We saw them popping up all over the area.

After waiting a few weeks, we finally got one and installed it at the turnoff to our house right below Lupaia. Previously, we had to go to the post office in Radda to pick up our mail. It is a nice convenience to have, and we like seeing a good kind of Americana permeate the culture here. Hopefully I won't ruin that feeling by looking too closely and finding a notation stamped on the mailbox saying "Made in China."

A woman was arrested during the summer of 2005 in Rome for an unusual escapade. Her crime? She lured men from a casino after they'd won money by offering them coffee. When the men accepted, she slipped pills into their coffee, causing them to pass out. The woman then proceeded to take all their winnings. The evidence was overwhelming as it was all caught on tape.

The kicker here was that the woman was eighty years old and had been linked to a Mafia organization, which, in turn, may have ties to the casino. This sweet *nonna* (grandmother, or I guess I should say godmother) is now incarcerated in a high security prison in Rome.

Speaking of crime, a few weeks later, it came to sleepy Lupaia. A car was stolen from a house near a hotel on a back road about half a mile from Lupaia. Another car was later stolen in Radda, and two thieves entered the house of Raffaello's daughter while she and her husband were out for a walk after dinner. The thieves were luckily scared away by a neighbor who heard them. The thieves were arrested a few days later and turned out to be two Albanian refugees living in Greve, about half an hour away.

Then in July that same year in Lupaia thieves tried to break into Maria's *bottega* at five thirty in the morning. Maria's sister, Gina, lives across from the *bottega* and heard a car idling in the center of the little piazza, a rare event at that hour in tiny Lupaia. She looked out and saw a group of men trying to pry open the lock on the door.

Gina, who's about 5'7" and built like an opera singer, weighing in at a hefty 180 pounds, let out a scream probably heard all the way to Radda, five miles away on the other side of the valley. Gina immediately called the Carabinieri and they "rushed" to Lupaia … arriving at eleven thirty in the morning. I can imagine the conversation among the thieves: "We better get outta here! The Carabinieri will be here in six hours!"

The thieves took off, but the Carabinieri later captured them in a station wagon they'd stolen from another town a two-hour drive from here. They were all Albanians, and it is believed they worked with Italians to plan these robberies.

The mini–crime wave continued a couple of months later when a large urn that was outside our neighbor's house was stolen. It was the first robbery of any kind that anyone ever remembers happening here. A small pickup truck was needed to take the urn, which was an antique that stood about five feet high.

The number of petty crimes being committed by Albanians is impacting the legendary tranquility enjoyed here. No longer can you leave your house without locking it up. We now have an alarm system, more as a warning to would-be thieves, since by the time the Carabinieri could respond, the perpetrators would be long gone.

Here at Ceppeto, our best crime deterrent is Pasquale. He's a big socializer now in Lupaia and Radda, where he is well known and liked. More importantly, he's made it known that he's always at Ceppeto, a fact not missed by the many Albanian migrant workers in the area who, I am sure, pass on information as to the best targets for theft.

But Pasquale has sent another message through these mostly Albanian workers: "If you enter Ceppeto, I will deal with you according to Muslim law. A thief will have his hands chopped off."

It is a shame there are simply no more oases left in the world to find a truly peaceful and gentle life. The expression for this in Italian, which I think is apropos, is "*Non si può lasciare la chiave nella toppa.*" ("You can no longer leave the key in the door.")

One of the local Carabinieri told us the Albanians are causing big problems and are responsible for a level of crime that had never existed here before now. Because Mica's father and brother were both career Carabinieri, the local officer offered as a courtesy to have our alarm at Ceppeto hooked up to their central office, something reserved for "sensitive" locations since they don't have the manpower to run around answering alarms everywhere. We accepted and feel certain that we are well protected.

The problem is that Italy's system of police is not nearly large enough to deal with the rising crime rates. The local Carabinieri office is only open from 9:00 a.m. to 6:00 p.m. and closed all day Sunday. They might as well post a sign outside the town saying "No robberies from 6:00 p.m. until 9:00 a.m. Monday through Saturday and all day Sunday."

When an emergency occurs, the calls go to a central station hours away from here, which is what happened in Lupaia. The closest fire station is in Siena, at least an hour away. So people here are left to their own devices, and yet no one is rushing out to buy guns.

In fact, a foreign resident cannot own a gun. Hunters can own shotguns but only if they are Italian citizens. No one is permitted to carry a sidearm, so one rarely hears of firearms being used by private citizens.

The reality is that the problems of the world are closing in everywhere. There is no place to hide. People are moving from one place to the next, while information is moving at lightning speed.

Not so long ago, oceans protected countries like the United States, and the borders of European countries were heavily guarded with restricted entry, preserving their integrity and culture. Walls and barbed wire fences isolated Eastern European countries.

Now, everyone is interdependent on everyone else. There's no one entity that can exist by itself in an isolationist manner. Thus the problems with Albania are now at the doorstep of Chianti, and everyone living here has to deal with it. There is no easy option, but now that awareness has been raised by these recent events, people here are more alert and cautious than before, which at least can help deter crime. Certainly, Pasquale is doing his part.

If I had to choose the best month to be at Ceppeto, I would say June. Not that the other months aren't great, but June seems to always stand out as the most beautiful. In June, we never tire of looking at the beautiful scenery: the earth-toned fields of grain being harvested next to the contrasting green vineyards and fields of multicolored wildflowers, all bordered by dense *bosco* (forests), and adding a little music to the background, almost twenty-four hours a day, are the *uccelli* (birds), the most lyrical-sounding birds I've ever heard.

The topaz-blue skies with just a few billowing white clouds are the perfect backdrop. Some days are so clear you can see for miles and miles. It was the middle of June when we went for a ride in our Jeep through some areas we'd never seen before.

Our 2002 Jeep Wrangler Sports model is all black and causes quite a stir whenever we drive into the small *borghi* (tiny villages). These *borghi* are usually tucked away on top of hills, and many are isolated from everyday life, so they are real throwbacks to what Italy was like before it became a modern country. I think the Jeep reminds many of the older residents of the US troops during and after the war. I know that when I was in Germany and rode in an army Jeep through small villages, people there would come out and wave. The children would run after us, yelling, *"Kaugummi!"* (the German word for chewing gum), the gift American GIs gave to the children back then.

No children were around in these villages in 2005, though, as most of the people were old and retired. The younger ones have all left for the bigger cities. The ride was definitely through areas not visited by tourists. There were no stores or bars of any type—just small houses clustered around a tiny piazza that usually had water flowing from a center fountain. Benches were invariably positioned around the piazza, where a few of the elderly people sat talking. They seemed to be waiting for something to happen, and when we appeared, they were clearly happy, waving at us with big smiles. It was as if we made their day. Each *borgo* looked as if there were no more than a dozen or so people living there. Actually, some were so tiny it looked as if just one family was living there. It took less than a minute or so to continue on past each one, where the open view of the stunning countryside reappeared. When Chianti is in full bloom—as it was in June—including the *girasole* (sunflowers), there's nothing like it anywhere else in the world.

September 11, 2005. None of us can ever forget exactly where we were and what we were doing on 9/11/2001, and it's hard to stop replaying those memories in our heads.

The news here on September 11, 2005, was filled not only with stories of 9/11 but also about Hurricane Katrina and how inept the United States had become. The one good thing the news highlighted was that Italy was sending food and supplies, but the most reassuring news bit was that Mexico had sent in troops to help us. Wow! Based on that information, we felt secure in returning to the States and therefore decided to return the next day.

Thus it was a wrap there at Ceppeto for that year. We left on September 11 for Milan, and our flight was the next day, Monday. Another reason for returning at this time—besides the security promised by Mexican troops—was we had just gotten back the laboratory results on our grapes, and the sugar content was too low to harvest; they needed to stay on the vine for at least another month.

We had hoped to be at Ceppeto for the *vendemmia* (harvest), but waiting until the middle of October was too late for us. So we packed it in and would return to Ceppeto for New Year's, which would be the critical point of time in the fermentation process, the point at which you can adjust the wine based on how much alcoholic content and how sweet or dry you want it to be.

Returning to Ceppeto in 2006, we arrived to find everything in tip-top shape along with a pot of *ribollita* (bread and vegetable soup) and *cinghiale* waiting for us, prepared by Raffaello's daughter, for our first few meals. Pasquale had continued to do an amazing job. Our first task the week after our return was to order the annuals, mostly red geraniums, for planting, and then I had until the end of the month to prune the olive trees. Olive oil production in October was a record. We produced over 350 liters of extra virgin olive oil.

The *pollaio* (henhouse) was empty. We had to have Pasquale get rid of all our chickens because of the bird flu scare. By law, all chickens needed to be raised indoors. As usual, few Italians were paying attention to it other than commercial vendors, but we did not want to take the risk. So Pasquale had himself seven free-range chickens while we were gone.

It looked as if he might have fed some to our cats, Fumo and Fiamma, as they were looking as chubby (and happy) as ever.

I tasted our wine, which was one of our first harvests. It was aging in an oak barrel, but it was not good enough to bottle. Well, in the interest of being candid, it was simply bad.

How bad? Let's just say I was looking for a hazardous waste facility to dispose of it, as it was too dangerous to pour down the drain. But we were not giving up and hoped to learn from our mistakes. We looked forward to trying again with this year's harvest.

One of the first things I did that year was go to an electronics store in Siena to check out video cameras. I ended up buying one that had a few more gadgets than I wanted, but the salesman convinced me that once I started using it, I would definitely want to use them. I asked him if there were instructions in English, and when he told me no, I impulsively thought, *No problem, I can read Italian.*

All excited, I paid for the camera, but as we were driving home, I suddenly realized, *Am I crazy or what? I can hardly understand instructions when they are written in* English! *My VCR and DVD players at home still have their clocks stuck on a blinking 12:00!*

When I arrived home, I opened the box and found two thick *libretti* (books) of instructions printed in every language I ever thought existed, including Suomi, Slovensky, Bahasa Indonesia, Magyar, Cesky, Polski, Japanese, Chinese, Korean, Arabic, and a bunch of other languages written from right to left and from top down or bottom up (I couldn't tell which way for sure) ... but no *English*!

I worked my way painfully through the instructions. After a few hours, I had figured out how to charge the battery and turn the camera on and off. At that rate, I was afraid that by the time I learned how to use the camera, it would be completely obsolete and the video cassettes no longer available.

In June, there was a mad dash to get chickens and eggs because my nephew and his wife arrived, somewhat unexpectedly, with their two adorable and smart children. Their little girl, Jordyn, was eight, and their son, Justin, was five. When we found out the children were coming, we ran out and bought six chickens (the avian flu scare had passed by this time), thinking it would be fun for the kids to collect eggs every morning for breakfast. The problem was chickens don't start laying eggs right away; they need time to get used to their new quarters. You also have to put fake wooden eggs in the nests so they get the idea that that is where they should lay their eggs.

Since our chickens weren't laying eggs in time, Mica ran out and bought a few dozen eggs from the store. She then started putting five or six in the nests each morning before the children awoke. There is a law in Italy, however, that you need to stamp a date on each egg sold in stores so you know how old they are. We didn't realize that until we put the eggs into the chicken nests, but having no other choice, we waited for the inevitable questions from our two little egg gatherers.

Justin, the youngest, questioned it first. While holding an egg in his hand, his lips moved as he silently pronounced the month, date, and year. When he finished, he turned to me with a puzzled look on his face and said, "Uncle Rich, why is there a date stamped on the egg?"

I, as forthrightly as I could, said, "These are special hens that date their eggs as they are laid." The look I got from both of them said that didn't go over with either of them, so for a fallback position, I said, "Actually, Pasquale dates them early each morning." That sort of went over. I knew it would only be good until their next visit, but by then, we would hopefully be back in regular egg-production mode.

Their first day here, we walked them all over the property. We checked out the chickens; then picked and ate cherries, fava beans, lettuce, and zucchini; went for a boat ride on our *laghetto* (small lake); and rode the big and little tractor … and that was all in the first two hours! What energy these little guys had! They could tire out an army.

We also took them to Florence for an evening party and afterward walked around the city, stopping, of course, for gelato. We didn't get to sleep until after one in the morning, but they loved it and were up the next day ready to start all over again.

I used my new video camera to interview Jordyn and Justin sitting together on our couch. I started off saying, "Justin, tell us where you are now."

Justin, looking straight into the camera, without a moment's hesitation, and with an absolutely deadpan expression, replied, "I'm on the couch."

My advice is to never get a toothache in Italy. Let me explain: I started having a toothache about midsummer in 2006. I spoke to the dentist I see in New York, and he suspected I needed root canal work done, though he couldn't be sure without seeing x-rays. Not knowing any dentists in Italy, Mica and I spoke to our local doctor, *Dottore* Dell'Anna, whom I call our quarterback GP because he is the one that recommends specialists when needed. He suggested I go to the dentist in Radda.

While sitting in the dentist's waiting room, I struck up a conversation with a gentleman of about sixty-five, who had an outdoor-worker's tan and who also looked very fit. He was the owner of a large *agriturismo,* a working farm where they rent out rooms to tourists during the vacation season. He introduced himself as Daniele Marino, and I told him there was a famous and wealthy American football player named Dan Marino. He laughed and said, "Just my luck. After my poor family members leave for America and become rich, I never hear from them again."

Daniele was also there for a toothache, and as we compared notes on our respective dental discomforts, he shared with me the view that the Italian medical system was in deep trouble.

He told me, "For routine matters, it seems to work well enough, particularly considering it is free for citizens, but anything that needs doing in a rush or is an emergency forces you to go to the *Pronto Soccorso* [emergency room] at the nearest hospital, in which treatment can get a bit spotty. As an example, if you have a broken bone, never go to the Siena Hospital. My wife did when she broke her arm, and they mistreated it so badly she ended up needing an operation. But for heart problems, it is a good place to go. You have to know these things before rushing off to just any emergency room."

I asked, "Who can tell you which one is best? I know there are a couple of hospitals in Siena and also in Florence."

"It is always best to get the information in advance so you are prepared. I make my list based on consulting with my regular doctor."

Then he continued, "But the biggest challenge to the Italian system is a combination of long lifespans and a low birthrate. Did you know it is only 1.4 children per family, one of the lowest in Europe?"

I was surprised at how low that figure was and said, "No, I had no idea it was that low."

"Now add the fact that Italians live longer than people in most any other country in the world. Consequently, an ever-decreasing number of younger workers are shouldering the tax burden to support the medical needs of an ever-increasing number of older, nonworking people. The high unemployment rate is only making the situation worse, with little possibility of a better future in view. It is an awful mess, and I just see it getting worse."

I thanked him for that information and said, "I never knew it was that bad here. We are grappling with the same problem in America right now, trying to come up with a system where everyone joins in and pays for health insurance starting at a young age. But the costs of medical care keep going up faster and faster, making it one gigantic money-losing proposition."

Daniele then said, "But the big difference between America and here is that you can print money to get yourself out of the problem. Italy, as part of the European Union, can't do that." Then Daniele added, "You know, as I think about this, my toothache gets worse." We both laughed and settled back to wait for the doctor to see us.

Daniele was soon called on by the doctor while I continued to wait for about another thirty minutes. It gave me time to digest all that Daniele had said. Boiling this all down, what it meant for me and my ill-tempered tooth was that taking care of certain kinds of medical problems could be problematic. Something that soon was to be proven true. To wit:

As it turned out, the Radda dentist didn't do root canals. His suggestion, however, was to keep the area around the tooth clean and see what happened. He gave me a bunch of mouthwashes to use. In football lingo, that would be called a "delay of game" and require a penalty. In this case, however, I was the one that paid the penalty. I always diligently cleaned my teeth, and I also started using the mouthwash he gave me several times a day. Nothing happened, other than that the pain kept getting worse.

On the advice of our friends in Siena, I saw a dentist there. He saw me three times, and each time, he put some medicine on the tooth and applied some strange device that heated up the tooth. It didn't help, and my discomfort was getting worse.

When we had dinner that week at Maria's in Lupaia, I noticed that she was wearing braces. I asked her about her dentist, and she raved about him, so I made an appointment with him in Florence. When I saw him, he took an x-ray and confirmed that I needed a root canal and said that he'd do it right then and there.

I was relieved, and after a healthy dose of Novocain, he went to work, finishing in about fifteen minutes. I was grateful to have the treatment finished so quickly but was a little skeptical, as I'd had root canal work done once before, and it had taken a couple of appointments to finish it.

Mica and her mother were with me, so we left the dentist's office and spent a few hours walking around Florence before heading home. When the Novocain finally wore off, the pain returned, which seemed strange to me. I always thought when you had a root canal, you may feel pain and soreness from the procedure, but the nerves themselves are gone, so the toothache should go away. If anything, my pain had become even worse.

In fact, it was so bad that I called my dentist in New York, and after I described the procedure done that day, he felt sure a root canal hadn't taken place. He suggested that I call the American embassy in Florence to recommend an American-trained dentist. Before I could do that, I received an e-mail message from my New York dentist giving me the name of a specialist in Florence who had been trained in root canal surgery at Boston University.

I saw that specialist the following week. He took x-rays and told me the dentist I had seen had not done a root canal procedure and had done nothing more than replace an existing filling with a temporary one and probably medicate the area. This new specialist told me that Italian-trained dentists aren't nearly as well trained as they are in the States. "If a root canal procedure took only fifteen minutes, I'd be a rich man, since it normally takes two hours," he said. So I made an appointment for the following week to have him do a "real" root canal, which by that time was a total of three weeks and four dentist visits since this all began. I thought, *With dentists like these, it's a wonder Italians have any teeth at all!*

Symbolically, I had the root canal done on July 4 and hoped that there would be no more fireworks, but alas, that wasn't meant to be. The odyssey with the lousy tooth continued. After a total of four hours in the dentist chair on two separate sessions—one without any anesthesia, which had me jumping out of the seat a few times—it appeared that the dentist had botched the job. I *still* had a toothache: it seemed he didn't get the whole nerve out. I could tolerate the pain during the day, but it was difficult to sleep at night. Can you imagine: it had now been one month, with eight visits to four different dentists, each one taking up most of the day? In hindsight, it would've been better to return to New York to have the work done there.

So back to the dentist yet again with the hope that he could get it right this time. It didn't pay to try to find another dentist at that point.

Whoever would've thought dentistry in Italy was so backward? There are backward things in Italy that are charming, but this sure wasn't one of 'em.

In fact, the tooth saga continued, and I was even more—pardon the pun—long in the tooth. The dentist decided that the root canal had been done correctly, but he found that my wisdom tooth had a crack inside that couldn't be detected by x-rays and had become infected. Result: I had it pulled out the next day.

That didn't end the issue either, as the pain continued and was probably stemming from a *third* tooth. I thought I would try to take care of that the following week. At that point, I had spent more time traveling to and from dentists and having teeth worked on than I've ever done in my whole life—and much of the time was actually spent on the wrong tooth. At that point, I would not have been surprised to return to New York toothless.

As the pain continued to increase, I went to *Dottore* Dell'Anna, who had recommended the first dentist I saw, and explained to him what had been going on with all the dentists I had seen and said that I would appreciate some sort of painkiller.

After listening to the saga, he asked a few questions and said he doubted that the problem was with any tooth. Instead, he thought it was probably an inflammation of nerves in that area. He said he had seen cases where patients had many teeth extracted, thinking they were the cause of the pain. He prescribed some medication for me, and, sure enough, the pain shortly went away.

When I got back to the States and saw my dentist, he confirmed the diagnosis and said he highly doubted I had a tooth infection requiring the tooth be extracted. He also said that the root canal work could have been avoided if the dentist had read the x-ray correctly. That said a lot for the dental school at Boston University.

The moral of the story, if there is one to be had, is this: don't go to an Italian dentist if you can avoid it. And be wary of a root canal diagnosis. By the way, I have never had a return episode of this pain.

As a coda to all this, about a month after everything had calmed down and was back to normal, there was a news report in Italy about two dental offices being closed by the government in Milan. Their employees were doing root canal work, fillings, extractions, and other procedures without formal training.

Alas, the Italian government came up with the perfect—and I must say ingenious—solution to combat the problem. A new law was instituted requiring certified dentists, as well as medical doctors, to wear green jackets when practicing, while dental and medical assistants had to wear white jackets.

Wow, if that law had been in effect when my toothache started, I might've been saved from all that aggravation!

In 2006 the Ceppeto Diet for the cats continued. Fumo, our resident cat—who we were seriously thinking of renaming Sumo, due to his size—had found a new sport that he spent hours a day playing. I guess you could have called it "Catch a Frog or Two as You Scare Them out of Their Hiding Place from under the New Dock." Or perhaps you could shorten it to "Pig Out on Frogs." Fumo's new habit was to go down to the dock right after breakfast and spend the whole morning playing this game. Unfortunately for the frogs, Fumo had found them to be quite a delicacy. Consequently, Fumo "the Sumo" was bulging again after having become moderately svelte. Between Rambo—Mica's mom's cat—constantly bringing home half-dead *lucertole* (lizards) and Fumo "the Sumo," I expected they'd be bagging *cinghiale* (wild boar) together before long.

In July 2006, we began the cultural season with the annual outdoor concert at the Piazza del Campo in Siena. To be sitting in the middle of this twelfth-century piazza, surrounded by medieval buildings with the famous clock tower silhouetted by a crystal-blue, cloudless sky while listening to none other than *Porgy and Bess* was as good as it gets. They could've played "Chopsticks," and the setting would have made it sound magical.

The songs were all sung in English and were as pure Americana as you can get. I can't imagine translating into Italian lines like

> Oh, I got plenty o'nuttin'
> An' nuttin's plenty fo' me

or

> Oh yo' daddy's rich and yo' ma is good lookin'
> So hush little baby don't yo cry.

For that matter, it wouldn't work in *any* other language. The English didn't seem to faze the almost three thousand people in attendance. They loved it, enough to call the performers back for five encores!

In 2007, we arrived at Ceppeto to start our eighth year there. One of the first things we did every year was get caught up on what had happened while we were away.

That year was a great one for Pasquale. He had rented an apartment in Montevarchi, about a half hour away, and had brought his family to live there with him. He moved from Ceppeto to the apartment. Even though he was still at Ceppeto six days a week, we missed him, knowing he was no longer sleeping here. His wife and children were all in Italy now. In addition, his eldest daughter was pregnant, and she and her husband were going to live in the apartment as well. When the new baby was born, they would be seven all together.

Still, these living conditions were vastly better than those in Albania. It brought to a close a long chapter in Pasquale's life. He left Albania that cold February night, seven years before, arriving in Italy shivering and wet after a harrowing boat trip across the Adriatic. It took not only courage but also perseverance during all those years when he never let go of his dream. It was a story of epic proportions with a real-life happy ending far better than any screenwriter could have created.

In Lupaia, it turned out, Ceppeto was also the talk of the town—among all thirty-two people living there. Everyone with whom we had spoken raved about how great Pasquale was and what a fabulous worker he was. It seemed they had kept tabs on what was being done at Ceppeto, and they reported to us that Pasquale had been outside working every day like clockwork, even in three feet of snow. Lupaia had been snowed in for several days, and, except for Pasquale, no one could get out.

Pasquale used our tractor to clear the road from our house to the main road. Then he plowed the road up to Lupaia and shoveled the snow in front of the apartments of all the older people. He even brought cut logs up to their apartments for their fireplaces and wood-burning stoves. To say the least, they had grown to love him. He could have probably run for mayor, and I bet he would have received at least thirty votes.

The next news item we heard was that there had been a problem with the bees. Ennis, the beekeeper, usually had plenty of honey—we bought from him every year. That year, though, there was none. According to him, it seemed the bees had been dissatisfied with their queen and had replaced her in a palace coup of sorts. They had crowned another queen who turned out to be no better. Well, she had gone the same way as the first one, and the result was that the bees had gone on strike and would not work without a queen. I was

CEPPETO

not a bee aficionado, but Ennis had been raising bees for decades, so I assumed there was truth to his explanation.

God, it's hard to find decent queen bees these days!

Mica and I celebrated our anniversary at Lake Como, which is one of the most beautiful places in Italy. After we returned, it seemed that Ceppeto had become more beautiful by the day, as if it had heard us raving about Lake Como and was saying, "So you thought that was beautiful today, just wait until tomorrow!" And sure enough, each day we woke up to the blossoming of new flowers. Our purple lilacs were in full bloom along with our lavender bushes, white lilies, the deep-red portulaca, the pink and blue hydrangeas, the roses of all different vibrant colors, and white blossoms on the linden trees surrounding the house. They all seemed as if they were competing with one another to be the most radiant. The trees were bursting with new leaves in every shade of green imaginable. Then there were the *fiori di campo* (wildflowers in the field), which were bursting in colors that defy description: violet, red, pink, blue all perfectly interspersed with accents of white blossoms. The yellow *ginestre* had blossomed all over the valley, looking like patches of gold in the sunlight.

We even had a few pollen showers from the early spring blossoms. If you're not a hay fever sufferer, they're spectacular to see; they look like snowstorms in the middle of a gorgeous spring day.

After our sense of vision was almost overwhelmed with color, the fragrant perfumes of the flowers began to awaken our sense of smell. It was such a delicious combination; it defied description and brought smiles to our faces.

As we looked out at the exquisite landscape, we were then struck by the silence. There were no cars, trucks, sirens, or the sound of any mechanical equipment in the early morning. If there was noise, it came from tractors working in the vineyards and was so muted it didn't disturb.

Instead, we heard the beautiful chorus of chirping birds, which sounded like the soundtracks they dub into documentaries during

243

the lulls in the action. With the gentle breezes that were almost constantly rustling the leaves in the trees and caressing our faces, we began to taste and smell the air infused by the exquisite fragrances of the flowers and trees. The topaz-blue skies with fluffy white clouds floating by all combined to tantalize our every sense.

When we looked at the valley from our vantage point, we could see what had to have been the innate architectural insight of the *contadini* (farmers) who built their farmhouses and cultivated the land by building walls and terraces down into the valley in perfect harmony with the natural beauty of the landscape.

I always thought I'd miss sailing and being by the open water when we moved here, but I haven't missed it for a moment. Ceppeto is just so spellbinding; I simply have never experienced being surrounded by nature in such perfect harmony like here. I now understand why the beauty of Chianti is so legendary.

All this beauty was not lost on Pasquale either, and our mutual respect and love of the land at Ceppeto as well as our shared vision for creating a place of utter beauty was what brought us together in our unique friendship.

That summer a lot of local people stopped by Ceppeto to say hello, and, without exception, they all were astounded by how beautiful it had become. As a result, we were invited to join the Counsel for the Beautification of Chianti, an organization dating back over a hundred years. The head of the counsel was Giovanni Ricasoli-Firidolfi, whose great-great-grandfather Bettino Ricasoli became the second premier of the new Italian Republic in 1859. He had also been the first to make Chianti wine into a major export for Italy.

We attended a number of meetings and social gatherings, but because we were not full-time residents, we couldn't continue to partake as much as we would have liked. It was an honor just to have been invited to join them and see so many residents acting to constantly improve the beauty of Chianti.

The summer of 2007, Mica was painting up a storm. She finished three paintings she had been working on for a while, and they were fabulous. She had developed a unique style that was distinctively hers. I loved seeing her work hung throughout the house. A few people recently had come by from Radda and asked Mica if she would like to have a show of her work at the city hall. It certainly was a great compliment, but she declined, as she preferred to keep her work private for our enjoyment and that of our visitors.

She painted a lot outside the house and underneath the *pergola* (arbor), where Pasquale had been noticing her work. One day, he asked her, "Signora, why you paint those things?" He was referring to a flower bed and surrounding trees she was depicting.

She told him, "It is a passion of mine to paint things that I think are beautiful." Mica and I had discussed his questions about her paintings before, so she knew it was a difficult concept for him to grasp. Then she asked him, "Pasquale, tell me, what are you really passionate about?"

He smiled and said without hesitation, "*Il mio lavoro.*" ("My work.")

And that it was. For him, making Ceppeto as beautiful as possible was his work of art, and like every great artist, it was his passion.

He really preferred to stay here and work rather than go home. He wanted to come and work on Sundays, and we had to insist he stay home with his family.

He usually spent the last hour or so of the day tending to the *orto* (vegetable garden). That, if anything, had also become his passion. He loved bringing us fresh vegetables each night: string beans, several types of lettuce, okra, onions, fava beans, garlic, and, later in the season, tomatoes, corn, and watermelons.

The garden had started out as a small patch of land, and each year he had expanded it until it had become more than a quarter of an acre. It was big enough that he proudly brought vegetables to his family and shared them with the older people in Lupaia. Oftentimes, before he went home, he stopped off to see Raffaello and his wife, Marina, and brought them some produce.

To have been able to share and show other people the literal fruits of his labor made him proud. He never had enough of anything to give to others; now, his horn of plenty included the vegetables; fruits from our apple, cherry, peach, and plum trees; nuts from our walnut trees; and eggs from our chickens.

He treated the plants and vegetables as if he were caring for a loved one. He examined all the plants on a regular basis, watered them when needed, and brought fresh black soil from the woods to provide nourishment for them. He pointed out to us how they were growing or when they had a problem. He treated them when they were suffering from insect infestations or other maladies. He had nursed countless plants and trees back to health, after we'd given them up for dead. Two peach trees that I thought had to be cut down he instead brought back to life, and a couple of years later, they were flourishing.

After he cut the grass around the main house, he pulled out all the crab grass and weeds by hand. No chemical weed killers were used here. A few times a week, he watered areas that hadn't been reached by our irrigation systems, so our lawn looked like a green carpet. Yes, he had elevated his job to an art, and it was indeed a passion of his to a point where, as was true of any real artist, he could not *not* do his art.

Notwithstanding Pasquale's wonderful *orto* (garden) and as surprising as it may be, it was difficult to get a variety of good veggies all summer, at least in this region. When a veggie was in season, it was great, but it meant, for example, that you were able to buy good broccoli and asparagus only in April and May. Zucchini was available most of the year and string beans from the middle of summer to September. When fresh seasonal vegetables were no longer available either from our garden or the stores, we just did without.

That changed when Tatiana, Raffaello's daughter, who is a fabulous cook, recommended we try Bo-Frost, a company that delivers frozen food right to your door. We called them, and they came to Ceppeto the following week.

Who can ever forget the excitement during the summer months of hearing the ding-a-ling of the Good Humor ice cream truck arriving in your neighborhood and the mad dash of all the kids into their houses to get money from their parents to buy ice cream? Picture that little white truck in a slightly larger version, with all the small refrigerator doors in the back opening up to reveal all sorts of delicious surprises, and that is the Bo-Frost delivery truck.

It arrived every two weeks. As it neared the house, Pasquale was usually the one who spotted it first. As if he were sitting in a ship's crow's nest and had spotted another vessel, he would yell out, "*Bo-Frost arriva!*" Then the word was passed between Mica and me: "Bo-Frost is here!" as we came running from wherever we were to meet the truck in our driveway.

Instead of running up to the truck with a fistful of loose change like in the old Good Humor days, we came running with credit card in hand. Yes, things have become modern; the drivers carried a handheld wireless computer to swipe your credit card and also to check if the item you wanted was in the truck and how many of them were stocked. For future orders, they left us a catalog, and we could call them a few days before their scheduled stop to order what we wanted. In addition to great gelato, they had truly delicious prepared fish and chicken dishes with healthy ingredients. Their vegetables and berries were excellent but would never be as good as just picked fresh vegetables and fruit when they were in season. Still, the rest of the time, it was an excellent alternative. The big bonus was that it saved us trips to the grocery store and supermarket. Bo-Frost had its own plants around Italy where the food was frozen immediately after being prepared or harvested so it really did lock in all the nutrients and flavor. In a country where home cooking was an ingrained tradition, they had to be good to be as popular as they were, especially with such a decidedly un-Italian name as Bo-Frost.

Paolo, the Bo-Frost driver, told us about an interesting psychological phenomenon: when the avian flu scare occurred, chicken parts, such as thighs, legs, breasts, and wings—which could easily be recognized as parts of a chicken—were not selling well (sales of chicken in Italy had plummeted 80 percent that year). But when the item didn't *look* like a chicken part—such as chicken burgers—they sold just fine.

One day after dinner we walked to Lupaia for some gelato and found Tina at the ancient water fountain in the piazza washing some pots. It was a scene from a hundred years ago. There were few people in the restaurants, and the bar had closed. Tina, whose daughter owned the bar, had the keys and opened it up for us so we were able to have some gelato, which she insisted we take without paying.

While we were standing outside, we noticed hundreds of *rondini* (swallows) circling around the tower of the castle. They flew incredibly fast and darted about, changing direction at lightning speed, catching insects on the fly. They were amazing to watch.

As we were watching them, thoroughly entranced by their speed and gracefulness, Fabio, Tina's husband, joined us and told us, "They are fascinating creatures. There are actually two types of *rondini*: small ones that make nests in the towers and rafters of buildings and the *rondoni*, or large *rondini*. They never stop flying. They soar to altitudes of ten thousand feet and higher, spreading their wings and sleeping as they glide through the air. They have very small feet, and if they landed on the ground, they wouldn't be able to take off again and would die. We love watching them and could sit here and spend hours seeing them fly while doing their acrobatic stunts."

I noticed that, after watching the birds for a while, they simply occupied one corner of my mind without interfering with my conversations, akin to pleasant background music that every now and then hits a sweet note or chord, bringing you into awareness for an instant that you are listening to music but not enough to stop you from speaking or expressing a thought. Perhaps this was one of the ways that multitasking developed.

Fabio continued with a twinkle in his eye, obviously delighted to have an audience, even if it was only the two of us: "The two species together—*rondini* and *rondoni*—not only eat massive quantities of insects but also pollen and other miniscule matter floating through the air. This keeps the air in the areas they inhabit remarkably clean." At that point, Fabio inhaled deeply and smiled as if he had just taken a puff of a delicious cigar. A look of complete satisfaction spread across his face.

He continued with a smile, "Scientists have conducted surveys in Lupaia because of this. In so doing, they've also discovered that the area has some of the finest specimens of *pipistrelli* [bats], which are also excellent for the environment and the air. Unfortunately, for some reason, the bats are vanishing, and studies are now being conducted to try to determine why." Then Fabio spread his arms wide apart and raised them up as if he were a conductor acknowledging an orchestra after they finished a virtuoso performance. "It is an interesting story, no?"

We of course agreed and thanked Fabio for imparting such enlightening information to us. Then we said *buona notte* to him and his wife and walked home while finishing our delicious gelato and watching the *rondini* and *rondoni* continue their show until they faded into the evening darkness.

During late September of 2007, unbeknownst to me, I apparently appeared to be a scary *spaventapasseri* (scarecrow). They are used here to chase birds away from vineyards and fruit orchards. It happened like this:

It was the beginning of the hunting season, and Ceppeto and the surrounding area had always been a favorite spot for hunters to shoot *cinghiale* (wild boar). Just after sunrise was a preferred time for hunters to chase their prey before leaving for work. As much as we didn't like the sound of gunshots, especially so early in the morning, they had a legal right to do so. This happened to be the same time when I usually started doing warm-up exercises outside. When it was hot, I would just roll out of bed and throw on a pair of shorts and sandals.

On one particularly beautiful morning at about six thirty, I was on the side of the house facing the rising sun when I heard two men talking close to our property line. I approached the fence at the top of our hill and looked over the bushes. There I saw below me two hunters dressed in fatigues and carrying rifles. They were certainly the legal distance from the house, so I couldn't object. Suddenly, they looked up at me and then quickly hurried off to their car, which was parked on the road, and drove off.

I had no idea why until I realized that as I'd walked over to see who they were, I'd never stopped doing my exercises, which entailed twirling my arms in different directions while rotating my torso. The bushes I'd looked over were low to the ground, but because they were standing considerably below me, they probably could only see me from the waist up, and I must've appeared to be nude to them. Because of the early hour, my considerably long and bushy hair had been uncombed and was standing up in all different directions as if I had put my finger in a lightbulb socket. I had no doubt they thought they were seeing a madman at that hour, far more dangerous than any *cinghiale*.

The word must have spread, as there weren't any hunters to be seen until a few days later, when the buzzer on our gate rang. A man spoke into the speaker, saying that he was a hunter and would like to talk to the owner. I opened the gate and went out to find the same two hunters, again dressed in fatigues and armed with rifles, sheepishly asking for permission to hunt in the woods at the bottom of our property.

We had been living here for eight years by that time, and no hunter had ever asked for permission to hunt on our property. The number of spent shotgun shells scattered around our grounds after every hunting season attested to that. Hiding my surprise, I gave them permission as long as they stayed well away from the house and our olive grove where Pasquale worked. Their faces lit up with delight, and they thanked me profusely. So one can add one more benefit to exercising outside early each morning: remember to just keep those arms flailing.

Every year when we first arrive at Ceppeto, usually in March, we start using the olive oil from the last harvest in the November of the previous year. We also begin giving it away to a growing list of locals who look forward to receiving it, including Raffaello and his daughter, Tatiana; Maria in Lupaia and her sister, Gina, as well as their parents; a few of the older people in Lupaia; and some of the merchants in town and contractors we've used. They all bring back the large bottles we originally gave them, which have been cleaned and are ready to be filled from our *fustini* (fifty-liter aluminum containers that look much like large milk cans used on dairy farms). The sharing of our olive oil production is much appreciated, and most gratifying for us is that each year we receive some wonderful praise for the quality of the oil.

After harvesting our olives, we immediately take them to a local mill that presses them for us. We only keep the extra virgin olive oil, which is collected after the first cold pressing of the olives, and in payment we let them extract and keep the additional regular olive oil from a hot pressing.

Gina, who is an expert of sorts on olive oil, as she worked previously for olive oil producers, said our oil was perfectly "balanced." Fabio, Gina's father, has lived here all his life and said that when it was a working farm, Ceppeto's olive oil was always considered the best around. I like to think the reason it tastes good again is that we've restored the health and condition of the more than 325 old olive trees on the property and that now they produce the same quality of olives they did before being abandoned many years ago.

In 2008 we started shipping our olive oil back to the States in a container by boat. We had been bringing some of it back with us in our luggage, packed in plastic bottles, but when one broke and the bag came out dripping in oil, we decided that was not a good idea. US Customs hadn't been thrilled about it either.

Once we began giving the oil to our friends and family, demand soon outpaced our shipments as our oil was being universally praised as the best olive oil anyone had tasted. When they also heard it contained natural ibuprofen, demand grew, especially from doctors we knew. We soon found that we had to ration it so we didn't run out of it ourselves, and we started shipping more and more each year. Demand continued to outpace supply, and people began to offer to pay us for it, which we refused. This was a fun hobby and not an enterprise. We were just happy we could bring something back from Italy that everyone enjoyed.

As an interesting side note, after years of closely monitoring our use of olive oil, which we now use at every meal, I have documented an interesting phenomenon. As you may know, olive oil has the tendency to splatter, no matter how carefully you pour it. We have used every type of table dispenser, but nothing helps. What is amazing, however, is its unerring ability to splatter clothes you're wearing *exactly* in places where you do not have a napkin. Move the napkin to the left, and it targets the unprotected area to the right, and vice versa. Tablecloths get hit the same way; any area outside of your plate is subject to laser-guided, pinpoint-accurate sneak attacks.

There was no question, however, that when our olive oil was added to our wine and Mediterranean diet, we felt better here than anywhere else we had lived. And it was no surprise, as much credit is given to the Mediterranean diet and lifestyle for why Italy has the longest life expectancy of any other European country and one of the highest in the world. Fast foods and snacks are not a big part of their diet. Lunches are usually eaten leisurely at home, and here in this region, at least two hours are taken for lunch, with most of the stores closing from twelve thirty until four in the afternoon. As maddening as that is for shopping, it evidently adds a decade to the average Italian life span.

When I started coming to Italy in 1997, I rarely saw an overweight Italian. Trips to the food markets pretty much told the story why. You could hardly find any sweets or sugar-loaded snacks and prepared foods. Most food was fresh. Even in the big supermarkets, there was hardly any space devoted to calorie-laden snacks—nothing like in the United States where there's aisle after aisle of junk food.

That has slowly been changing, and now we do see more overweight people, but for the most part, they are members of the younger generation, particularly young children. Regrettably, parents are tending to spoil their children, allowing them to indulge in more sweets, not realizing the health hazard that such foods present.

But if you maintain the traditional diet of fresh food eaten slowly with a glass of red wine, you inevitably will stay slim, have more energy, sleep better, and probably live longer. Raffaello, our former caretaker, is just one of many examples we see in these parts. He

- worked until he was eighty-three years old and is still going strong. Longevity is certainly a nice bonus to go with living in a place with such beauty. Tennessee Williams wrote that "No one is getting out of here alive," but I would add, "In the meantime, you might as well enjoy it as much as possible."

(Mica just read this and said she knows better why Italians live longer: "They don't pay taxes.") There's a lot of truth to that. Italians never had much faith in their central government. For more than a millennium prior to 1861, Italy was divided into many city-states that, at one time or another, were ruled over by Spain, Austria, the Napoleonic Empire, and the Vatican. In 1861, the country was liberated and unified into the Kingdom of Italy, which was the forerunner of Italy as it exists today.

Throughout the centuries, prior to the unification and right up to the present, Italy has maintained the culture and general geographic boundaries it has today. The inhabitants typically have a deep skepticism for centralized authority, having suffered under a number of authoritarian foreign regimes including, most recently, that of Mussolini, which ended in 1945. Then, in 1946 the monarchy was abolished, and a democratic government was established. Since that time, over fifty new governments have been formed, with a change in leadership each time. This has only fueled the misgivings the citizens already had for the central authority.

Corruption in the government and throughout the political process has added to the apathy and cynicism driving people back to their city-state roots and local communities. Nationalism is rarely displayed. The only time we have seen it is when the World Cup soccer matches are held. Then, Italian flags are proudly flaunted, especially when Italy wins. Afterward, however, the flags are put away.

While the central government expects its citizens to pay their taxes, a huge percentage of them just ignore it, right down to the little guy working for himself or owning a small shop. It is something few even try to hide. When we were closing on the purchase of Ceppeto, the sellers and their representatives were there, along with Mica and me and our Italian lawyer. The broker was there too. When it came time to issue checks in payment, including the broker's commission (half is paid by the seller and half by the buyer), the broker announced in front of everyone, "Does anyone object if my commission is paid in cash?"

I was shocked and turned to my lawyer, but before he could say a word, the seller's lawyer said, "No problem," and my lawyer nodded his approval. It was done in such a casual way that I realized this must be the way it is all over Italy.

Sure enough, tax evasion is a huge problem in Italy and is a primary reason why the economy suffers as much as it does. You can't have a stable government if the citizens do not voluntarily pay taxes. Simply put: Italians do not like being governed, and many won't pay taxes.

There may be another reason Italians live longer. I figured that out when I routinely went around the house resetting clocks due to power shortages and dead batteries. I used my computer to get the correct time, which was calibrated with Greenwich Mean Time (GMT). Shortly after setting the clocks, I couldn't help but notice when going to Radda to buy some things that the clocks there were around seventeen minutes slower than my watch, which I had just reset.

I didn't think much of it until the next day when we went to Poggiponsi to do our major supermarket shopping, and I noticed the time there was different by around five minutes. Then, on Saturday, we went to Lupaia, and I noticed the clock at Maria's restaurant was also different from my watch, which I, again, had calibrated with GMT time.

All this got me thinking, and I realized one of the stark differences between here and New York is that in Italy, no one really cares much about what the right time is. No one we know here makes appointments at a given time. Everything is *verso* (about) some part of the day. You make an appointment *verso* tomorrow morning, which means any time from eight o'clock until noon. Appointments *verso* the afternoon can be any time from two until six. Anytime you arrive within these approximate ranges is considered on time.

Most stores have signs in their windows showing the hours they're open and when they are closed, but these also mean *verso*. Typically in this region, stores close for a long lunchtime at twelve thirty to one, reopening any time from three to four.

The pharmacy in Radda is a good example. They *say* they reopen at four. When in need of medicine on several occasions, we've gone there at four and have waited up to an hour for them to open. The local customers and owners act as if this is perfectly normal, but the first time that this happened to me I was ready for a double dose of tranquilizers.

Imagine what it would be like not to have to make time such an important part of your life—to remove the stress caused by trying to get to an appointment on time and getting agitated with the cab driver, traffic congestion, or anyone or anything getting in your way of arriving on time. That seems to be the Italian way, at least in this area. I'd also bet that the number of watches and clocks sold in Italy per capita is one of the lowest in the Western world. I haven't seen any Tourneau-type watch stores thriving here. But most significantly, my conclusion to all this is not giving a damn about the time is a major reason that Italians live longer.

On another subject, I've always had difficulty throwing away old clothes. First, I feel that men's clothes rarely go out of style, and unless they're threadbare, I prefer to store them away somewhere, thinking I can use them in case I have to do some work requiring protective clothing, like cleaning the chimneys (which I have never done ... but hey, you never know!). The few times I have needed clothing for a particular messy chore, I've had a cache of stuff squirreled away big enough to clothe an army, and whatever I have used hasn't made a dent in the stockpile, much to the chagrin of Mica, who is always ready to give the clothes away or throw them out.

In 2007, I finally found a use for those old clothes, and my penchant for saving all that stuff was vindicated. It happened because the birds started eating our precious grapes in the vineyard, so Pasquale made eight *spaventapasseri* (scarecrows) using my old wardrobe. They were without question the best-dressed *spaventapasseri* in Chianti, some sporting garb by famous names, such as Ralph Lauren and Giorgio Armani, with a few Gap and Eddie Bauer items thrown in. I'm not sure how scary they looked, but then again, we just wanted to keep the birds away until after the harvest. Afterward, we hoped they would return, because we enjoyed the sounds of their chirping.

A few days after the scarecrows were up, it was still too early to tell whether they were working. I did, however, notice a few flocks of birds circling above the vineyard, kind of staking out the place. I have no doubt that they were talking among themselves. *"Che strani idioti laggiu' e che diavolo stanno indossando?"* ("What strange idiots down there—what the hell are they wearing?")

A month later, we had ten scarecrows spread throughout the vineyard, and they were definitely doing their job of keeping the birds away. For the most part, the *rondini* (swallows) were the ones kept at bay and away from the grapes. The *rondini,* however, also do a great job of eating bugs, particularly *tafani* (a cross between a horsefly and a yellow jacket). *Tafani* are prevalent wherever there are animals, and in our case, that would be the *cinghiale* (wild boar). *Tafani* are ferocious and attack you relentlessly in swarms. The more you try to wave them off, the more they attack. They bite and leave lumps that itch for days.

In late summer, the *rondini* start eating large quantities in preparation for their migration south, so they normally keep the *tafani* under control, but without them around, we were being eaten alive whenever we went out.

It was impossible to go swimming. When we tried, Mica and I had to run back to the house after having been bitten on our faces and bodies numerous times. Pasquale, who never complains, wasn't able to work in the fields because it was so bad.

As soon as the weather got colder in September, however, they disappeared. We decided after that, though, that unless our wine was terrific, our well-dressed scarecrows would be a thing of the past and we'd welcome the *rondini* back to eat all the grapes they wanted—as long as they had *tafani* as their main course.

That fall, a scandal rocked Radda when long-time resident Roberto Mescolino, a practicing accountant and real estate broker, was indicted and convicted of a conspiracy that included the secret purchase of cheap wine from Puglia, transporting it to Chianti, mixing it with a small amount of much more expensive Chianti Classico, and then reselling it as Chianti Classico. His sentence included a heavy fine, six months in jail, and loss of his accountant's license.

(It was Mescolino who wanted us to buy the villa with which we initially fell in love in 1998, but then our lawyer warned us not to purchase it, because the ownership was held by a company in Lichtenstein, in which Mescolino was a partner, that had never paid any real estate taxes.)

An anonymous tip followed by surveillance with helicopters and undercover agents broke up the operation. Mescolino had a tiny vineyard in Radda certified as producing Chianti Classico. The certification ensures a high price per bottle of wine. The agents calculated how much wine the small vineyard could produce, and then their surveillance uncovered truckloads of inexpensive wine from Puglia being unloaded at the vineyard. The total number of bottles of wine Mescolino was selling was comparable to the output of a vineyard fifty times bigger.

Pasquale continues to amaze everyone, even when we are away. We learned while we were away for a couple of weeks that some people in Lupaia, who can see Ceppeto from there, saw Pasquale out one day in the rain holding an umbrella in one hand while pushing a lawn mower with the other. They couldn't believe Pasquale found a way to work outside when it was raining. This was not news to us, as Pasquale had said in the past, "When rains, before grass too wet, is good time to cut. Much grass Pasquale need cut, no waste time because rain a little."

While we were away one time, we were expecting a delivery, so we gave the courier Pasquale's cell phone number to call as he got close to our house for directions and for Pasquale to open the gate for him. When we returned, the delivery still hadn't arrived. Frankly, we had forgotten about it until we got up one morning and found the package sitting outside our door.

When we asked Pasquale about it, he said, "Driver call at 7:00 p.m., and we make plan meet in Lupaia at 6:00 in morning." Well, that meant Pasquale had to get up by at least five in the morning to get there at that hour.

I asked Pasquale, "Why didn't you tell me? I could have called and told the courier to come later and given him directions."

He said, "No want disturb you and La Signora. No want you wake up early and disturb."

"Pasquale, thank you very much, but now you have been up since before 5:00 a.m. You can go home early today."

He looked at me as if I was crazy and said, "*Capo*, no, no, Pasquale want be here, not home. Pasquale work here. I do nothing home."

Pasquale often stops for coffee at Lupaia after finishing work and sits and chats for a while before heading home. In the mornings, he stops in Radda for coffee where all the workers congregate before heading off to their jobs. Both places are where local news or gossip is disseminated. No need for local newspapers here.

In Lupaia, Pasquale said he was talking to a man who said he thought La Signora—Mica—was very attractive. Pasquale said to him, "That kind of speak Pasquale no accept. You no never talk like that of *la padrona* [lady of the house] with disrespect."

Another time a person asked him what kind of deal he had at Ceppeto, meaning his salary. Pasquale told him, "You I talk about all things, but no about me with *Capo*, no. Keep nose out of that with my *Capo*."

We don't have a clue how Pasquale developed his inner being and sense of values, but we have never before in our lives met such a balanced person. He lives in a world completely different from ours, but within that world he has set parameters for his life and his immediate family based on a self-developed value system that is remarkably fair and enlightened, albeit, sometimes quite severe by our standards. He might have learned it from his stepfather, but his stepfather had a limited amount of time and influence with Pasquale before he died. Pasquale certainly didn't get it from his mother, who, by all accounts, abused her children and was extremely cruel. His siblings that are still living are constantly in trouble. It almost seems a bit like divine intervention, not unlike how we wonder how, throughout history, people have—on their own, with no apparent influence from any outside factors—developed inspirationally significant ways to better live their lives.

I will say that Pasquale is a person who lives without fear. He projects an inner and outer strength that few people dare to test. His physical prowess is legendary in terms of the Herculean tasks he does at Ceppeto. It is on display whenever workers come, as Pasquale intercedes as soon as they arrive and does the heavy work of lifting and carrying heavy items for them. It is his way of making sure he sees and understands everything they do. He constantly pokes fun at them while he does it. They are always laughing by the time they leave.

Not so long ago, two young, twentysomething electricians were here to fix an underground cable. To get to it, they had to move a heavy terracotta urn filled with soil and a large oleander bush. It had to weigh a few hundred pounds, so they were about to get a dolly to move it. Pasquale, as always, was watching nearby and said, "Hey, youngsters, let old man like me show you way to work. You don't know how work hard like me. When you grow up, maybe you learn; meantime you need Pasquale to show you." And with that he walked over and pushed the urn to one side without any problem. The young workers were in awe.

Whenever contractors come to Ceppeto, they don't bother bringing extra help, since they know Pasquale won't let them do anything without him there using his impressive strength to help get the job done—and faster to boot. With this tact, Pasquale has won the admiration of every contractor we have ever used.

For a simple man raised in a Muslim community with all its archaic beliefs to ignore many of those precepts and forge a novel way to live and integrate into Western society is remarkable.

Our first full week at Ceppeto in 2008, the weather was glorious. Each morning, Mica and I took an hour walk through our property, marveling at how much it's become a park, thanks to Pasquale's hard work for the last five years. We can now walk all through the woods where the chestnut, oak, walnut, and maple trees are blossoming as never before, since Pasquale cut away all the ivy that was sapping the life out of them. There are many olive, fig, cherry, prune, apricot, and apple trees mixed in as well—a feast for birds, and as a result Ceppeto has become a bird sanctuary. There are birds everywhere, including European robins, swallows, finches, sparrows, larks, and even egrets, owls, woodpeckers, and doves, all treating us to a concert from sunrise to sunset (these Italians really know how to sing!).

Italy is a place where you can slow down the pace of life. A recent survey of world cities found that, from 1994 until today, people rush around 10 percent faster. Singapore came in number one in the survey, and New York ranked in the top ten, but not one Italian city did. Italy has actually been making a concerted effort to slow things down.

The mayor of Greve in Chianti, Paolo Saturnini, with whom we've had dinner on several occasions, started a movement called Slow Food with a few other mayors. The idea was to get back to eating meals slowly—especially lunch—instead of running to fast food restaurants like McDonald's. The concept grew into Slow City, which encourages city planning and development that is designed to slow traffic down, especially in smaller towns, and encourage walking and biking instead of driving.

Restaurants that have joined the movement proudly display signs in their windows showing that they are a Slow Food member. The goal of these restaurants is to serve homemade-style Italian cuisine using local ingredients cooked and served at a leisurely pace, rather than to turn over the tables as many times a day as possible.

For Slow City, streets have been redesigned to provide bike lanes, and new walking paths are being created to encourage a slow movement of people that is far more environmentally friendly than using cars or even motorbikes.

Both Slow Food and Slow City movements try to conserve the traditional, centuries-old way of life in Italy, such as eating lunch slowly during the two- to three-hour lunch break in the afternoon and either walking or riding a bicycle to get from one place to the next. These healthy habits contributed to the Italian record of having one of the highest longevity rates in the world, but in recent years Italians had unfortunately been giving in to the fast-food craze imported from America. The mad rush to eat lunch and then either head back to work or, yes, even squeeze in some hurried shopping was becoming a health problem. For me, coming to Italy from New York City, one of the fastest-paced cities in the world, was a bit jarring at first, but once I settled in, it really turned out to be a charming way to live and certainly far less stressful. Since the inception of Slow Food and Slow City, over 150 countries have joined these movements.

That year I noticed how Pasquale's ideas and opinions were evolving in an interesting manner. He expressed his disgust with radical extremist Muslims. He laments the fact that the mullahs only take poor children into their religious schools, brainwashing them and turning many of them into suicide bombers. "It is wrong what do those mullahs. They take children with no education and teach hate. Then they make them suicide bombers. They should blow up the mullahs. I never see a suicide mullah. They are cowards." Pasquale is a perfect example of how a moderate from any religion can make a difference in society. In every religion or belief system, it's predominately the ultraorthodox and conservatives who are often radical, unable to adapt to modern times and accept anything different from their beliefs.

April 25 was an Italian holiday celebrating their independence day. It came on a Friday, and the weekend was considered a holiday weekend, much as it would be here in the United States. We, of course, gave Pasquale the weekend off starting on Friday. That Saturday night at around nine o'clock, he called me and asked if he could come to work on Sunday. I asked him why, and he said, "Pasquale sitting home all day today; I bored. I can't stay home. I have no thing to do. I can do things at Ceppeto and no make noise. Please, *Capo*, it pleases me to do." So he came in Sunday and worked in the *orto* (vegetable garden).

The next morning, Pasquale and I had our usual discussion. He started off, "*Capo*, now Pasquale have forty-seven years old, I realize I don't like spend time with old friends so much. When they come to find me, I have trouble understand their thinking. We grow in different places. They in one forest and me in another. I no know who they are and how they think. I know they have same problem with me. They angry and blame everyone; don't blame themselves. *Capo*, Pasquale no blame. That waste of time. What good do it does? It makes people angry. No, no, Pasquale no time to waste for that, and I no want to listen to them complain."

He told me a story about a close friend he had invited to his house for dinner in Albania shortly before he'd left for Italy. "Yes, I invite an old friend from when I was young to house mine for dinner. We had little food, but I know he hungry. We always serve three plates of food." It is their custom to have at least three courses for dinner.

Pasquale continued, "My wife make *fagioli* [beans], big pot of them she cook slow in fireplace. That is all we afford. So my wife serve first plate. After that finish, she clear all plates, wash and dry them, and make ready serve second plate. For that, she serve more of same beans. My wife do same for third plate. When she clear last of plates from table, my friend open up his big mouth and complain. He said, 'You invite me for dinner, and all you serve me are beans?' *Capo*, I get angry, pick up my broom, and with straw end, I smack him on back and chase him out the house. No, no, *Capo*, that is *disrespett*; I no tolerate *disrespett*. I no speak to him again, never. I invite him into my house because I know he has hunger and nothing to eat. I give him what I have, and it not good enough. No, no, enough friends like that. I become more *selettivo* [selective]."

I told him, "I understand, and I experience the same thing with old friends. As the years go by, we often grow in different directions and have less and less in common. It is normal, especially when you are experiencing and learning so much more than they are. The important thing is for all of us to be open to change and continue to learn and try new things in life. You are learning much about taking care of a farm like Ceppeto. It is not an easy task. It takes lots of planning. You need to be always learning, which you do by asking questions of experts. Then you are not afraid to try new things. Look at all the trees you saved, even when the professional arborists said they would die. You figured out how to save them. That is because you have a quality that most successful people have. You don't give up without trying, and you learn by listening and doing. Pasquale, you are a smart man who has learned about life the hard way and grown smarter and better because of it. Some people never do that; they just keep making the same mistakes over and over again and never grow. Bravo, Pasquale, we are very proud of you."

Pasquale looked so happy to hear this. He grabbed my hand and kissed the back of it. Holding my hand, he said, "*Capo*, you help me, and I always grateful. You have good heart."

A few days later, while I was walking the property and simply taking in the beauty I found wherever I set my eyes, I came across Pasquale turning the soil around each of the olive trees in one of the groves.

I stopped and said, "Pasquale, do you realize how magnificent this place is? Can you see the fruit of your work and what you have done here?"

He paused in his work and rested his arms on the handle of the spade he was using. "*Capo*, Pasquale see how beautiful Ceppeto is. It the most beautiful farm in the valley. I see every day, and it makes me happy. Ceppeto like raising a child, and I know for you it like a child too; we both take good care of Ceppeto for many years, and it show us appreciation growing into a beauty."

Then Pasquale turned around, waving one arm toward the nearby trees. "The trees, Pasquale look at them every day and remember how sad they were when I came first here. Now they smiling. The flowers, I smell them every day when they full with flowers; I see they happy too. Even when a day for me no go well, I look around Ceppeto, and it make me happy. It a gift from God."

CHAPTER 25

THE GREAT AND ENDLESS WOODLANDS WAR

I knew after my first, unpleasant meetings with Martino and Elisabetta Stenosa-Furbone, the couple who'd received ownership of most of Lupaia as a wedding gift, that we'd be crossing paths again. I just sensed inevitability about it. Damned if I wasn't right.

One small incident took place when we wanted to put a traffic mirror up at the corner of the road that leads to our house and the main road to Lupaia. The land there is owned by the Furbones, and at the junction, there is a blind curve preventing us from seeing oncoming cars, thus making it dangerous to turn onto the main road.

Mica wrote a nice note—in Italian, naturally—to the Furbones, explaining the problem and asking for permission to use a few square inches of their property in order to install a pole on top of which we wanted to mount a small traffic mirror. Receiving no response, Mica tried calling them.

Elisabetta, being advised by her secretary that Mica was calling, came to the phone. Without so much as a greeting she said, "I suppose you are calling about the traffic mirror you want to put up on my property."

Mica said yes and told her it would only take a few square inches.

With a regal breath of exasperation, Elisabetta replied, "Okay," and hung up the phone.

Not a big deal, granted, but it was typical of the are-the-little-people-bothering-us-again attitude of the Furbones. I drew little solace from learning, over time, that we were not being singled out for the Furbone brand of casual rudeness. For the few residents of Lupaia who owned their own places, it seemed that confrontations with the Furbones were not unusual over matters big and small, and their attitude was always the same.

Not all of our head bumpings were so minor. In the summer of 2007, Martino had begun to cut down trees on his property to sell for firewood. He owns a lot of the land that abuts our property and had already leveled fifteen acres of trees near our land where a freshwater brook defines our property line.

It is—I should say *was*—one of the prettiest corners in all of Ceppeto. A trail winds down below our olive grove, through the woods, and out into a vineyard before turning up the main road to Lupaia.

(When it comes to Ceppeto's scenic assets, okay, I'm biased, but that same trail was named one of the "9 Most Beautiful Walks in Europe" by the *New York Times* in 2013.)

Now, to the left of the trail and right up to it, everything had been leveled. It looked like a war zone. This kind of damage was being inflicted upon the countryside in order to make money that paled in comparison to the cost of reforesting the devastated acreage, making the razing even more egregious.

We tried to do everything we could to stop him, including calling the *Forestale* (government forestry service), which is empowered to protect the forests of Italy. This kind of thing is taken very seriously here, and to emphasize that fact, they are one of the few agencies where the personnel actually carry guns while on duty. The *Forestale* sent an inspector to see what Furbone was having cut, and the inspector said that since it was their property and he had secured permits to do the work supposedly *for the health of the woods*, there was little they could do. I, frankly, sensed they were not being totally candid. It seemed to me that there was cutting for the health of the woods, and then there was the kind of decimation the *Forestale* was supposed to prevent. It was clear to me that all the good trees were being cut down and the sickly ones left standing, in violation of existing regulations designed to protect *all* forests, public and private. Someone, for some reason, decided to look the other way. As the saying goes, particularly in Italy, "Go figure!"

We therefore decided to consult an *avvocato* (lawyer) in Siena. Our first meeting, scheduled for 3:00 p.m. with *avvocato* Duccio Garri, went off to a difficult start. He was close to an hour late. We kept forgetting appointments in Italy are *verso*. Garri was from the south of Italy, where people are known to be far more casual and humorous than their more-somber northern counterparts.

Garri was about 5'9" and slightly overweight, as evident from the size of his belly, which protruded over his belt line—a not-so-subtle clue that he probably spent more time at the table than at the gym. Still, he was always meticulously dressed in a suit and tie. He had dark hair and a round, pleasant face with a perpetual smile; angry or happy, it made no difference—that smile was always there.

My assumption about the nature of his great sense of humor was that he seemed to have resigned himself to the absurdity of the Italian judicial system, Kafkaesque by way of vaudeville, and to which we were soon to be exposed. As upset as I was that he was so late, he soon had me forgetting about it with his ingratiating manner and sense of humor. Other than a typical southern aversion to punctuality, he did have an excellent professional reputation, and after hearing our problem, he called Leonardo Botta, an expert in forestry matters, to come the next day to look at the area being cut.

Leonardo arrived early the next morning, and the two of us began walking through the Furbone-devastated area of the woods. Leonardo took lots of pictures and later wrote a full report of his findings that he gave to Garri.

Leonardo found a number of violations. When clearing and cutting down trees in the woods, you must leave sixty trees per acre evenly spread out, in other words, a space of about fifteen to twenty feet between trees. Although the company technically followed that procedure, they managed to sidestep the intent of the law by leaving trees that were dead, injured, sick, and dying, while cutting down all the healthy ones that produced more firewood. That was one reason why the area looked so ravaged. There were many other violations, enough that Leonardo felt confident that we'd be able to get them stopped from proceeding and doing more damage. He did say that clearing the woods—when done properly—was a good thing for the health of the trees and should be done once every fifteen years. We had no problem with that, but to do it properly meant that Furbone got less money per acre.

Duccio Garri sent a formal letter of complaint to Elisabetta Stenosa-Furbone, who was listed as the owner of the property. Enclosed with the letter was the full report from Leonardo, along with photos of the violations. Copies were sent to city hall and the *Forestale*. The consequences of not complying were severe penalties calculated from the value of the wood produced from the trees and the damage done to the land. That penalty amount could range from thousands to hundreds of thousands of dollars, depending on the decision of the courts, plus legal fees. As a result, the *Forestale* came by twice to inspect the work, and subsequently all cutting was stopped. Moreover, the Furbones were issued a fine, the amount of which I was never able to ascertain.

However, to borrow a line from Lewis Carroll, the Great Woodlands War then got "curiouser and curiouser."

I wanted to have a survey of Ceppeto done by our *geometra* (surveyor) to mark property lines between our land and the woods that Furbone intended to cut the following year. I wanted to be sure Furbone didn't cross our line and cut our trees. The forest service and our own surveyor told us not to worry, as Furbone only used very good surveyors, but I wanted to be sure, for our own peace of mind.

Most of the boundaries are marked with trails, little huts, or a geographic feature, such as a riverbed, rocks, and so on. Also, properties in this region are divided up into dozens of odd-shaped parcels with each assigned a number on a map. Altogether, the parcels look like a jigsaw puzzle, and ours is no different. I believe this was because parcels were added to the property over the centuries as the farmers cultivated new areas. There are even irregular plots in the middle of larger pieces, which designate stands of chestnut and oak trees found deep in the woods on our property. These areas can never be cultivated. Since buying Ceppeto, we relied on Raffaello to tell us where our property boundaries were. Based on his recollection, we went ahead and put fences up in certain areas and made walking trails throughout the woods for our private use.

The new surveyor successfully identified our property line and left me a copy of the map he was using. On examination, I realized it looked as if the property line at the base of our property was actually in the area Furbone had just slaughtered. I called the surveyor back and checked again to make sure. And sure enough, Furbone had cut almost three acres of *our* property, including a rare stand of beautiful oak trees. The enchanting trail we were heartsick about losing turned out to be on *our* property, not Furbone's. The surveyor Furbone had used had made a terrible—and heartbreaking—mistake.

Duccio Garri immediately filed a lawsuit but warned us that the average time a court case takes in Italy is ten years. At the time, I found this hard to believe, but the more time we spend in Italy, the more I come to realize the extent to which the government and judicial system are dysfunctional. Every encounter we have with the bureaucracy here reinforces our bewilderment at how Italy remains standing. Nothing functions normally, yet the country confounds outsiders by somehow continuing on.

I did not relish the idea of starting a lawsuit, but the fact was that they destroyed one of the most treasured walks on our property, which is something that cannot be replaced in our lifetimes. For Mica and me, it is gone forever. This is something we want to make sure never happens again for the sake of those who will follow us at Ceppeto.

We have always tried to respect our neighbors here and at home. As an example, when we received the surveyor's report, I realized that, by accident, we had built a fence to keep *cinghiale* out of our gardens and had planted some olive trees all on our neighbor's property. We hadn't overstepped by much, but it was enough for me to go to our neighbor Pietro Medele and apologize. I offered to either take the fence down and move it or pay him for the small parcel.

Pietro and his wife, Angela, are wonderful people. They only spend a few weeks a year in their home, shuttling between here and their homes in Milan and Spain. Pietro was an art dealer who knew Picasso, Picabia, and many of the great twentieth-century artists.

Pietro laughed at my offer and said, "Richard, what possible difference will it make in my life? Leave it; it is too much trouble to even bother with." Then he said, demonstrating the difference between being a member of the upper class and being someone *with* class, "While you are here, come in, and let's have a drink."

Our maiden voyage into the infamous Italian judicial system began in 2009. Our case was in the able hands of Duccio Garri. It took two years to get our *first* hearing where evidence was presented. All the photos and expert reports from Leonardo Botta, as well as surveys, appraisals of the damage, a videotape and narrative I had made of the entire area, correspondence between the parties, and a legal brief from Garri were submitted.

On the day of the hearing, the judge entered the courtroom and announced that all the papers and documents that had been presented to the court had been lost and would need to be replaced. The case was adjourned for another year.

The following year, our written testimony had to be resubmitted and notarized at the Italian consulate in New York City. It was written in Italian, and Mica's and my signatures were notarized there.

A notary in Italy is quite different from a notary in America. In Italy, a notary is almost on the same level as a lawyer, except they cannot try cases in court, but they are called on to authenticate documents and not just witness signatures, as is the main function of an American notary. To become a notary in Italy, one must have training similar to a lawyer, so when they notarize a document, they are confirming that it is authentic from the submitting party.

When our notarized testimony was submitted to the court, Furbone's attorneys claimed it was not valid because the woman that was the notary at the Italian consulate in New York City could not be verified as qualified and authentic herself. The judge then adjourned the matter until a new set of documents that could be properly authenticated could be submitted. When Mica told the notary at the Italian consulate what had happened, she was furious and an intrajudicial squabble ensued between the Italian consulate in New York City and the Italian judiciary. The result was that our testimony was resubmitted, and although accepted this time, the trial was not scheduled to reconvene for *another* year (which, for those of you keeping count, would make a total of four years).

Preliminary conferences were then held to gather yet more data from the experts on both sides. Then the judge would review that and reschedule a hearing about all the facts to be presented and make a decision shortly thereafter. But even after making a decision, he would need up to *another two years* to decide on what damages, if any, were to be assessed.

So it looks like our case will take at least ten years (just as Garri warned), as I am sure that we have not seen the end of additional delays. It is an example of the dysfunctional nature of the judicial system here in all its glory. It is also one of the reasons Italy today is in so much trouble. No business would ever want to come to this country and be faced with a court system that takes ten years to decide a case. The legal system favors corrupt and illegal activities by making it impossible to get a quick resolution of a matter that may be causing irreparable damage to a business. Who in their right mind would want to risk that, on top of all the normal risks a business faces when trying to become a successful operation? It is just one reason— among many, sadly—that has caused the Italian economy to collapse. The people have no faith in the central government, and after getting just a small whiff of the governmental machinery here, it is painfully clear that it is for good reason.

As the saying goes, "That's not all, folks!" In May 2013, we met with Garri in Siena for an update. It was by then the sixth—yes, sixth—anniversary of the lawsuit. Garri told us—all the while smiling as if he were telling a joke and about to come to its punch line—that the case was now in front of the *third* judge appointed to hear it (the first judge had gotten sick and couldn't continue, and the second judge had moved to Rome, out of the jurisdiction of our case). Garri thinks this new judge is a good one. I'm not sure what that means in Italy, but it is beginning to seem like an oxymoron.

Having said all that, in Italy a verdict can be appealed twice, so if the Furbones lose and decide to appeal, our case could drag on for even more than ten years, as each appeal usually takes another two years. The final decision ending our case will have to come in a sequel to this book.

In the meantime, this is a tragically common theme no matter where in the world one lives. Things may appear tranquil and peaceful from the outside—whether it be a family, a corporation, a government, a country—but once you lift the curtain and take a peek inside, there is always some turmoil, someone or something that, through greed, hunger for power, or sheer ignorance, will try to disrupt the lives of others for their own selfish desires.

Here at Ceppeto, this six-hundred-year-old paradise has seen it all—and many times over, considering all the human folly and foibles it has undoubtedly experienced, witnessed, and suffered in that time. Yet still it stands as a symbol that some places are impervious to the avarice of that most ravenous and dangerous of species: human beings.

CHAPTER 26

THE BAD, THE GOOD, THE CRAZY

In 2007, we hired a housekeeper whose name, by coincidence, happened to be Pasqualina. She was doing an excellent job inside the house. For the first time in seven years, we seemed to have the household help that we needed.

When we flew to Italy from the States, we usually had a car service pick us up at the airport at either Milan or Pisa. This last trip, we decided to fly to Florence after a stopover in Milan and asked Pasquale to drive our car to pick us up. He decided to have Pasqualina drive, saying that he thought she was a better driver than he was. When we arrived, waiting for us in the terminal were both Pasquale and Pasqualina: all 5'5" of Pasquale with his mustache and checkered golf hat and all 5'4" of Pasqualina in a dated skirt and blouse. Neither had ever flown, so they were excited to be in the terminal to greet us. The two of them, instead of us, looked like startled immigrants just arriving.

When I saw them waiting, I wanted to start singing, "Pasqualina, Pasqualee, tiny little things. Pasqualina dance, Pasqualee sing, Pasqualina, Pasqualee, what's the difference if you're so very small ..."

When Pasquale saw us, he ran toward us like a long-lost child. He threw his arms around me, kissed my hand and then Mica's, and didn't stop hugging and welcoming us for a few minutes, while

Pasqualina waved from the other side of the barrier. Moments like these made us realize how important we were to him.

Having been up for twenty-four hours, I wasn't ready to drive, but as it turned out, neither were Mica or I quite prepared for Pasqualina's driving. God only knows why Pasquale thought her driving was better than his, but if that was true, then he must drive like a maniac.

I was stomping on the imaginary brake on the passenger's side and had white knuckles grasping the armrest the whole trip. Mica was in the backseat, trying not to look, and I swear, despite having converted to Judaism years earlier, if she had had rosary beads with her, she would have had them out, praying for our salvation. How we got to Ceppeto in one piece is beyond me. The bigger question is how Pasqualina managed to drive our car to the airport.

Exiting the parking lot, she kept putting the car in first gear instead of reverse and then in reverse instead of first. Cars and people scattered to get out of the way. After running a red light, we finally settled down a little bit on the highway. Then came the tolls for entering the expressway. She couldn't reach the ticket from the automatic dispenser and had to back up and move closer, which wouldn't have been so bad if there hadn't been a car behind us and if she'd been able to tell reverse from first gear. Miraculously, she got the ticket with no one getting bumped, injured, or maimed. I was praying that my insurance would cover us when—not if—we got into an accident.

On the expressway, she didn't know how to shift into fourth or fifth gear, so we roared along at four thousand rpms the whole way in third gear. At that point, I was thinking, *Well, the car is already five years old anyway,* and I kept thinking—well, *hoping*—it had to get better.

It didn't. Still, we arrived in one piece.

It was the last time we asked Pasqualina to drive.

Now Pasqualina, at just 5'4", was a tiny bit shorter than Pasquale. She was a little plump and appeared to be the most timid person you were likely to ever meet. She had large, perfectly round blue-green eyes that welled up with tears at the drop of a hat. If you told her the cats needed fresh water in their bowls, she became teary-eyed, telling you how sorry she was for not having thought to do that herself. If I said something nice to her, like, "Pasqualina, that was a very good cake you made for us, thank you very much," she would get tears in her eyes and not be able to speak for a few minutes.

I had learned, however, that when she did start to speak, *she didn't stop*, going on and on and on. I started pretending that I didn't understand her, so that I wouldn't get caught up in any conversations with her. To make matters worse, she had a high-pitched, squeaky voice that hurt the eardrums, especially in the mornings when I was not yet fully awake. I know I have painted a terrible picture of her, which is not fair, because she was a good and dedicated housekeeper, the best to ever work for us. I am not sure if her condition was psychological, but there was definitely a condition there of some kind. That was why I did not want to intervene with her driving. She would have been devastated.

A number of weeks later, I realized how lucky we were to have gotten home safe that day when she drove us from the airport. I was enjoying a nice lunch by myself in the kitchen while reading, when suddenly I heard an earsplitting roar. I knew instantly it had to be a fighter jet flying low over our house, as they occasionally do from the NATO base in Pisa.

My first instinct was to duck, but in another split second, I realized I also heard music blasting over the roar of the jet engines, so it couldn't be a plane after all. I looked out the window, and lo and behold, I saw our timid little Pasqualina roaring out of the driveway in her Fiat Panda, which is the size of a Volkswagen Beetle. Pasqualina was fiercely gripping the steering wheel while bobbing up and down to the beat of the blaring rock music. I watched in utter awe as she sped out of the gate and down the road in a cloud of dust, the noise of her engine—which she apparently never shifted out of first gear— roaring and the blaring music slowly fading away.

Her almost bipolar personality soon took its toll on all of us, including Pasquale, and regrettably, Pasqualina left after a year. We have since found yet another housekeeper, who is decidedly much more well adjusted, calm, and capable. And so far, I have not been startled with the roar of jet engines and blaring hard rock music. Calm has returned to Ceppeto.

That summer, the social event of the year was Betti's wedding. Betti is the granddaughter of our original caretaker, Raffaello; her parents are Tatiana and Luciano Sori, with whom we've become very friendly. Betti was the runner-up in the Miss Italy contest a few years ago and is, as you'd expect, gorgeous. She's close to six feet tall, and today is a top model. Her husband is a local young man who is handsome and charming. They make a beautiful couple.

The wedding took place in the church in Castellina in Chianti. About two hundred people attended. Betti had attended our wedding in Radda, and she told Mica that she too wanted to walk down the street to the altar in her wedding dress the same way that Mica had. And that's exactly what Betti did. It was a spectacular entrance and brought back fond memories of Mica looking every bit as beautiful at our wedding, eight years ago.

In the church, there was a man standing behind the altar who I at first thought was the priest conducting the ceremony. I was told he was actually the altar boy. Now, I haven't been to many Catholic weddings, but I've been to enough to know that the altar boy is usually a young boy who lights candles and does various other things to help the priest with the service. This guy was at least fifty-five years old, short and stocky, with a three-day growth on his face, wearing a white jacket that looked like the ones butchers wear (I was too far away to see if there were any butcher-shop-type stains on it). He was balding, and what hair he had was cut very short. I swear he looked more like a hit man than an altar boy. I guess there's a shortage of young people interested in participating in church services these days.

The priest was old and bent over and had difficulty speaking loud enough for everyone to hear, although he was miked. The sound system had problems, so it kept shutting off or making noises that sounded like a shofar, the ram's horn that is blown in synagogues to announce the Jewish New Year and the end of Yom Kippur. In fact, the ceremony, for me, was indeed a lot like the Jewish high holy days in a synagogue: I couldn't understand a word, and there was a lot of standing up and sitting down. I must admit, the beautiful setting aside, after over an hour of this I was getting *spielghis* (Yiddish for "ants in your pants").

After the ceremony, we drove to the reception in an eighteenth-century villa overlooking San Gimignano, the medieval town famous for its towers, and watched a beautiful Tuscan sunset as appetizers and drinks were served. The sit-down dinner was a feast. On the terrace, there were tables set for eight people each. Spectacular views abounded, particularly of the towers in San Gimignano. Everything was lit by candlelight. Upon each table were bottles of locally produced Chianti Classico red wines as well as a variety of whites. There were trays of bread, cheese, and lots of olive oil. I lost count of the number of courses served, but it included chicken, *cinghiale*, veal, meatballs, pasta, vegetables, salads, hot *tortas* stuffed with cheese, fruits, and vegetables. Not to mention the ceremony of the cutting of the wedding cake, which was followed by grappa and vin santo. There were many toasts made throughout the evening and dancing to live music. We finally left at one in the morning. Raffaello; his wife, Marina; Tatiana; Luciano; Betti; and her new husband were thrilled we attended. They all made us truly feel like part of their family.

We learned that Furbone wasn't having his annual big bash this year. It was usually held on August 15 to celebrate Saint Lorenzo and was one of the biggest annual bashes in this area, with a band, food, fireworks, and teems of people converging on poor little Lupaia. It had been held annually for at least the last twenty-five years or more.

For us, it had always been a big nuisance because the noise traveled to Ceppeto and made it impossible to sleep. There were always problems with young people getting drunk, and two years ago, a gang attacked a Carabiniere. Last year a gang stood outside Furbone's house, taunting him, and the Carabinieri had to be called to disperse them.

Several years ago, when we were staying in Lupaia during the renovation of our house, we took our station wagon to Ceppeto and tried to sleep there during the night of the party. As romantic as it may sound, it was far from it. Yes, watching the falling stars on a beautifully clear night was spectacular, but trying to get comfortable in the back of the station wagon with all the seats folded down was not easy. Even with several layers of blankets to serve as a mattress, the seat buckle fittings still protruded enough to make it difficult to find a comfortable position. Then the mosquitoes discovered us and began having a feast. Finally, with little sleep, at around six in the morning, Mica decided to walk back to Lupaia, while I fed our cats. When I got back to our apartment, Mica was beside herself.

A drunken young man had stopped her and asked if she'd let him stay at her house so he could have a place to sleep. Understandably, she freaked out and ran to the apartment, locking herself inside. The man continued to knock on the door, pleading to be let in. I had no idea that this had happened, and when I arrived, I saw that very man walking away from our porch. He asked me if I could give him a place to sleep, and seeing he was quite drunk, I sent him away without giving him a second thought. When Mica told me what had happened and what he had done, I went back out looking for him, but by then, he'd disappeared.

It turned out that he'd started walking down the hill from Lupaia and, an hour or so later, had flagged down Raffaello, who was on his way to Ceppeto. He had asked Raffaello for a ride.

Raffaello had looked at the man's feet and asked, "What are you wearing?"

"Shoes," he had replied.

"Yes, and they're worn so a person can walk. Get moving."

With that in mind, we won't be sorry not to have to deal with Furbone's parties again.

CHAPTER 27

THE MENAGERIE

Mica and I both love animals. We have always wanted a dog, but living in New York City is a tough place to have one. Mica did have a dog before I met her, but it became too difficult for her to keep, so she brought it to Italy and gave it to her family. When I met Mica, we each had adopted cats. She had two, and I had three. Mine traveled with me everywhere, including on voyages on my sailboat as far away as the Caribbean. They actually handled brutal open-sea storms— some of which lasted as long as ten days—better than I did. I even had special life jackets for them that were hooked onto lifelines so they couldn't fall overboard. When Mica and I began living together, five cats became too much, and Mica again sent one to her family in Italy (I guess it kept her dog company), and I gave two away to my family. To this day, we still have two cats in New York City.

When we arrived at Ceppeto for the first time in March of 1999, we had no kitchen equipment, no stove, no refrigerator—nothing but a sink, as everything else had been removed by the previous owners when they left. We had to eat all meals out for about a month until we were able to replace everything we needed in order to start having meals at home. One evening, while having dinner at a restaurant in Radda, a newborn kitten kept playing at our feet. As are all newborn kittens, this one was adorable. We asked our waiter about it, and he told us he had just adopted it from a litter and that there were still kittens left that needed a home. We found out where the litter was and quickly finished our dinner before rushing a few blocks away to see them.

By the time we got there, only two were left, along with a surrogate mother cat that was still nursing them. The mother cat, for some reason, was unable to nurse these last two. A little gray fluff ball was all over us the moment we arrived next to the box in which they were being kept. The other one, hiding in the corner of the box and refusing to come out, was apparently the runt of the litter and was even tinier when compared to the meet-and-greet gray one. It was a female, with red streaks in its taupe-colored fur, and it had a constantly worried look on its face.

It is amazing to me to observe, whether in animals or human beings, how personalities are already formed by the time creatures are born. Often times, no matter what the upbringing, the personalities remain as they were at birth. For a parent, that can often be the source of great joy ... or quite the opposite.

I remember the scene in Peter Shaffer's play *Equus* where the mother, at one point, in so many words, asks the psychiatrist treating her son why he turned out the way he did, since she thought they were doing everything right for him. And the psychiatrist answers, while shrugging his shoulders, "It must be a matter of genes." After being a parent and watching the children of many of my friends turn out so completely different—in good and bad ways—I do believe, just like with animals, it is indeed a matter of genes, and we have less control over them than we care to accept.

We happily brought these two kittens back to Ceppeto that same night, and they became fixtures here for over ten years. The happy, friendly gray one we named *Fumo* (Smoke), and the shy taupe one we named *Fiamma* (Flame). As they aged, we became more concerned about their ability to survive at Ceppeto, given the number of fights they'd had with stray cats and other wild creatures.

Surprisingly, little Fiamma was far more adept at defending herself than Fumo, who grew into a big, strong, imposing creature but a real *pacifista* (pacifist). He hated to fight. As a result he was suffering from many battle wounds with pieces of his ears missing and with some nasty-looking scars on his body.

Fiamma, in contrast, just had one nick on an ear, but between the two cats, we decided we couldn't leave them at Ceppeto for long periods of time while we were back in the States. So we brought Fumo with us to New York and gave Fiamma to Mica's mother in Italy. It worked out well for both of them. By the way, Italian bureaucracy also extends to cats. In order to get permission to take Fumo out of the country, we needed to go to the government agency for animal control, where they issued him an Italian passport, complete with his photo.

When we returned to Ceppeto the following year, Pasquale greeted us with a surprise. He had saved a cat that was being abused by the children of a family living near his apartment. He felt bad for it and brought it to Ceppeto. He told us, "Ceppeto needs a cat, and I want it to be a *regalo* [gift] for you."

We were skeptical at first, especially because the cat was afraid of its own shadow and we couldn't get near it without it running off and hiding. But thanks to Mica's patience and love for animals, she finally gained its trust, and now, Ceppetina, as we call her, is a sweetheart of a cat, just as friendly and affectionate as any cat we have ever owned.

In March 2011, when we returned to Ceppeto, all seemed tranquil. One day, I looked out of my office window and saw what I swore was something akin to a Loch Ness monster: a long white neck was sticking out above the tall grass in our neighbor's field. His house was kept closed for all but two weeks per year, so I knew that they were not home. I had no idea what this serpentine thing was and immediately went to ask Pasquale about it. He said he had seen it a few times, as had some of the people from Lupaia, and that it was a llama, an animal hardly indigenous to Italy.

Pasquale said he'd heard that an animal preserve run by a local community about a forty-five-minute drive from Ceppeto had run out of funds. When some of their animals escaped, they didn't have the resources to try to recapture them. Apparently, a few llamas and monkeys had broken out and were now roaming about the countryside. The wolves in the area posed a threat to them, and it was reported that one of the llamas had already died. No one seemed to know what to do.

I didn't see the llama again for a week or so, and then one day I heard a dog barking incessantly on our neighbor's property. I went out to see what the commotion was all about and saw that a couple had wandered onto the neighbor's property with their small dog, which was barking like crazy at the poor llama. I yelled at them to get the dog on a leash and stop scaring the llama. They put a leash on the dog and hurriedly left.

As I got closer, I realized the llama had a rope around its neck and was dragging the end of it along the ground. I assumed that someone had probably tried to capture it at one point. Mica and I felt that the llama was in danger, so the next day Pasquale and I began trying to lure it onto our property by putting out water and grain for it to drink and eat. It took only a couple of days, and the llama seemed to be content to stay around our property. At that point it had somehow managed to slip off its rope.

By this time, Mica had called the veterinarian we use for the cats, and he put her in touch with a vet that specializes in large animals. He told her that llamas were very social, but if they hadn't been in contact with humans from birth, it would be difficult to domesticate them enough to even be able to touch them.

Our llama must have had plenty of human contact, because we soon found it appearing out of nowhere and following us as Mica and I took our daily walks through the woods on our property. It seemed to like the sound of Mica's voice (well, what's not to like?), and it soon began coming closer and eating leaves from the branches Mica held in her hand, even following her all the way back to the house, only to wander off again. We dubbed the llama Ceppettone.

As the days went by, Ceppettone would show up almost every day at the most unsuspecting times and places. One week, a repairman came to fix the heater in our swimming pool. When he finished, I asked him to wait on the patio outside our kitchen while I went inside to get money to pay him. When I returned to the patio, the repairman asked me, "Is it domesticated?"

I had no idea what he was talking about, and at first thought I misunderstood his Italian and that he was asking me if *I* was domesticated. I was about to answer with a snide retort, when I realized he was looking over my shoulder. I turned, and there was Ceppettone standing behind me on the patio, nonchalantly watching the two of us, with those great big beautiful blue eyes and Miss Piggy–length eyelashes, maintaining a stance that was unequivocally regal. The expression on her face (with lashes like that, it was hard not to think of Ceppettone as a she) seemed comically quizzical, as if she were about to ask, "So what are you guys doing here?" Then she casually turned and sauntered off toward some rosebushes that seemed to interest her more.

Ceppettone became something of an attraction for the locals, and they began coming by to try to get a glimpse of her. Mica and I were at a restaurant one day, and as we walked by the bar, we were stopped and asked, "Aren't you the people who have the llama on your property?" It was the subject of most conversations wherever we went.

It's delightfully amazing to see how an animal can change people's attitudes and make them, well—and I do appreciate the irony here—perhaps more human. When people talked about Ceppettone or saw her, they smiled and were clearly feeling happier. Ceppettone has a presence that radiates elegance and kindness in a spiritual way. I think we need more llamas in the world. Maybe we'll bring her back to New York City to visit the UN.

Having become very attached to Ceppettone, we decided she would be safer if we built a corral and kept her there. We had plenty of space and had Bini, our contractor, begin to build one that was over an acre in an area with many trees and terraces. It would be ideal for the llama to be able to get good exercise and contained the vegetation she liked to eat. But we also knew that if we didn't adopt her formally, there could be people complaining that we were preventing them from seeing her, so we called the city hall in the town of Cavriglia, which was in charge of the animal park from which Ceppettone had escaped, and made an appointment to meet the mayor there.

When we went to Cavriglia, we were expecting something on the order of the city hall in Radda, but it turned out to be much bigger, with an impressive palazzo housing all the town's offices, including the Carabinieri. The mayor, Enrico Corpini, looked like a young Al Pacino, dressed in a fashionable, perfectly tailored brown suit and tie, wearing wingtip shoes with hand-tooled leather tips, backs, and eyelets for the laces and a tan fabric in between the leather sections. I formed such a well-defined mental image of his footwear because His Honor was only about 5'4" tall. Every time I talked to him, I had to look down, so I couldn't miss seeing his shoes. His whole natty ensemble stood out even more so because all the other people in his office seemed to be dressed in a style that could best be described as "vintage sloppy," something we don't find unusual here.

The mayor greeted us warmly and ushered us into his towering conference room, easily fifteen feet high, with wood-paneled walls and a coffered ceiling from which hung three intricately carved gilded wood chandeliers running the length of the room. Heavy, faded-green, wool drapes framed three of the floor-to-ceiling windows. The inlaid dark wood floors were mostly covered by a threadbare, oriental-type rug. At one time, the room must have been majestic looking and an ideal setting for the signing of some very serious documents, which now seemed a bit paradoxical to be used for the signing of adoption papers for a llama. Mayor Corpini called in Eduardo, his vice mayor, and Fabio, the zoologist for the park from where the llamas had escaped. The mayor said, "We are grateful for you wanting to adopt the llama. We have a herd of seventeen llamas in the park, and oftentimes, when the males are rejected and get upset, they try to escape, and in this case three were successful." His mention that the escapees were males overturned our assumption that Maybelline-lashed Ceppettone was a female.

I said, "You know, we had assumed the llama was a female but weren't sure. However, when Ceppettone was kissing Mica's hand one day, Mica became suspicious of that assumption when she noticed that maybe Ceppettone had male equipment. We should have realized then that Ceppettone was, indeed, a clever male." Everyone laughed in agreement.

The zoologist added, "They are really great animals, and they can be very amusing. They do like company, however, and that can either be another llama or another animal, such as a donkey or a goat. Unless you want to start raising llamas, I would not suggest getting a female llama. You would have to keep them separated as the males want to mate constantly and can traumatize the females."

I replied most emphatically, "That is good to know because there is no way we want to start raising a herd of llamas. We like the idea of having just one as we think they are quite charming. We will try to find a goat or donkey as his companion. Right now, as we speak, we are in the process of building a large corral for him."

Fabio said, "It is important that it is big enough for him to roam around and have shelter from the cold and the rain, as well as adequate shade."

I replied, "It has lots of trees and terraces, so he can get good exercise going up and down. Altogether, it is about two acres, and we plan on building a stable for him once it is official that we can adopt him."

The mayor jumped in, "Oh, that will just be a formality. We are sure you will take good care of him. We will be sending out our veterinarian to see you and to examine the llama as well as give you pointers on how best to feed and care for him. If you have any questions at any time, you can call him."

Actually we knew before adopting Ceppettone that we had to lure her—ahem, him—into a corral, which, as of ten o'clock on the morning of our meeting, was not yet ready but was being worked on by Pasquale and Bini. While we were providing the information for the adoption papers, the zoologist, Fabio, took a telephone call in the next room and shortly returned to inform us, "I just received a call from an Ugo Rossi, who owns an inn, saying that he has a llama eating up his garden and wants the animal removed immediately. He knew that some llamas had escaped from our park, so he called us."

By coincidence, Mica and I knew Ugo Rossi quite well, as he lived a short distance from us.

Fabio said, "I have no choice but to have someone go there, and if they can't catch the llama, they will have to tranquilize it with a dart, and then we will be forced to return it to the zoo here by law and, unfortunately, cancel the adoption."

Mica and I looked at each other and read each other's minds. The thought of shooting and tranquillizing Ceppettone, who we now considered "our" llama, was a terrible development. I knew that such an action could harm the animal, as well as traumatize him. We knew we had to do something quickly. The mayor and Fabio were almost as anxious as we were, since they really wanted us to adopt the llama.

Mica, in front of everyone, called Ugo. "Hi, Ugo, Richard and I are coincidently here with the mayor and zoologist with whom you just spoke. We are adopting the llama and are sure it is the same one we want. If they have to come out to your place now and remove it, we will not be able to adopt it. Can you please just wait one more day? We are building a corral right now, and I am sure that by the end of today we will be able to get him in there so he won't cause you any more problems."

Mica held the phone away from her ear so we could all hear what Ugo's response was: "Mica, this is a big problem for us at the inn. It is the beginning of our season and I simply can't jeopardize it for the sake of a wild llama, who is eating all our flowers."

Mica replied, "Okay, I understand. We are coming right now, and I assure you that we will take care of it. It will take us about an hour to get there, but in the meantime, I will send Pasquale to see what he can do."

Ugo said, "I have little choice but to wait for either you or the park to get him out of here. Whoever gets here first will have to take the llama away."

Ugo hung up, and we turned to Fabio and the mayor and said we would come back to sign the papers if we were successful in getting Ceppettone corralled. They understood, but the mayor interjected, "Unfortunately, by law when we get a complaint like this we must send men from the park to either capture it peacefully or by tranquilizer. In either case, they are then required to return it to the park, and two men are on their way right now."

Fabio said, "What makes it worse is that there have been a number of calls from your area recently complaining about a llama eating vegetation, but then it would disappear so nothing could be done. Please understand that we would love for you to adopt the llama—it would be good for both the llama and our park—but our hands are tied. We must show we are doing our job and duty correctly."

We both nodded and said, "Yes, we understand. We will call you and let you know what happens." We said a hurried good-bye and raced to our car.

Mica immediately called Pasquale and said, "Pasquale, listen carefully: there is a problem with Ceppettone. He is eating the flowers at Ugo's inn, and the officials of the park have dispatched a team to capture him and return him to the park. If that happens, we won't be able to adopt him."

Pasquale responded, "But why can't they just wait?"

Mica was getting impatient. "Pasquale, please. There is no time to explain. Go to Ugo's house as fast as you can and make sure nothing happens until we get there. If the park people arrive before we do, keep them away from Ceppettone."

There was no doubt in our minds that Pasquale would lay down his life on orders like that, so we felt that the llama would be safe.

Why all this was happening at the very moment we were getting the adoption papers signed was beyond me, but we were happy to be there when it did so we could try to do something about it. A bit karmic, wouldn't you say?

As we drove to Ugo's inn, Mica kept trying to get in touch with Bini, who had not quite finished the corral. At this point, we had an emergency on our hands, and we needed it finished immediately. If we couldn't lure Ceppettone back to our place, there was a chance we would lose him.

Bini was not answering his cell phone. As we approached Radda, we knew he had a job nearby, so we went looking for him. Suddenly, he passed us, going in the opposite direction and waved at us, obviously unaware we were looking for him. I turned around and chased after him, catching up to him right outside Radda. He pulled over, and we told him the problem. He understood and got on his cell phone and dispatched his son and another worker to Ceppeto to get the unfinished corral quickly wired with an electrical fence that would keep Ceppettone safely inside, buying Bini the time to finish the corral.

That is, provided that we could get Ceppettone in there, which would be a tall order indeed.

Mica and I then drove toward Ugo's inn and called Pasquale, who was waiting for us there, telling him to go *back* to Ceppeto and wait for Bini and his crew.

When we arrived at Ugo's, Ceppettone was there, munching away on some beautiful ornamental bushes. The *guardiani*, as the employees from the park are called, had just left before Pasquale, who wouldn't let them touch Ceppettone. They thankfully didn't make a whole to-do about it, which I suspect was done with the tacit approval of Mayor Corpini. We found Ugo and his wife, Martina, anxiously waiting for us, along with their huge but gentle dog that looked more like a small lamb, with hair so long you couldn't even see its face. They were nervous and worried that Ceppettone could be dangerous but were understanding when we assured them that we would try to lure Ceppettone back to our place, even if we had to put a rope around his neck and gently coax him along. Ugo gave us a rope and gave some leafy vegetables to Mica, who tried to get Ceppettone to come to her. After a while, he did approach and kissed her hand. At that same moment, Ceppettone noticed the dog but instead of being spooked, he sauntered off toward it, apparently thinking anything that big and furry had to be a good candidate for a companion.

No matter what we did after that, we couldn't get Ceppettone's attention. Assuring Ugo and his wife that we would be back shortly with reinforcements, we drove the short distance back to Ceppeto.

We found Pasquale, Bini, and his crew finishing up the temporary corral. Bini left shortly thereafter, and about ten minutes later, he called to tell us to hurry and come up the back road from Lupaia toward Ugo's house: Ceppettone was on the road heading toward Lupaia.

Mica grabbed some sugar, and then she, Pasquale, and I jumped into my car, and off we raced. The road through Lupaia was blocked by construction just on the way to go toward Ugo's, but the crane that was in the way had raised its arm just as we arrived, and, without stopping, we raced under it. We cast quick glances at the scowling construction workers as we passed them and their sign declaring the road was closed.

A few hundred meters up the dirt road, we saw Ceppettone ambling toward us, with Bini walking behind him to make sure he continued to head in our direction. I stopped the car, turned off the ignition, opened my window, and held out the bag of sugar. Ceppettone stopped and stuck his nose in the bag but apparently lacked a sweet tooth, as he scooted away, continuing down the road toward Lupaia. Mica and Pasquale got out of the car and followed on foot.

I turned the car around and followed slowly, lagging far enough behind so as not to bother Ceppettone, while Bini continued on his way in the opposite direction. Just as Ceppettone got to a small path leading from the road to our property through the woods bypassing Lupaia, he started running, knowing he was close to Ceppeto.

As Pasquale followed him, Mica got in the car, and we drove back to Ceppeto. Once there, Mica tried to get Ceppettone to follow her toward the temporary corral, but to no avail. He seemed content to graze in the open field. Meanwhile, Bini's crew continued to work feverishly to complete the electric fence.

The situation seemed somewhat stabilized for the moment, so Mica and I both came back to the house, thankful for the opportunity to get warmed up. That day, of all days, had been bitterly cold, and as the day had worn on, it looked as if it would start raining momentarily. Just as we began getting a little warmer, we heard Pasquale yell up to us, "*Capo*, La Signora, Ceppettone is inside the corral."

Mica grabbed three apples and a dish of sugarcane, and we raced down to the corral. Pasquale and the other two workers had quietly surrounded Ceppettone in the field where he was grazing and gently urged him along until he entered the corral, which consisted of only electrical wires strung on wooden posts but was adequate to keep Ceppettone from escaping. They then hooked up the wires to close the opening and turned on the electricity. Ceppettone was now safely inside.

We notified the city hall in Cavriglia, and they sent a vet a few days later, by which time we had added wood posts and heavy fencing to the electrical wires. The vet complimented us on the corral and said it was ideal for the llama, as it had plenty of room for him to graze and good terraces where he could get plenty of exercise. He said Ceppettone was in good health but encouraged us to find some sort of companion for him. Since getting another llama was not an option for us, he suggested, as Fabio had, that a goat, lamb, or pony would do.

It took a few days more for Pasquale and I to make wooden gates big enough to get a tractor into the corral to move feed and, if the need arose, Ceppettone himself. Two weeks later, we had a stable built, and Ceppettone seemed very content.

My routine in the mornings was to feed the cat first and then go down to the corral to feed Ceppettone, but one morning before I even left the house to start that routine, the phone rang. I answered, and a woman pleasantly said, "*Buon giorno.* I am calling from the office of Castello di Lupaia."

I instantly thought that, despite as pleasant-sounding as she was, this could not be a good call coming from the office of our beloved Furbones.

She asked, "Are you Richard Hadar?"

I said, "*Sono io,*" and she continued, "Oh good. I am glad I found you. Our supervisor for the Castello, Simone, just called and told me that he has seen a llama a couple of kilometers down the hill from Lupaia, and he was wondering if it is yours."

My heart skipped a beat or two, but I selfishly was hoping against hope that perhaps this was another llama that had escaped from the animal park. I said, "I haven't been to the corral yet this morning, but if you give me your number, I will check it right now and call you back." I took her number and, with my heart in my throat, ran down to the corral and, to my surprise, found one of the gates wide open.

Ceppettone had escaped.

I ran back to the house, yelling for Pasquale, who was working nearby, to come right away. As I was running, I was struck by what a magnificent day it was, as clear and sunny as it had ever been since we'd arrived. Ceppettone at least had the good sense to break out on a nice day.

Arriving back at the house a bit out of breath, I hurriedly told Mica what was happening and called back the woman from Lupaia, telling her that it was our llama. She told me that the supervisor, Simone, had seen the llama on a road next to the new cantina at the bottom of the long winding hill from our house. It was a huge new cantina built by the Beretta family—the same Berettas that make the guns. The cantina was a spectacular facility, immodestly called "Castello di Radda in Chianti," something of a misnomer, as actually, it was built at the lowest point in the valley, not the traditional high point for a castle as was done for defensive purposes. However, I guess if you make the famous Beretta guns, who needs the high ground for defense?

Simone was a nice young man who was the one that, shortly after we had arrived here this year, had stopped us in the restaurant and asked if we were the people with the llama. As soon as he had seen the llama, he was pretty sure it was ours, but he didn't have our phone number, so he'd called his office, and they, in turn, had called me.

Having confirmed where the llama had been sighted, I ran to my Jeep with Pasquale close behind. I explained what had happened as we took off in the Jeep.

When we arrived at the cantina, several women and workers were outside, cameras in hand, and asked if we were there for the llama. I said yes, and they pointed to a field below the veranda where a crowd was standing. Pasquale and I ran to the field, and there, grazing quite peacefully and seemingly unperturbed, was Ceppettone.

Not being sure how we were going to get him back up to his

corral, we tried to coax him to follow us. He would have none of it and instead went around the cantina to the veranda where the cantina workers were and began eating the flowers. It was not a popular move, but after a bit of waving my arms and saying some gibberish, I was able to get him headed down the dirt road, at least in the general direction of Ceppeto, which was about four miles away up the steep road.

While I herded Ceppettone along the road by jogging behind him, I told Pasquale to get the Jeep and go ahead of us. He did, and Ceppettone began following the Jeep, while I loped along behind, herding him back on the road whenever he began to wander off on either side. As the hill became steeper, I began to get winded and knew that there was no way that I was going to be able to jog up that hill. It was hard enough just walking up it, which Mica and I had done before.

Just at that moment, Simone drove up behind me in the Castello di Lupaia Range Rover. He told me to hop in, and we continued to follow Ceppettone up the hill, swerving from one side of the road to the other in order to keep him following the Jeep. When he wandered too far off the road, I jumped out and herded him back behind the Jeep.

We then came to a house with three huge German shepherds—luckily, all behind a fence—that began barking ferociously at Ceppettone. The llama stopped in his tracks, and at that point, Pasquale jumped out of the Jeep, and we exchanged places. I jumped in the Jeep and called Ceppettone, who then followed me up the hill. Pasquale continued to trot behind, keeping him on the road every time he tried to wander off.

At that point, we had traffic stopped in both directions (not that there is ever much traffic going or coming from Lupaia), but it was quite a scene, with Ceppettone running at a horse-gallop pace behind the Jeep, Simone swerving from one side of the road to the other in the Range Rover, honking his horn if Ceppettone started to wander off, and Pasquale jogging behind, also helping to keep the llama on the road. We started to get cheers from the workers in the fields and waves from the people stopped in their cars as we made our way up the long, winding road.

As we got farther along, it seemed that Ceppettone was enjoying the attention, and he continued to gallop closely behind the Jeep. Maybe he thought that he had finally found a companion, but, whatever the reason, he followed the Jeep through the front gates of Ceppeto, which we quickly closed after us.

At that point, Simone turned around and drove back to Lupaia. I called him later to thank him for all his help. As for Pasquale, he followed at a trot matching the llama's easy lope. I think it might be a vestige of those days that Pasquale spent dodging border guards and thieves as he crossed back and forth from Albania into Greece. He trotted up the four-mile uphill slope after Ceppettone, an incline I'd seen bicyclists have a hard time tackling. Pasquale was drenched from his marathon run—yet another remarkable feat of strength and dedication from the little iron man.

Once inside the grounds of Ceppeto, our next task was to get Ceppettone back into the corral. Mica hadn't left yet, so she, Pasquale, our housekeeper, and I all tried to direct Ceppettone down to the corral below our vineyard, located about three hundred meters from the front gate. Easier said than done; each time we headed him in the right direction, he would veer off onto a different one. Finally, after running all over Ceppeto, through the vineyard, and back up to the front gate, then down by the pool and vegetable garden, I decided to once again try the Jeep.

Sure enough, as soon as I turned on the motor and started down the hill toward the corral, Ceppettone came running. From there, it was a snap. I stopped the Jeep at the entrance to the corral. Ceppettone waited for me to get down from the Jeep and then followed me into the corral. Mission accomplished—for real this time.

Mica, who had dressed to go to Florence, had just enough time to freshen up before her ride picked her up, and our housekeeper was a bit stunned at having been pressed into service to round up a llama. I was relieved because I never thought we would be successful getting Ceppettone back to Ceppeto.

We were later informed that Ceppettone wanted to get out because he was looking for a mate. So I assume that Ceppettone thought that our cute little Jeep Wrangler with an open-air Bimini top—which always gets compliments from the locals—was a possible mate for him. Why else would he chase after it up a daunting, winding, hardtop road for four miles?

We had ruled out getting a female llama because they would have to be kept separated most of the time, but as previously suggested, the company of another animal would do the trick—not for mating, but just for Ceppettone to have company and keep him occupied with things other than mating. So that next week, Pasquale found a goat that seemed to fit the bill perfectly. The llama and the goat got along swimmingly (a nice, if comical symbol of coexistence), and Ceppettone was decidedly happier. What we didn't know was that damned goat was already pregnant, and a few months later, we had *two* goats! Our plans for a stable just got bigger, as did our family of animals.

The aftermath of all this was to figure out how Ceppettone escaped in the first place. Pasquale and I had built the gates, and they were certainly strong enough to keep Ceppettone inside. How the gate was opened remained a mystery, as it was tightly secured and took a great deal of effort to unbolt. It appeared to me, upon further examination, that someone had to have actually forced it open with enough muscle to crack the wood holding the deadbolt.

My first thought was someone had opened it during the night, but then again, I am inclined to quickly think conspiracy whenever I can't figure out why something happened. I knew some of our neighbors weren't happy about us adopting Ceppettone, as they had enjoyed seeing him wander around, even after learning that our taking him in had probably saved his life.

We had also had a run-in with a hunter from Lupaia who kept two hunting dogs locked up near Ceppeto that barked incessantly every night. He refused to move them, and we finally went to the Carabinieri, who had warned him that what he was doing was illegal and that he would receive a big fine if he didn't move them and keep them from barking all night. He did so but was not pleased, to say the least. Anyway, I had ample grounds to conjure up all sorts of conspiracies, even if some were decidedly on the fringe.

In the meantime, Pasquale immediately put a chain and lock around the gate after Ceppettone was inside, and we decided to reinforce it the next morning with locks so that no one could open it. The next morning, I went to the corral first thing to check on Ceppettone. I found him comfortably lying down next to the gate and realized that if he had rolled himself into the gate, he did have the weight—over three hundred pounds—and the strength to have forced the gate open.

Since then, all has been calm. With the addition of two goats, we had to double the size of the corral as we soon learned that goats are eating machines, so we alternate them from one corral to the other in order to give the grass a chance to grow. Ceppettone is plainly content, and when we drive our Jeep by the corral, he comes running to greet it, preening by bending his head and long neck backward until his head touches his back. He obviously has a thing for our Jeep.

CHAPTER 28

THE CHANGING OF THE GUARD

The inhabitants of Ceppeto and Lupaia witnessed, made, and survived Italian history together for over six centuries. Of the thirty-two people still living there, Lina Salvano is the descendant of the longest-living family in Lupaia, having settled there over 320 years ago. Living next door to Lina is Raffaello's older sister, Carmela, who is now in her late nineties. She and Raffaello were both born in Lupaia. Today, as Lina and Carmela look out over what were the ancient fortress walls of Lupaia, they can see the house and fields of Ceppeto.

More than neighbors, they shared their lives with the *contadini* (farmers) who lived at Ceppeto, just as their ancestors did for hundreds of years beforehand. Carmela married, lived, raised children, and worked there for many years. Raffaello, as a young boy, played and later worked there. Lina's family held a coveted license from the government, authorizing them to sell tobacco, alcohol, and matches, and they managed the only *bottega* in Lupaia that sold staples to the area residents from the late 1600s until the 1990s when Lina sold the license to Tina and Fabio, whose daughters now run a restaurant and lunch bar there. The *bottega* was the place where the *contadini* were able to buy the few items they were not able to make themselves. It was conveniently within walking distance for them, when the only means of traveling were by foot or horse. When Lina was a little girl, she remembers over three hundred *contadini* living and working on the farms around Lupaia.

The most important gatherings were every Sunday at the village churches, all three of them. That was when most of the three hundred *contadini* came to the center of Lupaia, called by the ringing of the bells from the tall church tower that to this day still beckon the few remaining area residents just one Sunday morning a month to the only one of the three churches that is still active (as the other two have been converted to wineries).

For hundreds of years, this was the place where the people prayed together and shared their joys and sorrows, becoming one large family whose common goal was to live and work on their farms while raising families to take over for succeeding generations.

Raffaello was born into that social structure in which the importance of the farms surrounding Lupaia was the lifeblood of this communal existence for centuries. For him and his sister, there was no farm more important than Ceppeto. When Carmela lived there, Raffaello was still a youngster, and he loved being there with her and playing with the other children living on the farm. As a child and later a young working boy, he came to know all eighteen people for whom Ceppeto was both a home and a place of work. It was only natural for Raffaello to take on the job of custodian when it was turned into a private residence.

Ceppeto was a symbol he felt compelled to preserve. It was more than a job; it was a duty. It was not about money: we know—in fact, we saw—that he would work without pay to ensure that his beloved Ceppeto survived.

Raffaello met Pasquale that first day when Pasquale arrived at Ceppeto, claiming to be "strong like Superman." When Raffaello handed Pasquale a rake, no one knew that Pasquale would one day be the one to take over and return Ceppeto to its original splendor. It would take several years before Raffaello fully accepted the fact that Pasquale was his last hope to see Ceppeto restored to its full potential beauty. He at first begrudgingly worked with the Albanian immigrant, who, little by little, showed him how good a worker he was, willing and anxious to learn from *Babbo*, showing him all the respect of his status as the elder overseer. At the age of eighty-four, urged by his family, Raffaello finally willingly retired and turned over the full reins of Ceppeto to Pasquale.

It had been a long run for Raffaello, spanning decades, all the way back to the 1920s. He had witnessed Ceppeto going from a thriving farm that raised cows and produced milk, wheat, fruit, nuts, wine, and olive oil to abandonment after WWII to its subsequent resurrection when Mica and I became the owners. He now knew that Ceppeto, which had existed for over six hundred years, would continue to last long into the future. His task, then, was complete, and as his eighty-four-year-old body and mind began to inevitably erode, he at long last believed that it was time to leave, content in the knowledge that the person now in charge was capable of carrying on—of not only maintaining but also protecting Ceppeto—long after he was gone.

After he retired, Raffaello continued to drive up to Ceppeto once every week or so, and Pasquale would stop by his house to visit once or twice a week to report to Raffaello what was happening at the farm. An unlikely friendship developed between the two of them over the years, borne from mutual respect that came from working side by side, which, in turn, had nurtured a growing affection, confirmed by the birthday gifts they exchanged over the years.

In 2010, Raffaello drove to Ceppeto to pay one of his visits. As always, on these unannounced drop-ins, he brought a cake his daughter had made. He sat with Mica and me and had coffee. He then handed us the keys to Ceppeto, a set we had always wanted him to have in case of an emergency while we were gone. He announced, "I have to tell you that I will not be visiting again, as I have to turn in my driver's license, so it is best that you take the keys." Then, with a tinge of sadness but mostly courage, he said, "You see, I have cancer, and I am no longer permitted to drive."

Mica and I both were stunned. Mica, with tears rolling down her cheeks, got up and gave Raffaello a hug. Tears welled up in his eyes, and I swallowed hard, holding back mine.

What Raffaello didn't say, and what we found out later from his family, was that he was also in the first stages of Alzheimer's disease.

He thanked us for all we had done for him, and we hugged and thanked him for all he had done for us—and Ceppeto. Pasquale was waiting for him outside. He intuitively knew something was not right when he saw Raffaello arrive and waited close by enough to have overheard the conversation. Pasquale hugged him as well and said, "*Babbo, ti prendi cura.*" ("Pop, take care of yourself.") Raffaello smiled and slowly walked to his car, driving away from Ceppeto for the last time.

In 2012, Raffaello—who had for so long seemed to live outside the passage of time—succumbed to the ravages of Alzheimer's and cancer. He had just turned ninety-one. We were in New York and were therefore not able to attend his funeral, but Pasquale was there and bade him good-bye on our behalf.

His name translates as "God has healed." It was a singularly appropriate name for a man who cared for this little corner of the world when others had forgotten it and left it unworked, neglected, and overgrown. He was tireless in his dedication to these few acres, and as much as any man he was responsible for bringing it back to life—not only through his own sweat but also through what he taught Pasquale and myself.

He was as much a part of this farm as are the olive trees and the walls he built with the stones dug out of the Ceppeto dirt. We lost a part of this place with his passing, and no artisan is good enough to repair that wound.

CHAPTER 29

RUMINATIONS

It is now 2013, and we are in our fourteenth year at Ceppeto. Pasquale has been working here full-time since 2002.

When I drive up the long hill toward Lupaia and Ceppeto, I pass hundreds of cypress trees planted by the Furbones, marking the sides of the road. These trees were mere saplings when we first came here, and they are now majestically tall, most over thirty feet high—including the two planted in celebration of our wedding. They escort me up the long road that winds from the bottom of the valley to the top, over two thousand feet above sea level.

As I slowly climb higher, the views become breathtakingly beautiful. The ancient stone bell tower stands guard above Lupaia on one side of the valley, and our villa at Ceppeto looks out from the other side. Beneath both are vineyards, wild forests, and silver-leafed olive groves in a painter's palette of every shade of green imaginable. As I gaze out over this landscape, I am struck by the topaz blue of the sky with billowy white clouds slowly floating across the horizon, casting great patches of shadow that ripple over the ground below. The gentle wind causes the cypress trees to slowly sway back and forth in perfect unison, and as I drive by the olive, oak, chestnut, and linden trees, I can see their leaves fluttering and anticipate hearing the sweet rhythmic sound I'll hear when I finally stop and get out of my car.

Ahead of me is the twenty-foot-high wall surrounding tiny

Lupaia, a remnant of its days as a fortified castle centuries ago. A weather-beaten dark-blue sign with large wide white letters spelling LUPAIA hangs above a niche in the wall in which is nestled a statue of the Madonna, surrounded at its base by fresh flowers. At the foot of the wall, marking the entrance to the dirt road that leads to the gates to Ceppeto, is our green American-style mailbox, complete with its metal-hinged red flag to indicate when mail has arrived. It's an odd contrast to see this cultural artifact from an episode of *The Andy Griffith Show* standing next to village walls that were already ancient when the Pilgrims landed at Plymouth Rock.

Farther along between the road and our little lake is a small chapel with beautiful frescoes on its ceiling and walls, probably dating back to the 1500s. No longer used, it is owned by descendants of the Medicis. At one point, I thought it would make a wonderful addition to our property and was willing to have it restored as it was in a state of disrepair. That chapel would become my first lesson in local Italian diplomacy.

In hindsight, I must have appeared like an arrogant wealthy American real estate investor (which is, unfortunately, the norm in an industry where egos are grotesquely inflated) who cavalierly wanted to buy up everything in sight. I, in fact, had even asked our neighbor if he might be interested in selling his property.

The Medicis turned down what I, in a rather self-serving assumption, felt was a good offer, with a simple and unequivocal no. As they say, *no* can be a complete sentence, and that was exactly what it was in this case. Not even a glimmer of possibility for negotiation, which was a true comeuppance for a real estate guy, a reminder that this wasn't New York City where real estate wheeling and dealing had been born when the Dutch scooped up Manhattan from the locals for a small bunch of beads.

This was Italy, and what I didn't know, and have since learned, was that I hadn't been offering to buy a piece of property; I had unknowingly asked them at what price they would be willing to sell part of being a Medici. Of course they said no. There's no amount large enough.

(As a footnote to all this, a year later, while Mica and I were having dinner one summer evening following a horrific thunderstorm, we heard what sounded like a huge explosion. I ran out of the house and saw a big cloud of dust rising from the area where the chapel was. The roof had collapsed, sadly ruining much of the fresco work inside. The Medicis repaired it, but it somehow lost much of its character in the process.)

As I continue driving along the road, I reach a small, wooden, handcrafted sign right outside our front gate, which is set low in the ground with CEPPETO chiseled onto the surface. Next to the gate is the beginning of an open-faced fence made from hand-hewn narrow logs forming an X between each section of heavier wood posts. At about five feet high, it is just tall enough to deter wild boar from entering the grounds around the main house where they would otherwise forage for roots and dig up the ground, ruining all the vegetation. They have been so persistent that we have added a few lines of electrically charged wires to the fence, which gives them enough of a harmless shock to discourage them from entering.

That works most of the time, although a few years ago, during a prolonged drought, they even broke through that and started digging up the vineyard, getting to the roots of the grapevines. It got so bad that Pasquale spent all night sleeping outside near the vineyard, armed with a flashlight and small firecrackers. When he heard them breaking through the fence, he quickly got up and threw some firecrackers in the direction of the noise, scaring them off. Unfortunately, they still did damage to some of the vines.

Our vineyard has several types of grapes, mostly Sangiovese, which is an Italian grape indigenous to this area and the primary grape used in Chianti and Montepulciano wines. I still remember Raffaello getting upset when we also planted merlot. His complaint was "Merlot isn't Italian; it's French," followed by *"Porca miseria!"* ("For God's sake!") for added emphasis.

The siege by the wild boars lasted over two weeks, and toward the end of that time, Mica and I arrived to find Pasquale looking exhausted for the first time ever. We understood why when he explained his all-night vigils, only to continue to work as hard as ever during the day to get the place in tip-top shape for our arrival. Typically, he never complained, and after we learned what was going on between him and the boars, we told him he didn't have to do that.

He shrugged his shoulders and said, "*Capo*, whether it is animals or people that enter Ceppeto without permission, it is my job to protect it, even if I have to stay up twenty-four hours at a time."

Fortunately, the siege ended a day later when it rained for several days and the drought was finally over. When Pasquale and I inspected the vineyard together to survey the damage, we discovered that the only vines the wild boars had damaged were the French merlots. When we told Raffaello what had happened, he grinned like a Cheshire cat after nabbing a mouse.

As I drive through the iron gates, fashioned by the hands of the local *fabbro* (blacksmith) and see our *laghetto* (small lake), I am filled with pride—not the pride of ownership but something akin to the pride of authorship. The *laghetto* is now surrounded by a mix of wild vegetation, a variety of trees, and a rose garden. In the middle of the rose garden is a wooden bench that Mica's brother and I made—on which we sit to watch the thousands of goldfish that now populate the forty-foot-deep lake.

Providing shade over the bench is a beautiful chestnut tree that Pasquale transplanted from the surrounding *bosco* (woods) when it was just a sapling. He cared for it in the same way that one would a child, doting on it with absolute loving care, and it is now a magnificent specimen, providing an ideal shady place to sit and meditate.

Pasquale is gifted with a love for plants and an innate ability to care for them. He is untrained as a gardener or arborist, but his affinity for plant life is like a sixth sense for him. He actually tells me he can feel when the plants are thirsty or when they need to be trimmed and pruned. He told me, "*Capo*, young plants are like children; when they are young, they need lots of attention and loving care, but also they need from time to time to be *castigato*," which for him meant trimmed in the sense of being disciplined.

Pasquale raises his children with the same remarkable amount of sensibility. He knows he faces challenges as a Muslim parent raising his children in a culture that is new and very different from the one in which he grew up. He grants them a fair amount of freedom, but if they cross over a certain line, he doesn't hesitate to let them have it: "You can go out and have fun, but no drugs, no drinking, and you must be home by a certain hour. If you can't abide by those rules, you can't live in this house." That seems to work as well as any other fatherly code.

But he has also had occasion to express his frustrations, as all parents do, at the lack of appreciation his children have for the life they now have, and he has stumbled his way—as all parents do—through the usual parent-child conflicts as his children began dating and eventually got engaged, married, and had children of their own.

Make no mistake: he loves his children and now has two grandchildren, and he looks forward to being with them on his days off.

When I see him doting on his kids, particularly his grandchildren, it's a reminder to me of the danger of making snap judgments. On that "Me strong like Superman" day when I'd first met Pasquale, my first assumption had been that this comical little big-mouthed man was going to be a pain in the ass. But since then, in the same way Raffaello taught him to rebuild the old farm walls stone by stone and day by day, Pasquale built his connections to us. He feels it is his responsibility to take loving care of us along with this farm that he helped bring back to life. We are family to him, and he has become family to us. Pasquale will often say to me, "*Capo,* if someone insults you or La Signora, it is same as insulting me. If someone hurts Ceppeto or either of you, it is the same as hurting me. As long as I live and breathe, I won't let that happen. *Mai, mai* [never, never]."

As much as the value of loyalty and hard work, Pasquale has also taught me something about the generosity of heart and spirit. Many of our friends and family have passed through these grounds, and Pasquale remembers each and every one of them, as well as where they stayed, what they looked like, and what he thought about them. He may not remember their names, but even years later, when I have completely forgotten about their visits, Pasquale can rifle through his mental catalog and come up with them:

"She seemed nervous and smoked outside all the time but never in the house."

"He was slim, had dark hair, an Italian name but only spoke a little Italian, had a bicycle he rode everywhere."

"He was very serious, a little chubby but nice."

"Her brain seemed to go in circles, nice but not there when she looked at you."

The result is that when he calls me in New York, after we've finished our discussion, he'll end by saying *"Salutami tutti ..."* ("My regards to everyone ..."), and then he will take what feels like forever to complete the list of people, from my kin to Mica's relatives to our damned cats.

But the thing is, it's not just a ritual of politeness. He really does care. He calls Mica's eighty-four-year-old mother more than Mica's six brothers do all together!

When Raffaello's health began to fail, Pasquale stopped by his house almost every evening after work to cheer him up and help Raffaello's wife. In Lupaia, he helps aging Fabio with his vegetable garden and takes clothes to the cleaners for the elderly and brings them back when they're ready. For the aged and infirm that have trouble getting about, Pasquale is there. Pasquale learned that the word for *Good Samaritan* in Italian is *buon samaritano.* He now often says, *"Capo,* it is necessary to be *un buon samaritano. Perche no?* [Why not?] If I can help, I help."

And that he does. There is hardly a day that goes by that he hasn't helped someone. Just about every person in Lupaia, all thirty-two of them, have his cell number. To them, Pasquale is Superman, always flying to help those in need: whether by taking their laundry to the cleaners in Montevarchi twenty miles away, clearing the roads and their steps when it snows, or bringing cut firewood to their apartments and setting it up in their fireplaces so they only have to light a match to get a fire going. Many have small vegetable gardens, and Pasquale takes time to help them weed, water, and harvest them.

He does all this and more without missing a beat at Ceppeto. When there was an attempted robbery in Lupaia, the first person they called was Pasquale, who responded far faster than the Carabinieri were able to. To bring all the residents solace, he began sleeping at Ceppeto a couple of minutes away by car and told everyone to call him at any hour if they needed help. That continued until things finally calmed down and was comforting to everyone at Lupaia. They talk about it all the time when we see them.

One day he came to work late, a rarity for him. He was driving to work when a huge truck train hauling gravel passed two bike riders and cut them off, knocking one off his bike. Pasquale was following and saw all this happen. He immediately called 118 (the Italian 911) on his cell phone and then rushed to the aid of the fallen bicyclist, who apparently had hurt his arm. The man was an American, and his wife had screamed when she saw him being knocked over by the truck. Pasquale assured him and his wife that an ambulance was on the way and told them just to stay put until it arrived.

He then ran to the cab of the truck, which had stopped, and confronted the driver, saying, "What is wrong with you? Those people are old people. You didn't have to pass them on the curve. What are you trying to do, get to where you are going five minutes faster? That is stupid." The driver, a hefty muscular type, didn't argue at all. He gave Pasquale all his identification, including his phone number, and apologized.

Pasquale then returned to the couple to try to comfort them. The wife had calmed down, and the man, although hurt and in need of a doctor for his arm, seemed okay as well. They were American tourists from California and spoke no Italian. How Pasquale communicated and got all this information is beyond me. But that is Pasquale: somehow he always manages to make himself understood. He did that from the first time we met. When someone meets Pasquale, they immediately recognize that he can be very funny, but at the same time they understand that they are dealing with a powerful and forceful person, one that you just *know* you better stop and pay attention to.

He has that rare quality that instantly commands respect. Pasquale waited for the ambulance, and by that time, the tour guide for the American bicyclists arrived and took over from there. Before leaving, Pasquale gave the couple his cell number and told them to call him if they needed any help. He told them his daughter spoke English, as did the people he worked for, so if they needed someone who spoke English, they should call him. They were grateful and wanted to give Pasquale some money, but he refused, saying it was his pleasure to be able to help.

Mica and I visited the office of the Carabinieri in Radda to get some documents for our car issued. While there, the commander came over and introduced himself to us. He was about six feet tall, thin and broad shouldered, with a full, round face, blue eyes, and brown hair. His distinctive features were a Roman nose and a strong chin. In his uniform he looked imposing and said, "Hello, I am Maresciallo Lucio Sentori. I wanted to finally meet the owners of Ceppeto, whom I have heard so much about, primarily from Pasquale. I know, Signora Hadar that your father and brother were both career Carabinieri, so it is a particular pleasure to meet you. Pasquale loves the two of you, and there is virtually nothing he won't do for either of you. All of us have gotten to know Pasquale quite well. He is one of the most unusual and likable men any of us have ever met. I can tell you from all that I know he has done for other people, he is a true saint. The people in Lupaia love him. He takes such good care of anyone there that needs help at any time of day or night. Who else would sleep every night at Ceppeto to calm the fears of the people in Lupaia when they had a robbery there? He actually slept outside in the cold, wrapped in blankets, so if something did happen, he could get to Lupaia faster. No question he is a saint and is *stupefacente* [amazing]. We have been to Ceppeto, and the work he has done there is incredible. Everyone thinks Ceppeto is the most beautiful farm in Chianti."

I said, "Thank you, Maresciallo; we really appreciate your kind comments. Yes, Pasquale is a wonderful human being with a value system that is truly remarkable. I agree; he is like a saint."

Mica added, "He is such a wonderful and unusual person that my husband is writing a book about him."

Mareschiallo excitingly responded, "Well, I am sure it will be a very interesting book. From what I know of Pasquale's story, it probably reads like a novel."

I agreed. "That is what makes him so special. He hasn't one ounce of regret in anything that has happened to him. Just happiness to be where he is in life now. It is a rare quality that we enjoy witnessing."

He replied, "Yes, I agree. Well, nice meeting you both, and if there is anything we can do for you, please let me know."

As he returned to his office, Mica leaned over and whispered to me, "Wow! You must put that into the book."

I really think the most unusual relationship Pasquale has cultivated, besides with us, is with the Carabinieri. When he first came to Ceppeto, he was frightened the minute he saw a Carabiniere or policeman for fear of being discovered as an illegal immigrant and being deported. Remember that he hid in the woods when he saw a policeman come to Ceppeto to inspect our home during the processing of his papers to become a legal immigrant. Amazingly, today, Pasquale counts the Carabinieri among his best friends. He has slowly befriended them and, in turn, they him over the years. Today, they have nothing but praise and respect for Pasquale, as does just about everyone that gets to know him. He really has a rare quality of respecting others first and expressing himself in a way that is not offensive but, rather, with great candor, sincerity, and often humor.

One of the younger Carabinieri, Piero, asked Pasquale if he could swim in our pool when we went back to the States. Without a moment's hesitation and putting his quick thinking on display, he said, "I tell you what, Piero: You come up to swim in the pool, and when you take off your uniform, hat, and gun, I will put the uniform and hat on and put the belt and gun around my waist. Then, while you are swimming, I will go into Radda and walk around acting like a Carabiniere, waving to everyone." As Pasquale said that, he strutted around as if he had on the uniform. "How does that sound?"

Piero couldn't help but laugh, and then Pasquale said seriously,

"As long as I am at Ceppeto, no one uses the pool or goes there for anything other than business. And when my *Capo* and La Signora are not there, no one enters unless I am there to give them permission to enter. When they are away, I don't even use the pool. I would never think of it. It is not mine to use, and it is not mine to give you or anyone else permission to use it. We are friends, but don't take advantage of that by asking me for things that you know I should not do."

Piero sheepishly apologized. Pasquale had made his point, and the two continue to be friends.

There is nothing fake about Pasquale, and over time, people have come to realize that and slowly begun trusting, liking, and respecting him more and more. It has been truly an amazing accomplishment for someone who came to live and work in Italy with only a few clothes on his back in 2002.

Yes, the only thing our Superman is missing is his cape. In every other way he has lived up to his initial claim, "Me strong like Superman."

It is Pasquale's unfailing love of plants that has turned Ceppeto into the beautiful place it is. Imagine nursing ailing trees—thousands of them—back to health after they were overgrown with vines that were strangling them to death. He personally cut the vines at the base of every tree, some as big as tree trunks, and when the vines died after a year or two, he pulled them off the trees. He then waited until the foliage returned so that he was able to see what branches had died, and then he carefully pruned them, giving the trees new vitality. I watched him nurse some back to health that I had given up as hopelessly lost, including what turned out to be beautiful fruit-producing apple, cherry, and plum trees.

He meticulously weeds the gardens and lawn. No weed killers or chemical products needed. He removes the weeds by hand, one by one, with the same intensity and focus with which he had impressed me on his first day at Ceppeto with the squad of Italian workers whose task was to pick up all the stones on this same ground so that we could plant grass. Today, that lawn, covering several acres, rolls out from the house in a lush green carpet.

This—all this—is the product of a man whose botanical concerns sixteen years ago were limited to hoping that the small patch of ground allowed him by the Albanian government might provide enough food to keep his family from starving.

He never buys plants and instead cultivates them from seedlings. He has grown and transplanted so many flowers and ornamental bushes indigenous to this area that when visitors come, they are astonished at the beautiful panoply of red, blue, yellow, and shades of green artfully placed throughout the grounds. All this is thanks to a man who couldn't see the purpose in Mica's painting yet who is, himself, very much an artist, with an artist's passion for what he does and an artist's vision driving him.

As I pass through the iron gates onto our driveway, now lined with tall cypress trees, and drive around a bend to the parking area, the entire vista comes into sight. I first see the rich green lawn, which originally had been an orchard. There are still plum, apricot, cherry, and apple trees there, many very old ones that Pasquale has nursed back to health. The apple trees are an almost extinct variety and produce apples in the fall, which, after being picked, last throughout the winter.

Next to the lawn is the main house with its *pergola* (arbor) outside the kitchen, covered with an American grapevine. It provides shade for our outdoor meals and in September produces a wonderful grape from which Mica makes and jars a delicious marmalade that lasts a full year.

Under the arbor is where we spend lots of time during the summer months, enjoying Tuscan-style meals of which Mica is a master chef and drinking our wine at lunch and dinner, often with guests, while watching the valley change colors and hues from one moment to the next as the sun sets and darkness takes over.

I walk past the main house, by the vineyard and the first rows of olive trees. We produce about three hundred bottles of wine a year, just enough to enjoy the process of making wine and more than enough to give away to friends. Our wine cellar now contains over a thousand bottles, more than we will ever drink.

Taking care of the vineyard and making wine is something Pasquale learned from scratch, first from Raffaello and then from an oenologist. For the last several years, he has been doing everything himself. He looks after every single vine with the same loving care he gives all the plants, taking samples to a laboratory for analysis throughout the process from vine to fermentation to aging in oak barrels to finally bottling and labeling.

Fourteen years ago, I stood on this very spot and saw the woods choked with undergrowth, the crumbling walls, the vine-strangled olive trees, the weedy terraces. I remembered a childhood dream, one fostered on weekend drives out to the Pennsylvania farm country. My mother got what any mother wishes for her children: she lived long enough to see my dream come true … and then some.

Like our wine, Ceppeto has matured as beautifully and as gracefully as I could ever have imagined possible when I first stepped onto the grounds on that gray, unpromising day, all those years ago. It is an idyll—a lovely word, so close to *ideal*—complete with a bird sanctuary and many private walking trails through beautifully restored forests. The locals now refer to Ceppeto as *Paradiso*.

How is it possible that those years have gone by so quickly? Though I am filled with memories of those times, they come nowhere close to representing the thousands of days we've spent here. That raises the following questions: Did we waste a lot of time? Or have we just forgotten so many of those days?

We all have selective memories when it comes to our pasts, and I often wonder what causes the mind to store some events for later recall while throwing others away, never to be thought of again.

My hypothesis is that the less we remember, the faster the years seem to slip by. In order to slow down time, it would seem important to do things that are memorable—even more than memorable, things that are *worth* remembering. Who wants to remember the bad things, the tedious things, the times of pain and unhappiness? As I see it, we need to keep doing things to make our lives interesting.

The key is to occupy yourself with things about which you are passionate, whether it be painting, writing, taking long walks not just for the exercise but also to relish spectacular scenery, or climbing a daunting hill or mountain. It may even be to take some overgrown piece of ground and return it to the beauty it once knew.

I find I enjoy and remember things that involve as many senses as possible. Sight, sound, smell, touch, and taste is my preferred hierarchy, but any combination will do. For me, there is no better place to do that than here at Ceppeto, where the scenery is gorgeous, the sound of the wind and the birds are symphonic, and the sweet smell of fresh air laden with scents of flowers, trees, and grass—a fragrance so thick and rich you can taste it—is a constant during spring, summer, and fall.

By comparison, New York City tends to be comparatively one-dimensional. The sights are grand, but the sounds are not particularly pleasing—nor are the smells. Therefore, the daily walks I take there are often simply functional, only to get from one place to the next. In fact, looking at the store windows takes my mind off the crowds, the noise, and the jostling one needs to tolerate when out on the streets of Manhattan. When I reflect upon my days there, I have no recollection of any part of those forays, as they are better forgotten than to clutter up whatever storage capacity I have left in my brain. That is not to say that New York isn't an exhilarating place to live. There is more to do in New York City than any place I know of, and we wouldn't want to be without it, but you can't walk out your door and find the good stuff waiting for you. You have to *work* at enjoying life in the Big Apple; it is more of a contrived life than the simple one lived here.

Our extended Italian family here has all aged with us and gone through many moments of joy and sadness. We have shared many of those times with them. Those events are the markers reminding us of the years—so many, now—that have passed for us here and of the changes that we have all witnessed and lived through. Without those moments—those markers—the years would have been a meaningless, weightless blur.

Many of those memorable moments involve Pasquale, as I witnessed his emerging, unique personality take shape once we were able to communicate better. That image of him became more defined as time progressed and we spent more time working together and conversing.

His toughness and fearlessness are easy to recognize, but he has never flaunted them. Instead, he has garnered respect by not being afraid to be direct and honest with everyone. Add to this his desire to help as much as he can and you have the ingredients of an amazing individual. He is incredibly loyal to us and would lay down his life if necessary to protect and help us. Of that, I have absolutely not one iota of doubt. That message has been heard loud and clear by everyone that has met Pasquale. It never comes across as a threat or a boast but rather a statement of fact, and anyone who knows Pasquale knows he means every word of it.

As I stand near our little lake, a beautiful body of water surrounded by many of the trees and flowers Pasquale planted, I am reminded of how Pasquale arrived in Italy by crawling through the bone-chilling surf to reach the beach and then scurrying as fast as he could through the forest to change his clothes and start his journey in Italy that took him to Ceppeto.

Then there is the joy of having my mother meet Mica's parents here in Ceppeto. The fun of having her teach them Yiddish while they taught her Italian. The sadness of losing both my mother and Mica's father one year later. Betti's wedding and her grandfather Raffaello's death. The births of many babies among our friends and watching those babies grow into their distinctive personalities. Our wedding and, of course, the tragedy of 9/11, the mourning performed not only by us but also by our many Italian friends. Celebrating Christmas in the tiny ancient church of Lupaia and listening to a few beautiful voices sing Christmas songs in Italian, echoing off the ancient walls of the tiny church. Yes, some big and some small events, but all indelibly etched among our most cherished memories.

They all stand as reminders of the importance of sharing our lives, of doing things together with people we care about and who care about us to create those markers of times gone but cherished. They are what allow us to relive those times and how we felt about them, what we felt *in* them, whether happiness or sadness or the bitter sweetness that sometimes resides in between. Those markers form the basis of our conscious existence, provide grist for the mental mill as we ponder what Plato said was the most important thing to consider about one's life: "Whether we have lived a life of a good man or bad."

I sometimes wonder if that question ever plagues Pasquale, though he probably has less reason to ask it of himself than any man I know. Sometimes, at the end of the day, I stand, holding a glass of wine made from our grapes, and look down at the valley, the now manicured and productive terraces, the grounds restored to a parklike beauty and elegance, nearly all of which are the immediate results of Pasquale's handiwork. I watch as he drives home in his car—*his* car, to *his* home, to the family he never forgot when he left them to cross the Adriatic on that frigid February night so long ago … I am not only proud of him but also proud to know him.

Though he still makes me laugh with his wild gestures and his unfailing good humor, he's no longer the vulnerable comic Chaplinesque waif he was then. He dresses quite well now, even when he's in his street clothes. Tomorrow morning, before he comes to work, he'll stop in Radda, treat Bini to a coffee, pick up fresh bread to bring to Ceppeto, and chat with the familiar faces. That icy night he made his crossing, those seemingly trivial acts—buying a friend a cup of coffee, a friendly exchange with a neighbor in the *bottega*—were as much a fantasy of riches to him as this farm was to me as a child.

We have each traveled far and each found a treasure here among the hills of Tuscany.

I have done much with my life. I've made and lost and made another fortune, I found a woman who has filled any of those voids a man alone might have, and we discovered and restored this place.

And I took a chance on a funny-looking little guy who introduced himself with the less-than-modest moniker of "Superman." He has never stopped thanking me with his words, with his actions, and with his dedication and loyalty, but when I look out over these grounds, I'm not always sure who should be thanking whom.

When I work Plato's question over in my mind and am tempted

to appraise myself a little too grandly, I remember that Ceppeto is over six hundred years old and we have only been here for fourteen of them—barely 2 percent of all its years. This is a humbling thought, one that makes me feel ... insignificant. Lupaia, Radda, and some of the farms nearby are even older, well over a thousand years. There is no question that these already ancient places will be here for another thousand years. I am not sure about the people, but that is another story.

ILLUSTRATIONS

Entrance to Ceppeto today

WINEMAKING

Pasquale and crew harvesting grapes by hand

Pasquale and Simone harvesting grapes by tractor

CEPPETO RENOVATIONS

Pasquale and Rafaello clearing the overgrowth of land abandoned for fifty years

Raffaello (*left*) and Pasquale (*right*) with Fumo the cat working on clearing the land. Fumo always followed them and watched as they worked but then insisted on being carried back to the main house.

One of the many trails for which Pasquale and Raffaello cleared
the undergrowth and rebuilt the stone walls, as it looks today

CEPPETO TRAILS AND WALLS

The trail before the stone walls were repaired

Oliviero, a stonemason, working on one of the walls

Raffaello working on part of the miles of stone walls that were restored

Mica on one of the trails after Pasquale and Rafaello restored
the stone walls and cleared the area from overgrowth

THE CANTINA

The hut used to store feed for the cows as it was found in 1999 (prior to our renovation of it) after it had been abandoned for fifty years

The hut today, made into a cantina to make Ceppeto wine

THE KITCHEN

The kitchen before it was renovated. This is where
the pigs were kept up until the late 1940s.

Oliviero renovating the kitchen

The kitchen after renovation. Bini built a steel bridge to frame the opening in the wall in order to support the upper floors.

The living room and library today. This area was used to keep the cows until the late 1950s.

CEPPETO AND ITS ENVIRONS

View of the valley from the front of the villa

View of main house. This shows Pasquale's extraordinary handiwork: the lawn without a weed, trees perfectly pruned and maintained, and the orchard on the left, where he saved many of the dying trees. The orchard now has flourishing mulberry, cherry, apple, plum, and pear trees. To the right are a few of the 350 olive trees Pasquale nursed back to health. The wagon we found at Ceppeto is an artillery wagon from the First World War that we restored.

Pasquale cleared and restored the vegetation around the lake. He transplanted trees and bushes from other areas of the property. Bini built the dock.

The grape arbor outside the kitchen of the main house under which meals are served

PASQUALE

Pasquale cultivates one of the many walnut trees on the grounds. There are several over seventy years old that he has nursed back to health.

Pasquale standing in front of one of his prized possessions, his new car

Pasquale shortly after we hired him to live and work at Ceppeto

CEPPETO FRIENDS

The Sages, *from left to right*: Richard, Saul, Bill, and Joe

Bill, Joanna, Liane, Joe, Mica, and Richard
watching the news on TV on 9/11/2001

Ceppettone the llama and his companion, Ceppe the goat

RICHARD AND MICA'S WEDDING

Richard and Raffaello, who gave Richard the rosebud for
his lapel and then drove him to the wedding

Mica arrived separately to the wedding after staying the night
before with her matron of honor. As she walked to the city hall,
people stopped in their tracks to look and take pictures of her.

The mayor of Radda (wearing the *tricolore* sash), who officiated the wedding with Nadia, the city hall administrator who helped us get the wedding documents together. As a wedding gift, she provided the flower arrangements for the ceremony.

Richard with Joe LaRosa, who was a witness and best man for the ceremony

The mayor of Radda, Richard, Mica, and Nadia after the ceremony

The postwedding procession from Radda

Richard and Mica in front of the cypress trees Raffaello planted in honor of their marriage in 1999 (an Italian tradition). The trees are named Richard and Mica.

Richard and Mica with the cypress trees in 2013. Richard's tree is shorter because it was eaten by deer and had to be replanted.

ABOUT THE AUTHOR

Richard Hadar was born during the Great Depression years in rural Pennsylvania, worked his way through college, and after two years in the army launched a number of innovative and successful businesses, culminating in a real estate investment company. He and his wife, a theater actress, divide their time between New York City and Italy.

CPSIA information can be obtained at www.ICGtesting.com
Printed in the USA
BVOW07*0000101114

374219BV00001B/2/P